Tree & Shrub
Gardening
for
Michigan

Tim Wood
Alison Beck

The Publisher: Lone Pine Publishing
10145 – 81 Avenue
Edmonton, AB, Canada T6E 1W9
Website: www.lonepinepublishing.com

1808 – B Street NW, Suite 140
Auburn, WA, USA 98001

National Library of Canada Cataloguing in Publication Data

Wood, Timothy D., 1960–
    Tree and shrub gardening for Michigan / Tim Wood and Alison Beck.

    Includes index.
    ISBN 1-55105-347-0

    1. Ornamental trees—Michigan. 2. Ornamental shrubs—Michigan.
    I. Beck, Alison, 1971– II. Title.
SB435.52.M5W66 2003   635.9'77'09774   C2003-910294-7

Editorial Director: Nancy Foulds
Project Editor: Dawn Loewen
Editorial: Dawn Loewen, Shelagh Kubish
Illustrations Coordinator: Carol Woo
Photo Editor: Don Williamson
Production Manager: Gene Longson
Book Design: Heather Markham
Layout & Production: Ian Dawe, Heather Markham
Cover Design: Gerry Dotto
Image Editing: Ian Dawe, Jeff Fedorkiw, Arlana Anderson-Hale, Heather Markham
Illustrations: Ian Sheldon
Scanning, Separations & Film: Elite Lithographers Co.

Photography: all photos by **Tim Matheson** or **Tamara Eder**, except **Agriculture and Agri-Food Canada** (**Morden Research Station**) 157b, 166b; **Alison Beck** 47, 155a, 317a; **Janet Davis** 329b; **Don Doucette** 15a, 211b, 253a, 264, 310; **Lynne Harrison** 96b, 183a, 205a; **Dawn Loewen** 164; **Steve Nikkila** 159b, 183b, 195b, 270a&b, 271a, 327b; **Kim O'Leary** 55a, 73; **Allison Penko** 26, 120, 126b, 128a, 150b, 180a, 181b, 220, 233a, 260, 278, 281b, 300, 302, 314; **Robert Ritchie** 42b, 64, 68, 80, 88, 89a&b&c, 95a, 96a, 97&c, 98, 99b, 104, 105a, 167a, 171a, 176, 177a&b, 184a&c, 195a, 241a, 242a&b, 259a, 289a, 319a, 320, 321a&b, 326, 330a; **Mark Turner** 82, 83a, 225a&b; **Tim Wood** 12a, 13b, 17a, 18b, 21b, 22a&b, 23a&b, 75a, 77a, 78a&b, 79a, 81a&b&c, 83b&c, 87a&b&c, 92a, 99a, 101a, 102a&b, 105a, 107a, 108a, 109a, 111a&b, 113a&b, 116a&b, 117a, 121b, 122b, 123b, 125a, 129a, 131a&b, 132b, 135a, 137a&b, 139a&b, 140, 141b, 143a&b, 144a&b, 145a&b, 149a&b, 153a, 155b, 156, 157a, 163a, 165a&b, 166a, 167b, 169a&b, 171b, 175a, 189a, 191b, 192a&b, 193b, 197a, 199a&b, 200a, 201, 202, 204, 205b, 209b, 217a&b, 221a&b, 222a&b, 227a&b, 228b, 237a&b, 239b, 251a&b, 255a&b, 262a&b, 265b, 266a&b, 267b, 269a&b, 272, 273a&b, 275a, 279a&b, 280, 281a, 287a&b, 291a&b, 294, 295a&b, 299a&b, 303a, 304b, 305a&b, 306b, 307a&b, 311a&b, 312, 313a&b, 318a, 323a&b, 325b, 327a, 328b, 329a, 333a

Front cover photos: elderberry by Tim Wood; maple and euonymus by Tim Matheson; viburnum by Tamara Eder

Back cover author photos: Alison Beck by Alan Bibby, Tim Wood by Tim Wood

Map: based on USDA plant hardiness zone map (1990)

We acknowledge the financial support of the Government of Canada through the Book Publishing Industry Development Program (BPIDP) for our publishing activities.

PC: P4

CONTENTS

ACKNOWLEDGMENTS

We express our appreciation to all who were involved in this project. Special thanks are extended to the following individuals and organizations: Mark Carfae, Elisabeth Eder, Lesley Knight, Todd Major and Pension Fund Realty at Park and Tilford Gardens, Heather Markham, Tim Matheson and assistant Dawna Ehman, Nancy Matheson, Paul Montpellier and the Vancouver Board of Parks and Recreation, Bill Stephen, J.C. Bakker & Sons Ltd., the Devonian Botanic Garden, Free Spirit Nursery, Gibbs Nurseryland and Florist, Niagara College Horticulture Program, Niagara Parks Botanical Gardens and School of Horticulture, Niagara Parks Commission, Riverview Arboretum, the Royal Botanical Gardens in Hamilton, Spring Meadow Nursery, UBC Arboretum, VanDusen Botanical Garden.

I would like to acknowledge my wife, Tracy, who is my inspiration and my guiding star. She is a gift from God.—*Tim Wood*

THE TREES & SHRUBS AT A GLANCE

A Pictorial Guide in Alphabetical Order, by Common Name

Aralia
p. 74

Arborvitae
p. 76

Aronia
p. 80

Barberry
p. 82

Bearberry
p. 84

Birch
p. 94

Beautyberry
p. 86

Beauty Bush
p. 88

Beech
p. 90

Black Jetbead
p. 98

Boxwood
p. 100

Butterfly Bush
p. 106

Bush Honeysuckle
p. 104

Caryopteris
p. 110

Cherry
p. 112

Cotoneaster
p. 120

Crabapple
p. 124

Daphne
p. 130

Dawn Redwood
p. 134

Deutzia
p. 136

English Ivy
p. 146

Euonymus
p. 148

Dogwood
p. 138

Elderberry
p. 142

False Cypress
p. 152

False Spirea
p. 156

Fir
p. 158

Firethorn
p. 160

Flowering Quince
p. 162

Forsythia
p. 164

Fothergilla
p. 168

Fringe Tree
p. 170

Ginkgo
p. 172

Goldenchain Tree
p. 174

Golden Rain Tree
p. 176

Hawthorn
p. 178

Hazel
p. 182

Heather
p. 186

Hemlock
p. 188

Holly
p. 190

Hydrangea
p. 198

Hornbeam
p. 194

Horsechestnut
p. 196

Japanese Hydrangea
Vine, p. 204

Japanese Pagoda-Tree
p. 206

Kalmia
p. 212

Kerria
p. 216

Juniper
p. 208

Katsura-Tree
p. 214

Larch
p. 218

Lilac
p. 220

Linden
p. 224

Magnolia
p. 226

Maple
p. 230

Mock-Orange
p. 236

Ninebark
p. 238

Oak
p. 240

Oregon-Grape
p. 244

Potentilla
p. 254

Peashrub
p. 246

Pieris
p. 248

Pine
p. 250

Redbud
p. 258

Rhododendron
p. 260

Rose-of-Sharon
p. 264

Serviceberry
p. 268

Seven-Son Flower
p. 272

Silverbell
p. 274

Smokebush
p. 276

Spirea
p. 278

Spruce
p. 282

St. Johnswort
p. 286

Sumac
p. 288

Summersweet Clethra
p. 290

Sweetgum
p. 292

Sweetspire
p. 294

Thornless Honeylocust
p. 296

Trumpetcreeper
p. 298

Tulip Tree
p. 300

Viburnum
p. 302

Virginia Creeper
p. 308

Weigela
p. 310

White Forsythia
p. 312

Wisteria
p. 314

Witchhazel
p. 316

Yew
p. 322

Yellowwood
p. 320

Yucca
p. 324

Zelkova
p. 326

INTRODUCTION

Trees and shrubs are woody perennials. They live for three or more years, and they maintain a permanent live structure above ground all year. In cold climates, a few shrubs die back to the ground each winter. The root system, protected by the soil over winter, sends up new shoots in spring, and if the shrub forms flowers on new wood it will bloom that same year. Such plants act like herbaceous perennials, but because they are woody in their native climates they are still classified as shrubs. Butterfly bush falls into this category of perennial-like shrubs.

A tree is generally defined as a woody plant having a single trunk and growing greater than 15' tall. A shrub is multi-stemmed and no taller than 15'. These definitions are not absolute because some tall trees are multi-stemmed, and some short shrubs have single trunks. Even the height definitions are open to interpretation. For example, a Japanese maple may be multi-stemmed and may grow to about 10' tall, but it is often still referred to as a tree. Furthermore, a given species may grow as a tree in favorable conditions but be reduced to a shrub in harsher sites. It is always best to simply look at the expected mature size of a tree or shrub and judge its suitability for your garden accordingly.

Vines are also included in this guide. Like trees and shrubs, these plants maintain living woody stems above ground over winter. They generally require a supporting structure to climb upon, but many can also be grown as trailing groundcovers. Again, the definition is not absolute, because some vines, such as wisteria, can be trained to form free-standing shrubs with proper pruning. Similarly, certain shrubs, such as firethorn, can be trained to grow up and over walls and other structures.

Woody plants are characterized by leaf type, whether deciduous or evergreen, and needled or broad-leaved. Deciduous plants lose all their leaves each fall or winter. They can have needles, like dawn redwood and larch, or broad leaves, like maple and dogwood. Evergreen trees and shrubs do not lose their leaves in winter and can also be needled or broad-leaved, like pine and rhododendron, respectively. Semi-evergreen plants are generally evergreens that in cold climates lose some or all of their leaves. Some types of viburnum fall into the semi-evergreen category.

Swiss stone pine

Firethorn

The climate of Michigan is considered temperate, which means generally moderate. Still, the winters are cold enough, the summers are warm enough and the rainfall is dependable enough to make our state a great place to grow a variety of woody plants. The cold winters allow a good dormancy period for plants that need cold in order to produce flowers. The warm summers allow plants plenty of time to grow.

Despite the overall similarity in climate, our weather and precipitation patterns do vary significantly across Michigan. The Great Lakes have a strong moderating influence, so that gardeners near the lakes enjoy cooler summers, milder winters and increased cloud cover and precipitation. The hardiness zones map on p. 15 reveals that the western edge of the Lower Peninsula is categorized as one zone higher than the interior of our state, meaning its average lowest winter temperatures are higher than in the interior. Similarly, the eastern shoreline, particularly the Detroit metropolitan area, is moderated by the presence of Lake Huron, Lake St. Clair and the Detroit River, and by the 'heat island' effect of the city of Detroit. Gardeners in these warmer zones can grow a greater variety of trees and shrubs than gardeners in the northern and interior sections of Michigan.

Soil conditions also vary widely. Once completely glaciated, Michigan encompasses a diverse patchwork of soil types. Clay, loam, muck, gravel and pure sand can all be found in the state, often with several types in very close proximity. Western areas near Lake Michigan tend to have mainly sandy soils. Gardeners in the southeast will most likely encounter clay and loam. Many regions of the north have sandy or rocky soils of poor fertility.

No matter what challenges you face in your garden, you will find a tree, shrub or vine that will thrive in your space. Hardiness zones, though not the final word on what will or will not grow, are useful in helping you decide what to put in your garden as well as where to put it.

Don't be put off because a catalog or book says a plant is hardy only to a certain zone. Part of the fun and challenge of gardening is experimenting with unusual and out-of-zone plants. Keep in mind that local topography in the garden creates microclimates, small areas that may be more or less favorable for growing different plants. Buildings, hills, windbreaks, low spots,

Dwarf Alberta spruce & Japanese maple

Flowering dogwood

White spruce

in your garden for that tender shrub, and you just may be surprised at how well it does.

You'll find a trip to a nearby park or botanical garden, where the trees are labeled and unusual specimens grown, invaluable for showing you trees, shrubs and vines that thrive in Michigan. Also, keep your eyes open when walking through your neighborhood. You may see a tree or shrub that you hadn't noticed before or that you were told wouldn't grow in your area. What is actually growing is a better guide than what is supposed to or not supposed to thrive.

drainage patterns and prevailing winds all influence your garden and the microclimates that occur in it (see 'Getting Started,' p. 24, for more information on assessing conditions in your garden). Pick the right spot

Many enthusiastic and creative people are involved in gardening in Michigan. From one end of the state to the other, individuals, growers, societies, schools, publications and public and private gardens provide information, encouragement and fruitful debate for the novice or experienced

A colorful mixed planting

gardener. Michigan gardeners are passionate about their plants and will gladly share their knowledge and opinions about what is best for any little patch of ground.

Outstanding garden shows, public gardens, arboretums and display gardens in our state (see the list in *Perennials for Michigan,* by Nancy Szerlag and Alison Beck) attract gardeners and growers from all over the world. Seek them out as sources of inspiration and information. Open yourself to the possibilities, and you'll be surprised by the diversity of woody plants that thrive in our varied climate. Initially, you may want to plant mostly tried and true, dependable varieties, but don't be afraid to try

Red-osier dogwood

something different or new. Gardening with trees and shrubs is fun and can be a great adventure if you're willing to take up the challenge.

HARDINESS ZONES MAP

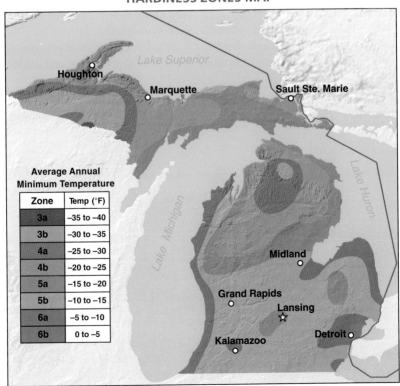

Average Annual Minimum Temperature

Zone	Temp (°F)
3a	−35 to −40
3b	−30 to −35
4a	−25 to −30
4b	−20 to −25
5a	−15 to −20
5b	−10 to −15
6a	−5 to −10
6b	0 to −5

WOODY PLANTS IN THE GARDEN

Trees and shrubs create a framework around which gardens can be designed. These permanent features anchor the landscape, and in a well-designed garden they create interest all year round. In spring and summer, woody plants provide shade and beauty with flowers and foliage. In fall, leaves of many tree and shrub species change color, and brightly colored fruits attract attention and birds. In winter, the true backbone of the garden is revealed; the branches of deciduous trees and shrubs are laid bare, perhaps dusted with snow or frost, and evergreens take precedence in keeping the garden colorful.

Carefully selected and placed, woody plants are a vital and vibrant element of any landscape, from the smallest city lot to the largest country acreage. They can provide privacy and keep unattractive views hidden from sight. Conversely, they can frame an attractive view and draw attention to particular features or areas of the garden. Trees and shrubs soften the hard lines in the landscape created by structures such as buildings, fences, walls and driveways. Well-positioned woody plants create an attractive background against which other plants will shine. Trees and shrubs can be used in groups for spectacular flower or fall color shows, and a truly exceptional species, with year-round appeal, can stand alone as a specimen plant in a prime location.

Woody plants also help moderate the climate in your home and garden.

As a windbreak, trees provide shelter from the winter cold, reducing heating costs and protecting tender plants in the garden. A well-placed deciduous tree keeps the house cool and shaded in summer but allows the sun through in winter, when the warmth and light are appreciated. Woody plants also prevent soil erosion, retain soil moisture, reduce noise and filter the air.

Attracting wildlife is an often overlooked advantage of gardening. As cities expand, our living space encroaches on more and more wildlife habitat. By choosing plants, particularly native plants, that are beneficial to local wildlife, we provide food and shelter to birds and other animals, fulfilling our obligation as stewards of the environment. We can bring nature closer to home. The only difficulty is that the local wildlife may so enjoy a garden that they consume it. It is possible, though, to find a balance and attract wildlife while protecting the garden from ruin.

When the time comes to select woody plants, think carefully about the various physical constraints of your garden and the purposes you wish the plants to serve. First and foremost, consider the size of your garden in relation to the mature size of the plants in question. Very large plants are always a bad idea in a small garden. Remember, too, that trees and shrubs not only grow up, they also grow out. Within a few years what started as a small plant may become a large, spreading tree. Spruce are often sold as very small trees, but many eventually grow too large for a small garden.

Woody plants can help soften hard lines in the landscape (above).

Birds and squirrels are frequent garden visitors.

Another consideration that relates to size is placement. Don't plant trees and shrubs too close to houses, walkways, entryways or driveways. A tree planted right next to a house may hit the overhang of the roof, and trying to fix the problem by pruning will only spoil the natural appearance of the tree. Plants placed too close to paths, doors and driveways may eventually block access completely and will give the property an unkempt appearance.

Consider, too, the various features of trees and shrub species. A feature is an outstanding element, such as flowers, bark or shape, that attracts you to the plant. Decide which of the features that follow are most important to you and which will best enhance your garden. Many plants have more than one feature, providing interest over a longer period. A carefully selected group of woody plants can add beauty to the garden year-round. Whether you are looking

Woody plants offer such features as shade (above) and fall color (burning bush cultivar, below).

for showy flowers, fall color, fast growth, unique bark or a beautiful fragrance, you can find trees or shrubs with features to suit your design; consult the individual plant entries and the Quick Reference Chart at the back of the book.

Form is the general shape and growth habit of the plant. From tall and columnar to wide and gracefully weeping, trees come in a variety of shapes. Similarly, shrubs may be rounded and bushy or low and ground hugging. Form can also vary as the year progresses and leaves are developed and lost. Often a unique winter habit makes a tree or shrub truly outstanding.

You should be familiar with some growth form terminology when considering a purchase. A 'shade tree' commonly refers to a large deciduous tree but can be any tree that provides shade. An 'upright,' 'fastigiate' or 'columnar' plant has the main branches and stems pointing upward and is often quite narrow. 'Dwarf' properly refers to any variety, cultivar or hybrid that is smaller than the species, but the term is sometimes mistakenly used to mean a small, slow-growing plant. The crucial statistic is the expected size at maturity; if a species grows to 100', then a 30–50' variety would be a dwarf but might still be too big for your garden. 'Prostrate' and 'procumbent' plants are low growing, bearing branches and stems that spread horizontally across the ground. These forms are sometimes grafted onto upright stems to create lovely, weeping plant forms.

'Skyrocket' juniper has a columnar form.

Weeping beech

Oakleaf hydrangea
White fir

'Golden Guinea' kerria (below)

Foliage is one of the most endur-ing and important features of a plant. Leaves come in a variety of colors, shapes, sizes, textures and arrange-ments. You can find shades of green, blue, red, purple, yellow, white or sil-ver. Variegated types have two or more colors combined on a single leaf. The variety of shapes is even more astounding, from short, sharply pointed needles to broad, rounded leaves the size of dinner plates. Leaf margins can be smooth, like those of many rhododendrons, or so finely divided the foliage appears fern-like, as with some Japanese maple culti-vars. Foliage often varies seasonally, progressing from tiny, pale green spring buds to the vibrant colors of fall. Evergreen trees provide welcome greenery even when winter is at its snowiest and coldest.

Growing plants with different leaf sizes, textures and colors creates con-trast and makes your garden more interesting and appealing. An entire garden can be designed based on var-ied foliage. Whether it forms a neutral backdrop or stands out in sharp con-trast with the plants around it, foliage is a vital consideration in any garden.

Flowers are such an influential feature that their beauty may be enough reason to grow a shrub or tree, such as goldenchain tree, that is dull or even unattractive the rest of the year. Flowering generally takes place over a few weeks or occasion-ally a month; only a few woody plants flower for the entire summer. Keep this limitation in mind when selecting woody plants. If you choose species with staggered flowering periods, you will always have some plants in bloom. You can achieve different but equally striking effects by grouping plants that flower at the same time, or by spreading them out around the garden. A simple and effective way to create a garden with a season-long progression of blooms is to visit your garden center on a regular basis. Because many people shop for plants only in spring, their gardens tend to be dominated by spring bloomers.

Fruit comes in many forms, including winged maple samaras, dangling birch catkins, spiny horse-chestnut capsules and the more obviously 'fruity' serviceberries and apple pomes. This feature can be a double-edged sword. It is often very attractive and provides interest in the garden in late summer and fall, when most plants are past their prime. When the fruit drops, however, it can create quite a mess and even odor if allowed to rot on the ground. Choose the location of your fruiting tree carefully. If you know the fruit can be messy, don't plant near a patio or a sidewalk. Most fruit isn't terribly troublesome, but keep in mind that there may be some cleanup required during fruiting season.

Bark is one of the most overlooked features of trees and shrubs. Species with interesting bark will greatly enhance your landscape, particularly in winter. Bark can be furrowed, smooth, ridged, papery, scaly, exfoliating or colorful. A few species valued for their bark are birch, ninebark, London planetree, cherry, sevenson flower, paperbark maple, beech and hornbeam.

Lily magnolia
'Early Amethyst' beautyberry

Paperbark maple (below)

'Crimson & Gold' flowering quince
'Cardinal' red-osier dogwood

Fragrance, though usually associated with flowers, is also a potential feature of the leaves, fruit and even wood of trees and shrubs. Flowering quince, summersweet clethra, witchhazel, arborvitae, viburnum and of course lilac are examples of plants with appealing scents. Site fragrant plants near your home, where the scent can waft into an open window.

Branches as a feature fall somewhere between form and bark, and, like those two features, they can become an important winter attribute for the garden. Branches may have an unusual gnarled or twisted shape, like those of corkscrew hazel; they may bear protective spines or thorns, like those of firethorn; or they may be brightly colored, like those of red-osier dogwood and kerria.

Growth rate and **life span,** though not really aesthetic features of woody plants, are nonetheless important aspects to consider. A fast-growing tree or shrub that grows 24" or more a year will mature quickly and can be used to fill in space in a new garden. A slow-growing species that grows less than 12" a year may be more suitable in a space-limited garden.

A short-lived plant appeals to some people because they enjoy changing their garden design or aren't sure exactly what they want in their garden. Short-lived plants, such as sumac, usually mature quickly and therefore reach flowering age quickly as well. A long-lived tree, such as a sugar maple, on the other hand, is an investment in time. Some trees can take a human lifetime to reach their mature size, and some may not flower for ten years after you plant them. You can enjoy a long-lived tree as it develops, and you will also leave a legacy for future generations— your tree may very well outlive you.

FAST-GROWING TREES & SHRUBS

Birch
Butterfly bush
Elderberry
Forsythia
Hydrangea (except *H. quercifolia*)
Katsura-tree
Lilac
Linden
Red-twig dogwood
Staghorn sumac
Thornless honeylocust
Trumpetcreeper
Virginia creeper
White forsythia
Wisteria

SLOW-GROWING TREES & SHRUBS

Aronia
Bearberry
Beech
Boxwood
Daphne
Euonymus
Fir
Fothergilla
Fringe tree
Ginkgo
Holly
Hornbeam
Kalmia
Paperbark maple
Pieris
Rhododendron
Yew

'Fiesta' forsythia

'Tauntonii' yew

GETTING STARTED

Before you fall in love with the idea of having a certain tree or shrub in your garden, it's important to consider the growing conditions the plant needs and whether any areas of your garden are appropriate for it. Your plant will need to not only survive, but thrive, in order for its flowers or other features to reach their full potential.

All plants are adapted to certain growing conditions in which they do best. Choosing plants to match your garden conditions is far more practical than trying to alter your garden to match the plants. Yet it is through the use of trees and shrubs that we can best alter the conditions in a garden. Over time a tree can change a sunny, exposed garden into a shaded one, and a hedge can turn a windswept area into a sheltered one. The woody plants you choose must be able to thrive in the garden as it exists now, or they may not live long enough to produce these changes.

Light, soil conditions and exposure are important factors that will guide your selection. As you plan, look at your garden as it exists now, but keep in mind the changes trees and shrubs will bring.

LIGHT

Buildings, trees, fences, the time of day and the time of year influence the amount of light that gets into your garden. Light levels are often divided into four categories for gardening purposes: full sun, partial shade (partial sun), light shade and full shade. Some plants adapt to a variety of light levels, but most have a preference for a narrower range.

Full sun locations receive direct sunlight most of the day. An example would be an open location along a south-facing wall. Heat from the sun

may be more intense in one spot than another, depending on, for example, the degree of shelter from the wind. **Partial shade** locations receive direct sun for part of the day and shade for the rest. An east- or west-facing wall gets only partial shade. **Light shade** locations receive shade most or all of the day, but with some sun getting through to ground level. The ground under a small-leaved tree is often lightly shaded, with dappled light appearing on the ground underneath the tree. **Full shade** locations receive no direct sunlight. The north wall of a house is usually in full shade.

SOIL

Plants have a unique relationship with the soil they grow in. Many important plant functions take place underground. Soil holds air, water, nutrients and organic matter. Plant roots depend upon these resources for growth, while using the soil to hold the plant body upright. In turn, plants influence soil development by breaking down large clods with their roots and by increasing soil fertility when they die and decompose.

Soil is made up of particles of different sizes. Sand particles are the largest. Water drains quickly from a sandy soil, and nutrients can be quickly washed away. Sand has lots of air spaces and doesn't compact easily. Clay particles are the smallest, visible only through a microscope. Water penetrates clay very slowly and drains away even more slowly. Clay holds the most nutrients, but there is very little room for air and a clay soil compacts quite easily. Most soils are made up of a combination of different particle sizes and are called loams.

Tamarack grows best in full sun.

Virginia creeper grows equally well in full sun & full shade.

Rhododendrons and azaleas need an acidic soil.

organic matter to the soil or by building raised beds. Avoid adding sand to clay soil, or you may create a substance much like concrete. Working some gypsum into a clay soil along with organic matter will help break it up and allow water to penetrate and drain more easily. Water retention in sandy or rocky soil can also be improved by adding organic matter.

Another aspect of soil that is important to consider is the pH, or the measure of acidity or alkalinity. Soil pH influences the availability of nutrients for plants. A pH of 7 is neutral; higher numbers (up to 14) indicate alkaline conditions; and lower numbers (down to 0) indicate acidic conditions. Most plants prefer a neutral soil pH of between 6.5 and 7.5. Soils in Michigan tend to be alkaline, but some are more acidic. Ask your Michigan Cooperative Extension Agent about the local soils. The agent can make general recommendations or help you test your soil.

If a soil test reveals a pH problem, your soil can be made more acidic with the addition of horticultural sulfur, or it can be made more alkaline with the addition of horticultural lime. The test results should include recommendations for the proper rates of application when using amendments to adjust your soil pH.

Keep in mind that it is much easier to amend soil in a small area than in an entire garden. The soil in a raised bed or planter can be adjusted quite easily to suit a few plants whose soil requirements vary greatly from the conditions in your garden.

Particle size is one influence on the drainage and moisture-holding properties of soil; slope is another. Knowing how quickly the water drains out of your soil will help you decide whether you should plant moisture-loving or drought-tolerant plants. Rocky soil on a hillside will probably drain very quickly and should be reserved for those plants that prefer a very well-drained soil. Low-lying areas tend to retain water longer, and some areas may rarely drain at all. Moist areas suit plants that require a consistent water supply; constantly wet areas suit plants that are adapted to boggy conditions.

Drainage can be improved in very wet areas by adding sand, gravel or

EXPOSURE

Exposure is a very important consideration in all gardens that include woody plants. Wind, heat, cold, rain and snow are the elements to which your garden may be exposed, and some plants are more tolerant than others of the potential damage these forces can cause. Buildings, walls, fences, hills and existing hedges or other shrubs and trees can all influence your garden's exposure.

Wind can cause extensive damage to woody plants, particularly to evergreens in winter. Plants can become dehydrated in windy locations because they may not be able to draw water out of the soil fast enough to replace that lost through the leaves. Evergreens in areas where the ground freezes frequently face this problem because they are unable to draw any water out of the frozen ground. For this reason it is important to keep them well watered in fall until the ground freezes. Because the broad-leaved evergreens, such as rhododendron and holly, are most at risk from dehydration in winter, grow these plants in a sheltered site.

Strong winds can cause physical damage by breaking weak branches or by blowing over entire trees. However, woody plants often make excellent windbreaks that shelter other plants in the garden. Hedges and trees temper the effect of the wind without the turbulence created on the leeward side of a more solid structure, such as a wall or fence. Windbreak trees should be species that can flex in the wind or should be planted far enough from buildings to avoid extensive damage to homes or sheds should branches or trees fall.

Hedges are excellent windbreaks.

Blue holly does best in a sheltered location.

Hardiness zones (see map, p. 15, and Quick Reference Chart, p. 334) indicate whether species will tolerate conditions in your area, but they are only guidelines. Daphnes are generally listed as Zone 4 plants but often thrive in sheltered spots in Zone 3. Don't be afraid to try species that are not listed as hardy for your area. Plants are incredibly adaptable and just might surprise you.

Here are some tips for growing out-of-zone plants:

- Before planting, observe your garden on a frosty morning. Are there areas that escape frost? These are potential sites for tender plants.
- Shelter tender plants from the prevailing wind.
- Plant in groups to create windbreaks and microclimates. Rhododendrons, for instance, grow better if they are planted in small groups or grouped with plants that have similar growing requirements.
- Mulch young plants in fall with a thick layer of clean organic mulch, such as bark chips, composted woodchips, composted leaves or compost mixed with peat moss. You can also use special insulating blankets available at garden centers. Ensure that organic mulches have a minimum depth of 6–8" for good winter protection. Mulch over at least the first two winters.
- Water thoroughly before the ground freezes for the winter.
- In regions with plenty of snow, cover an entire frost-tender shrub with salt-free snow for the winter. You can also cover or wrap it with a layer of burlap or horticultural cloth. If the plant is being grown in a container or planter, place it under shelter or against a house for protection.

Katsura-tree (top), boxwood & Japanese maple (center) & daphne (bottom) can often be grown in areas outside their zone rating.

PURCHASING TREES & SHRUBS

Now that you have thought about the features you like and the range of growing conditions your garden offers, you can select the plants. Any reputable garden center should have a good selection of popular woody plants. Finding a more unusual specimen may require a few phone calls and a trip to a more specialized nursery. Mail-order nurseries are often a great source of the newest and most unusual plants.

Many garden centers and nurseries offer a one-year warranty on trees and shrubs, but because trees take a long time to mature it is always in your best interest to choose the healthiest plants. Never purchase weak, damaged or diseased plants, even if they cost less. Examine the bark and avoid plants with visible damage. Observe the leaf and flower buds. If they are dry and fall off easily, the plant has been deprived of moisture. The stem or stems should be strong, supple and unbroken. The rootball should be soft and moist when touched. Do not buy a plant with a dry rootball. The growth should be even and appropriate for the species. Shrubs should be bushy and branched right to the ground. Trees should have a strong leader. A healthy tree or shrub will have the best chance in your garden.

Woody plants are available for purchase in three forms.

Bare-root stock has roots surrounded by nothing except moist

Avoid purchasing root-bound plants.

Purchasing container stock in fall lets you see the fall color.

sawdust or peat moss within a plastic wrapping. The roots must be kept moist and cool, and planting should take place as soon as possible in spring. Avoid planting stock that appears to have dried out during shipping.

Balled-and-burlapped (B & B) stock comes with the roots surrounded by soil and wrapped in burlap, often secured with a wire cage for larger plants. The plants are usually field grown and then dug up, balled and burlapped the year they are sold. It is essential that the rootball remain moist. Large trees are available in this form; be aware that the soil and rootball are often very heavy and there may be an extra expense for delivery and planting.

Container plants are grown in pots filled with potting soil and have established root systems. This form is the most common at garden centers and nurseries. Container stock establishes very quickly after planting and can be planted almost any time during the growing season. It is also easy to transplant. When choosing a plant, make sure it hasn't been in the container too long. If the roots densely encircle the inside of the pot, then the plant has become root-bound. A root-bound tree or shrub will not establish well, and as the roots mature and thicken, they can choke and kill the plant. Note that sometimes field-grown stock is dug and sold in containers instead of burlap; ask if you aren't sure. Such plants must be treated like balled-and-burlapped stock when planting (see 'Planting Trees & Shrubs,' p. 32).

Winter storage technique for container plants

Bigger is not always better when it comes to choosing woody plants. Research and observation have shown that smaller stock of a given species often ends up healthier and more robust than larger stock, particularly in the case of field-grown (as opposed to container-grown) plants. When a plant is dug up out of the field, the roots are severely cut back. The smaller the plant, the more quickly it can recover from the shock of being uprooted.

Woody plants can be damaged by improper handling and transport. You can lift bare-root stock by the stem, but do not lift any other trees or shrubs by the trunk or branches. Rather, lift by the rootball or container, or if the plant is too large to lift, place it on a tarp or mat and drag it. Even a short trip home from the nursery can be traumatic for a plant.

If you are using a truck for transport, lay the plant down or cover it to shield it from the wind. Traveling down a freeway at 80 miles per hour in an open truck isn't good for any plant. Avoid mechanical damage such as rubbing or breaking branches during transport. Remember, too, that the heat produced inside a car can quickly dehydrate a plant.

Once home, water the plant if it is dry and keep it in a sheltered location until you plant it. Remove damaged growth and broken branches, but do no other pruning. Plant your tree or shrub as soon as possible. A bare-root tree or shrub should be planted in a large container of potting soil if it will not be planted outdoors immediately. If you must store container plants over a cold winter before planting, bury the entire container until spring.

PLANTING TREES & SHRUBS

Before you pick up a shovel and start digging, step back for a moment and make sure the site you are considering is appropriate. The most important thing to check is the location of any underground wires or pipes. Even if you don't damage anything by digging, the tree roots may in the future cause trouble, or if there is a problem with the pipes or wires you may have to cut down the tree in order to service them. Most utility companies will, at no charge, come to your house and locate any underground lines. Prevent injury and save time and money by locating utilities before you dig.

Check also the mature plant size. The plant you have in front of you is most likely pretty small. Once it reaches its mature height and spread, will it still fit the space you have chosen? Is it far enough away from the house, the driveway and the sidewalk? Will it hit the overhang of the house or any overhead power lines?

If you're planting several shrubs, make sure that they won't grow too close together once they are mature. The rule of thumb for spacing: add the mature spreads and then divide by two. For example, when planting a shrub with an expected spread of 4' next to another shrub with an expected spread of 6', you would plant them 5' apart. For hedges and windbreaks, the spacing should be one-half to two-thirds the spread of

Nicely planted and well-maintained shrub beds

the mature plant to ensure there is no observable space between plants when they are fully grown.

Finally, double-check the conditions. Will the soil drainage be adequate? Will the plant get the right amount of light? Is the site very windy? Remember, it's easier to start with the plant in the right spot and in the best conditions you can give it. Planning ahead saves time and money in the long run.

WHEN TO PLANT

For the most part, trees and shrubs can be planted at any time of year, though some seasons are better for the plants and more convenient than others. Spring is a great time to plant. It gives the tree or shrub an entire growing season to become established before winter sets in, and gets it started before the weather turns really hot. Many gardeners avoid planting during the hottest and driest period of summer, mainly because of the extra work that may be involved in terms of supplemental watering. However, even a spring-planted tree or shrub will require watering during hot, dry weather.

Bare-root stock must be planted in spring because it is generally available only at that time, and it must be planted as soon as possible to avoid moisture loss.

Balled-and-burlapped and container stock can be planted at any time, as long as you can get a shovel into the ground. They can even be planted in frozen ground if you had the foresight to dig the hole before the ground froze. Keep the backfill (the dirt from the hole) in a warm place so it won't be frozen when you need to use it.

Sizing up the hole

Digging the hole

Adding organic matter to backfill (below)

The time of day to plant is also a consideration. Avoid planting during the heat of the day. Planting in the morning, in the evening or on a cloudy, calm day will be easier on both you and the plant.

It's a good idea to plant as soon as possible after you bring your specimen home. If you have to store the tree or shrub for a short time before planting, keep it out of direct sunlight and ensure the rootball remains moist.

PREPARING THE HOLE

Trees and shrubs should always be planted at the depth at which they were growing, or just above the roots if you are unsure of the depth for bare-root stock. The depth in the center of the hole should be equal to the depth of the rootball or container, whereas the depth around the edges can be greater than this. Making the center higher will prevent the plant from sinking as the soil settles and will encourage excess water to drain away from the new plant.

Be sure that the plants are not set too deep. Planting even 2–4" too deep can cause problems. Most potted field-grown trees are planted deeply in the pot in order to help keep the freshly dug tree from tipping over, and there may be mulch on top of the soil as well. Planting such a tree to the same depth as the level in the pot may not be a good idea. Scrape off the soil until you find the root mass, and then plant to just above it.

Make the hole for bare-root stock big enough to completely contain the expanded roots with a bit of extra room on the sides. Make the hole for balled-and-burlapped and container stock about twice the width of the rootball or container.

The soil around the rootball or in the container is not likely to be the same as the soil you just removed from the hole. The extra size of the hole allows the new roots an easier medium (backfill) to grow into than undisturbed soil, providing a transition zone from the rootball soil to the existing on-site soil. It is good practice to rough up the sides and bottom of the hole to aid in root transition.

A couple of handfuls of organic matter can be mixed into the backfill. This small amount will encourage the plant to become established, but too much creates a pocket of rich soil that the roots may be reluctant to move beyond. If the roots do not venture beyond the immediate area of the hole, the tree or shrub will be weaker and much more susceptible to problems, and the encircling roots could eventually choke the plant.

Such a tree will also be more vulnerable to blowdown in a strong wind.

PLANTING BARE-ROOT STOCK

Remove the plastic and sawdust from the roots. Fan out the roots and center the plant over the central mound in the hole. The mound for bare-root stock is often made cone-shaped and larger than the mound for other types of plants. Use the cone to help spread out and support the roots. Make sure the hole is big enough so the roots can fully extend.

PLANTING BALLED & BURLAPPED STOCK

Burlap was originally made out of natural fibers. It could be left wrapped around the rootball and would eventually decompose. Modern burlap may or may not be made of natural fibers, and it can be very difficult to tell the difference. Synthetic fibers will not decompose and will eventually choke the roots. To be sure your new plant has a healthy

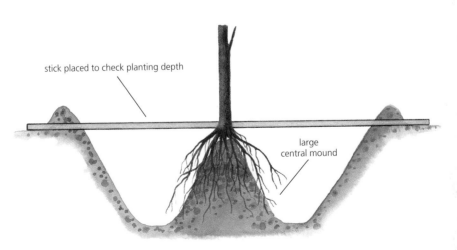

stick placed to check planting depth

large central mound

Planting bare-root stock

future, it is always best to remove the burlap from around the rootball. If roots are already growing through the burlap, remove as much as you can while avoiding damage to these new roots.

If there is a wire basket holding the burlap in place, it should be removed as well. Strong wire cutters may be needed to get the basket off. If the tree is very heavy, it may not be possible to remove the base of the basket, but cut away at least the sides, where most of the important roots will be growing.

With the basket removed, sit the still-burlapped plant on the center mound in the hole. Lean the plant over to one side and roll the burlap down to the ground. When you lean the plant in the opposite direction, you should be able to pull the burlap out from under the roots. As with the basket on a heavy tree, just remove as much burlap as you can if the tree is difficult to move once in the hole. If you know the burlap is natural and decide to leave it in place, be sure to cut it back so that none shows above ground level. Exposed burlap can wick moisture out of the soil, robbing your new and vulnerable plant of essential water.

Past horticultural wisdom suggested removing some top branches when planting to make up for the roots lost when the plant was dug out of the field. The theory was that the roots could not provide enough water to the leaves, so top growth should be removed to achieve 'balance.' We now know that the top growth—where photosynthesis occurs and thus where energy is produced—

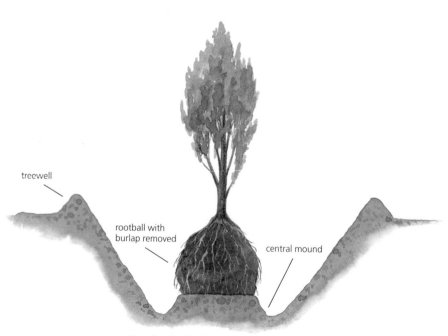

treewell

rootball with
burlap removed

central mound

Planting balled-and-burlapped stock

is necessary for root development. The new tree or shrub might drop some leaves, but don't be alarmed; the plant is doing its own balancing. A very light pruning will not adversely affect the plant, but remove only those branches that have been damaged during transportation and planting. Leave your new plant to settle in for a year or two before you start any formative pruning.

PLANTING CONTAINER STOCK

Containers are usually made of plastic or pressed fiber. All should be removed before planting. Although some containers appear to be made of peat moss, they do not decompose well. The roots may have difficulty penetrating the pot sides, and the fiber will wick moisture away from the roots.

Container stock is very easy to plant (see photos, p. 38). Gently remove or cut off the container and observe the root mass to see if the plant is rootbound. If roots are circling around the inside of the container, they should be loosened or sliced. Any large roots encircling the soil or growing into the center of the root mass instead of outward should be removed before planting. A sharp pair of hand pruners (secateurs) or a pocketknife will work well for this task.

BACKFILLING

With the plant in the hole and standing straight up, it is time to replace the soil. If you have amended the soil, ensure it is well mixed before putting it into the hole. Backfill should reach the same depth the plant was grown at previously, or just above the rootball. If planting into a heavy soil, raise the plant about 1" to help improve surface drainage away from the crown and roots. Graft unions of grafted stock are generally kept above ground to make it easy to spot and remove suckers sprouting from the rootstock.

When backfilling, it is important to have good root-to-soil contact for initial stability and good establishment. Large air pockets remaining after backfilling could result in unwanted settling and excessive root drying. Use water to settle the soil gently around the roots and in the hole, being careful not to drown the plant. It is a good idea to backfill in small amounts rather than all at once. Add some soil, then water it down, repeating until the hole is full. Stockpile any remaining soil after backfilling and use it to top up the soil around the plant as the backfill settles.

If you are working with a heavy clay soil, ensure that the surface drainage slopes away from your new transplant. If your soil is sandy or well drained, build a 2–4" high, doughnut-like mound of soil around the perimeter of the hole to capture extra water. This ring of soil, sometimes called a **treewell,** is an excellent tool for conserving water, especially during dry spells. Once the tree or shrub has become established, after a year or two, the treewell will no longer be needed and should be permanently removed.

To conserve water, mulch around the new planting. Composted wood chips or shredded bark will stay where you put them, unlike pebble bark or peat moss. Two to four inches of mulch is adequate. Do not use too

1. Gently remove container.

2. Ensure proper planting depth.

3. Backfill with amended soil.

4. Settle backfilled soil with water.

5. Ensure newly planted shrub is well watered.

6. Add mulch.

much, and avoid mulching directly against the trunk or base of the plant; otherwise, you may encourage disease problems.

STAKING

Some trees may need to be staked in order to provide support while the roots establish. Staking is recommended only for bare-root trees, for tall, top-heavy trees over 5' tall and for trees planted in windy locations, particularly evergreens because they tend to catch winter winds. Stakes should be removed as soon as the roots have had a chance to become established, which normally takes about a year.

Growing trees and shrubs without stakes is preferred because unstaked trees will develop more roots and stronger trunks. Most newly planted trees are able to stand on their own without staking.

There are two common methods for staking newly planted trees. For both methods you can use either wood or metal stakes.

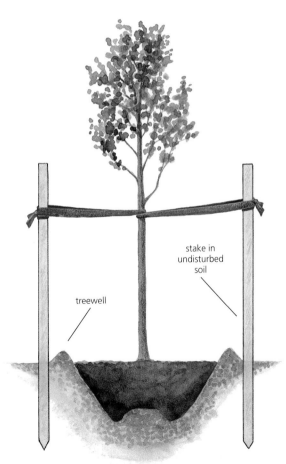

stake in
undisturbed
soil

treewell

Two-stake method

The **two-stake** method is suitable for small trees (about 5–6' tall) and also for trees in low-wind areas. Drive stakes into the undisturbed soil just outside the planting hole on opposite sides of the tree, 180° apart. Driving stakes in right beside your newly planted tree can damage the roots and will not provide adequate support. Tie string, rope, cable or wire to the stakes. The end that goes around the trunk should be a wide, belt-like strapping material that will not injure the trunk. Your local garden center should have ties designed for this purpose. Attach the strap to the tree at a height of about 3–4' above the ground.

The **three-stake** method is used for larger trees and for trees in areas subject to strong or shifting winds. The technique is much the same as the two-stake method, but with three stakes evenly spaced around the tree.

Here are a few points to keep in mind, regardless of which staking method is used:

- Never wrap a rope, wire or cable directly around a tree trunk. Always use non-damaging material. Ensure you re-adjust the strapping every two to three months to prevent any rubbing or girdling injury.
- Never tie trees so firmly that they can't move. Young trees need to be able to move in the wind to produce strong trunks and to develop roots more thickly in appropriate places to compensate for the prevailing wind.
- Don't leave the stakes in place too long. One year is sufficient for almost all trees. The stake should be there only long enough to allow the roots some time to grow and establish. The tree will actually be weaker if the stake is left for too long, and over time the ties can damage the trunk and weaken or kill the tree.

TRANSPLANTING

If you plan your garden carefully, you should only rarely need to move trees or shrubs. Some woody plants (indicated as such in the individual species entries) resent being moved once established, and you should avoid transplanting these species whenever possible. For all species, the younger the tree or shrub, the more likely it is to re-establish successfully when moved to a new location.

As a general rule, you can transplant evergreens in spring before growth starts or later in the season after it stops, as long as it is not during spells of hot weather. Deciduous plants should be transplanted only while dormant, or in other words when the branches are bare of leaves in spring, fall or early winter.

When woody plants are transplanted, they inevitably lose most of their root mass. Care should be taken to dig a rootball of an appropriate size. The size of the tree or shrub will determine the minimum size of the rootball that must be dug out in order for the plant to survive. As a general guideline, for every 1" of main stem width, which is measured 6–12" above the ground, you need to excavate a rootball at least 12" wide, and preferably larger.

Rootballs are heavy, and a 24" rootball is probably the most the average gardener can manage without heavy equipment. Trees with trunks more than 2" wide should be moved by professionals. Shrubs cannot always be measured as easily as trees, so you will need to use your best judgment. Because shrubs mature fairly quickly, it may be easier to start with a new one rather than try to move a very large specimen.

If it is necessary and feasible to transplant a shrub or small tree, follow the steps on the next page.

treewell

Three-stake method

Magnolia (above) and redbud (below) dislike being transplanted.

1) Calculate the width of the root-ball to be removed, as described on p. 40.

2) Water the proposed rootball area to a depth of 12" and allow excess water to drain away. The moist soil will help hold the rootball together.

3) Wrap or tie the branches together to minimize branch damage and to ease transport from the old site to the new one.

4) Slice a long spade or shovel into the soil vertically, cutting a circle around the plant as wide as the calculated rootball width. Cut down to about 12". This depth should contain most of the roots for the size of tree or shrub that can be transplanted manually.

5) At this point, most small, densely rooted trees and shrubs can be carefully removed from the hole by leaning on the spade or shovel and prying the plant up and out. If you encounter resistance, you may have missed some roots and should repeat step 4. Once the plant has been freed, place it on a tarp and continue with step 10. Larger trees and shrubs will require additional steps; continue with step 6.

6) Cut another circle one shovel-width outside the first circle, to the same depth.

7) Excavate the soil between the two cut circles.

8) When the appropriate rootball depth is reached, carefully cut horizontally under the rootball. When you encounter a root, cut it with a sharp pair of hand pruners. The goal is to sculpt out a rootball that is standing on a pedestal of undisturbed earth.

9) Spread a tarp in one side of the hole. Gently remove the pedestal and lean the rootball over onto the tarp. Carefully cut any remaining roots in the pedestal. Lift the tree and rootball out of the hole with the tarp, not by the stem or branches.

10) Lift or drag the tarp to the new location and plant immediately. See planting instructions given in preceding sections for information on when to plant, how to plant, staking, etc. Transplanted trees and shrubs can be treated as balled-and-burlapped stock.

CARING FOR TREES & SHRUBS

The care you give your new tree or shrub in the first year or two after planting is the most important. During this period of establishment, it is critical to keep the plant well watered, to remove competing weeds and to avoid all mechanical damage. Be careful with lawn mowers and string trimmers, which can quickly girdle the base of the plant. Whatever you do to the top of the plant affects the roots, and vice versa.

Once woody plants have established, they generally require minimal care. A few basic maintenance tasks, performed regularly, will save time and trouble in the long run.

WEEDING

Weeds can rob young plants of water, light and nutrients, so keep weeds under control to encourage optimum growth of your garden plants. Avoid deep hoeing under woody plants because it may damage shallow-rooted shrubs and trees. A layer of mulch is a good way to suppress weeds. If you must use commercial weed killers, consult your local nursery or extension agent for advice and follow the label directions carefully.

MULCHING

Mulch is an important gardening tool. It helps soil retain moisture, it buffers soil temperatures and it prevents soil erosion during heavy rain or strong winds. Mulch prevents weed seeds from germinating by blocking out the light, and it can deter pests and help prevent diseases.

Keep mulch from the base of your tree or shrub.

It keeps lawn mowers and line trimmers away from plants, reducing the chance of damage. Mulch can also add aesthetic value to a planting.

Organic mulches can consist of compost, composted wood chips, bark chips, shredded bark, composted leaves and grass clippings. These mulches are desirable because they add nutrients to the soil as they break down. Because they break down, however, they must be replenished on a regular basis.

Inorganic mulches, such as stones, crushed brick or gravel, do not break down and so do not have to be replenished. These types of mulches don't provide nutrients and they can also adversely increase soil temperatures. Some books recommend using black plastic or ground cloth under the mulch. These products should be avoided with organic mulches, but ground cloth can be used under stone and rock mulches to keep them from sinking into the soil.

For good weed suppression, the mulch layer should be 2–4" thick. Avoid piling mulch up around the trunk or stems at the base of the plant because doing so can encourage fungal decay and rot. Try to maintain a mulch-free zone immediately around the trunk or stem bases.

WATERING

The weather, type of plant, type of soil and time of year all influence the amount of water your shrubs and trees will need. If your area is naturally dry or if there has been a stretch of hot, dry weather, you will need to water more often than if you live in a naturally wet area or if your area has received a lot of rain recently. Pay attention to the wind; it can dry out soil and plants quickly. Different plants require different amounts of water. Some, such as willows and some birches, will grow in a temporarily waterlogged soil; others, such as pines, prefer a dry, sandy soil. Heavy, clay soils retain water longer than light, sandy soils. Plants need more water when they are on slopes, when they are flowering and when they are producing fruit.

Plants are good at letting us know when they are thirsty. Wilted, flagging leaves and twigs are a sign of water deprivation, but excessive amounts of water can also cause a plant to wilt. It is best to test for soil moisture by checking at least 1" down with your fingers or with a soil probe. If you feel moisture, you don't need to water.

Make sure your trees and shrubs are well watered in fall, especially before the ground freezes. You should continue to water as needed until the ground does freeze. Fall watering is very important for evergreen plants because once the ground has frozen, the roots can no longer draw moisture from it, leaving the foliage susceptible to desiccation.

Once trees and shrubs are established, they will likely need watering only during periods of excessive drought. To keep water use to a minimum, avoid watering in the heat of the day because much will be lost to evaporation. Work organic matter into the soil to help the soil absorb and retain water, and apply mulch to help prevent water loss. Collect and use rainwater whenever possible.

FERTILIZING

Most garden soils provide all the nutrients plants need, particularly if you use an organic mulch and mix compost into the soil before planting your garden. Simply allowing leaf litter to remain on the ground after the leaves fall in autumn also promotes natural nutrient cycling of nitrogen and other elements in the soil.

Not all plants have the same nutritional requirements, however. Some plants are heavy feeders, while others thrive in poor soils. Pay attention to the leaf color of your plants, and they will tell you if they are lacking in essential nutrients. Yellowing leaves, for example, may be a sign of a nitrogen deficiency.

When you do fertilize, use only the recommended quantity because too much can be very harmful. Roots are easily burned by fertilizer applied in too high a concentration. Chemical fertilizers are more concentrated and therefore have the potential to cause more problems than organic fertilizers.

Granular fertilizers consist of small, dry particles that can be spread with a fertilizer spreader or by hand. Consider using a slow-release type of granular fertilizer. It may cost a bit more but will save you time and reduce the risk of burn. It will also prevent overapplication because the nutrients are released gradually over the growing season. One application per year is normally sufficient; applying the fertilizer in early spring provides nutrients for spring growth. In garden beds you can mix the fertilizer into the soil.

Tree spikes are slow-release fertilizers that are quick and easy to use. Pound the spikes into the ground around the dripline of the tree or shrub (see diagram, p. 46). These spikes work very well for fertilizing trees in lawns, because the grass tends to consume most of the nutrients released from surface applications.

If fertilizer is not applied correctly or not needed, your plant will not benefit. In fact, it will make a tree or shrub more susceptible to some pests and diseases and can accelerate a plant's decline. Fertilizing should be done to correct a visible nutrient deficiency, to correct a deficiency identified by a soil and tissue test, to increase vegetative, flower or fruit growth or to increase the vigor of a plant that is flagging.

Do not fertilize trees or shrubs
- when there are sufficient nutrients in the soil as determined by a soil and tissue test
- if your plants are growing and appear healthy
- if your plants are sufficiently large and you want to reduce pruning and shearing
- during times of drought, as roots will not absorb nutrients during drought.

If you do not wish to encourage fast growth, do not fertilize. Remember that most trees and shrubs do not need fertilizer and that fast growth may make plants more susceptible to problems. In particular, fall fertilizing with chemical fertilizers is not recommended because they can encourage new growth late in the season. This growth is easily damaged in winter. Organic fertilizers can be applied in fall because they are activated by soil organisms that are not as active in cool weather.

Unnecessary or excessive fertilizer can pollute your local lakes, streams and groundwater. Many homes in Michigan obtain their drinking water from wells, which can be contaminated by fertilizers. Use fertilizers wisely, and we all benefit. Misuse them, and we all pay the price.

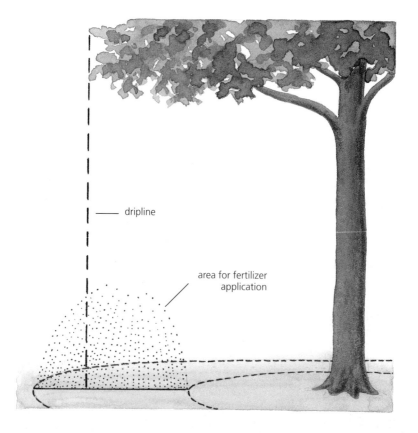

dripline

area for fertilizer application

PRUNING

Pruning helps maintain the health and attractive shape of a woody plant. It also increases the quality and yield of fruit, controls and directs growth, and creates interesting plant forms and shapes, such as espalier, topiary and bonsai. Pruning is quite possibly the most important maintenance task when growing trees and shrubs—and the easiest to mess up. Fortunately for new gardeners, it is not difficult to learn and can even be enjoyable if done correctly from the beginning and continued on a regular basis.

Proper pruning combines knowledge and skill. General knowledge about how woody plants grow and specific knowledge about the growth habits of your particular plant will help you avoid pruning mistakes that can ruin a plant's shape or make it susceptible to disease and insect damage.

If you are unsure about pruning, take a pruning course or hire a professional, such as an arborist certified by the International Society of Arboriculture (ISA)(see 'Resources,' p. 342). Pruning courses may be offered by a local garden center, botanical garden, community college or master gardener program. Excellent books are also available on the subject. Certified professionals understand the plants and have all the specialty pruning equipment to do a proper job. They might even be willing to show you some pruning basics. You should **always** call a professional to prune a tree growing near a power line or other hazardous area, or to

prune a large branch that could fall and damage a building, fence, car or pedestrian.

Genetically programmed to grow to a certain size, plants will always try their best to reach that potential. If you find yourself doing a lot of pruning to keep a tree or shrub in check, the plant may be too large for that site. We cannot emphasize enough how important it is to consider the mature size of a plant before you put it into the ground.

WHEN & HOW MUCH TO PRUNE

Aside from removing damaged growth, do not prune for the first year after planting a tree or shrub. After that time, the first pruning should develop the plant's structure. For a strong framework, leave all branches that have a wide angle at the crotch (where the branch meets the trunk or another branch), as these branches are the strongest. Prune out branches with narrower crotches, while ensuring an even distribution of the main (scaffold) branches. These branches will support all future top growth.

Trees and shrubs vary greatly in their pruning needs. Some plants, such as boxwood, can tolerate or even thrive on heavy pruning and shearing, while other plants, such as flowering cherry, may be killed if given the same treatment.

The amount of pruning will also depend on your reasons for doing it. Much less work is involved in simply tidying the growth, for example, than in creating elaborate bonsai specimens. Inspect your trees and shrubs annually to see if there are any dead, damaged, diseased or awkwardly growing branches and to determine what pruning, if any, is necessary.

Professional tree service

Many gardeners are unsure about what time of year they should prune. Knowing when a plant flowers is the easiest way to know when to prune. See p. 53 for information on pruning conifers.

Trees and shrubs that flower before about July, such as rhododendron and forsythia, should be pruned after they are finished flowering. These plants form flower buds for the following year over summer and fall. Pruning just after the current year's flowers fade allows plenty of time for the next year's flowers to develop and avoids taking away any of the current year's blooms.

Trees and shrubs that flower in about July or later, such as Pee Gee hydrangea and rose-of-Sharon, can be pruned early in the year. These plants form flower buds on new growth as the season progresses, and pruning in spring just before or as the new growth begins to develop will encourage the best growth and flowering.

Some plants, such as maple, have a heavy flow of sap in spring. As long as proper pruning cuts are made, these trees can still be pruned in spring. If the excessive bleeding is aesthetically unappealing or is dripping on something inappropriately, wait until these species are in full leaf before pruning.

Take care when pruning any trees in early spring, when many canker-causing organisms are active, or in fall, when many wood-rotting fungi release their spores. These are times when the weather is cool and plants are fairly inactive, making it difficult for them to fight off invasion.

Always remove dead, diseased and damaged branches as soon as you discover them, at any time of year.

Proper hand pruner orientation

THE KINDEST CUT

Trees and shrubs have a remarkable ability to heal themselves, but it is critical to make proper pruning cuts. A proper pruning cut, while still a wound, minimizes the area where insect and disease attack can occur and takes advantage of the areas on a plant where it can best deal with wounds. The tree or shrub can then heal as quickly as possible, preventing disease and insect damage.

Using the right tools makes pruning easier and more effective. The size of the branch being cut determines the type of tool to use.

Hand pruners, or secateurs, should be used for cutting branches up to $3/4$" in diameter. Using hand pruners for larger stems increases the risk of damage, and it can be physically strenuous.

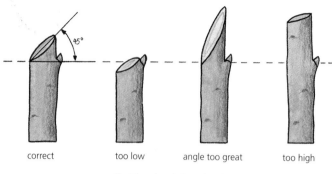

correct   too low   angle too great   too high

Cutting back to a bud

Loppers are long-handled pruners used for branches up to $1^1/_2$" in diameter. Loppers are good for removing old stems. Hand pruners and loppers must be properly oriented when making a cut (see photo, p. 49). The blade should be to the plant side of the cut and the hook to the side being removed. If the cut is made with the hook toward the plant, the cut will be ragged and slow to heal.

Pruning saws have teeth specially designed to cut through green wood. They can be used to cut branches up to 6" in diameter and sometimes larger. Pruning saws are easier to use and much safer than chainsaws.

Hedge clippers, or shears, are intended for shearing and shaping hedges.

Make sure your tools are sharp and clean before you begin any pruning task. If the branch you are cutting is diseased, you will need to sterilize the tool before using it again. A solution of 1 part bleach to 10 parts water is effective for cleaning and sterilizing.

TYPES OF PRUNING CUTS

You should be familiar with the following types of pruning cuts.

Cutting back to a bud is used for shortening a branch, redirecting growth or maintaining the size of a tree or shrub. The cut should be made slightly less than $^1/_4$" above a bud. If the cut is too far away from or too close to the bud, the wound will not heal properly. Cut back to buds that are pointing in the direction you want the new growth to grow in.

Cutting to a lateral branch is used to shorten limbs and redirect growth. The diameter of the branch to which you are cutting back must be at least one-third of the diameter of the branch you are cutting. As with cutting back to a bud, cut slightly less than $^1/_4$" above the lateral branch and line up the cut with the angle of the branch. Make cuts at an angle whenever possible so that rain won't sit on the open wound.

Removing limbs can be a complicated operation for large branches. Owing to the large size of the wound,

Ensure the bud beneath each cut is pointing in the direction you want the branch to grow.

Cutting back to a bud   Cutting to a lateral branch

it is critical to cut in the correct place—at the branch collar—to ensure quick healing. The cut must be done in steps to avoid damaging the bark. The first cut is on the bottom of the branch a short distance from the trunk of the tree. This cut should be 12–18" up from the crotch and should extend one-third of the way through the branch. The purpose of the first cut is to prevent bark from peeling down the tree when the second cut causes the main part of the branch to fall. The second cut is made a bit farther along the branch from the first cut and is made from the top of the branch. This cut removes the majority of the branch.

The final cut should be made just above the branch collar. The plant tissues at the branch collar quickly create a barrier against insects and diseases. Do not make flush cuts and do not leave stubs; both may take longer for the tree to heal.

The use of pruning paint or paste has been much debated. The current consensus is that these substances do more harm than good. Trees and shrubs have a natural ability to create a barrier between living wood and dead and decaying sections. An unpainted cut will eventually heal over, but a cut that has been treated with paint or paste may never heal properly.

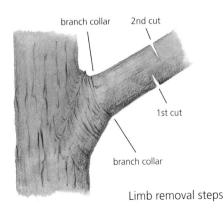

branch collar   2nd cut

1st cut

branch collar

3rd cut at branch collar

Limb removal steps

To prune or cut down large trees, it is best to hire a certified arborist. These professionals are trained for the task and have all the necessary equipment. Many fences, cars and even houses have been damaged by people who simply didn't have the equipment or the know-how for removing a large branch or tree.

Shearing is used to trim and shape hedges. Only plants that can handle heavy pruning should be sheared because some of the normal pruning rules (such as being careful where you cut in relation to buds) are disregarded here.

Informal hedges take advantage of the natural shape of the plant and require only minimal trimming. These hedges generally take up more room than formal hedges, which are trimmed more severely to assume a neat, even appearance. Formal hedges are generally sheared a minimum of twice per growing season. Make sure all sides of the hedge are trimmed to encourage even growth. The base of your hedge should always be wider than the top to allow light to reach the entire hedge and to prevent it from thinning out at the base. Remember that a hedge will gradually increase in size despite shearing, so allow room for this expansion when planting your hedge.

Thinning is a rejuvenation process that maintains the shape, health and productivity of shrubs. It opens up space for air and light to penetrate and provides room for younger, healthier branches and selected suckers to grow. Thinning often combines the first two cuts discussed above, and it is the most frequently performed pruning practice. Plants that produce new growth from ground level (suckers) can be pruned this way.

A shrub that is thinned annually should have one-quarter to one-third of the growth removed. Cutting the oldest stems encourages new growth without causing excess stress from loss of top growth. Although some plants can be cut back completely to the ground and seem to suffer no ill effects, it is generally better to remove only up to one-third of the growth.

incorrect

correct

Hedge shape

Follow these steps to thin most multi-stemmed shrubs:

1) Remove all the dead, diseased, damaged, rubbing and crossing branches to branch junctions, buds or ground level.
2) Remove about one-third of the growth each year, leaving a mix of old and new growth, and cutting unwanted stems at or close to the base. Do not cut stems below ground level because many disease organisms are present in soil.
3) Thin the top of the shrub to allow air and light penetration and to balance the shape. This step is not always necessary because removing one-third of the stems generally thins out the top as well.
4) Repeat the process each year on established, mature shrubs. Regular pruning of shrubs will keep them healthy and productive for many years.

Thinning cuts

Mugo pine candles

PRUNING CONIFERS

Coniferous trees and shrubs, such as spruce, pine and juniper, require little or no pruning other than to fix damage or correct wayward growth. Prune conifers in mid- to late spring after the danger of frost has passed, and once the new growth, called candles, has fully extended.

Growth can be shaped and directed when it is in this candle stage. To encourage upright growth, remove all candles but the longest one. For bushy, dense growth, pinch all candles by half. Pinching should be done by hand and not with shears or hand pruners.

When removing a coniferous branch, cut it back to the branch collar at the trunk. Take a good look at a few branches before you start cutting because the collar can be difficult to find on a coniferous plant. There is no point in cutting a branch back part way because most coniferous species, including pine, spruce and fir, will not regenerate from old wood. Make sure you really need to remove a branch before you do so to avoid disfiguring the plant. Here is another reason to think about mature size before you plant any tree or shrub.

Juniper can regenerate from old wood, but it takes a long time and may result in an oddly shaped plant. Juniper and arborvitae can be lightly sheared for hedging. It is best to begin training hedge plants when they are very young.

If the central leader on a conifer is broken or damaged, it is important to cleanly remove it and to train a new leader in its place. In doing so you reduce the chance of infection and prevent many opportunistic leaders from attempting to form. Gently place a straight stake next to the main trunk. Do not insert the stake into the ground. Tie the stake to the main trunk. Bend the new leader as upright as possible and tie it to the stake. Remove the stake when the new leader is growing strongly upright. Remove any other leaders that attempt to form.

Topping disfigures and stresses trees.

TREE TOPPING

One pruning practice that should never be used is tree topping. Topping is done in an attempt to control height or size, to prevent trees from growing into overhead power lines, to allow more light onto a property or to prevent a tall tree from potentially toppling onto a building.

Topped trees are ugly and weak and can be hazardous. A tree may be killed by the stress of losing so much of its live growth, or by the gaping, slow-to-heal wounds that are vulnerable to attack by insects and wood-rotting fungi. The heartwood of a topped tree rots out quickly, resulting in a weak trunk. The crotches on new growth also tend to be weak. Topped trees, therefore, are susceptible to storm damage and blowdown. Hazards aside, topping trees spoils the aesthetic value of the tree and of its surrounding landscape.

It is much better to completely remove a tree, and start again with one that will grow to a more appropriate size, than to attempt to reduce the size of a large, mature specimen.

English ivy on wire frame topiary

SPECIALTY PRUNING

Custom pruning methods are used to create interesting plant shapes.

Topiary is the shaping of plants into animal, abstract or geometric forms. True topiary uses hedge plants sheared into the desired shape. Species that can handle heavy pruning, such as boxwood, are chosen.

A much simpler form of topiary involves growing vines or other trailing plants over a wire frame to achieve the desired form. Small-leaved ivy and other flexible, climbing or trailing plants work well for this kind of topiary.

Espalier involves training a tree or shrub to grow in two dimensions instead of three, with the aid of a solid wire or other framework. The plant is commonly trained against a wall or fence, but it can also be free-standing. This method is popularly applied to fruit trees, such as apples, when space is at a premium. Many gardeners consider the forms attractive and unusual, and you may wish to try your hand at espalier even if you have lots of space.

Bonsai is the art of developing miniature versions of large trees and landscapes. A gardener prunes the top growth and roots and uses wire to train the plant to the desired form. The severe pruning creates a dwarfed form of the species. There are many books available on this subject and courses may be offered at colleges or by horticultural or bonsai societies.

Boxwood true topiary

Apple espalier

Pine bonsai (below)

PROPAGATING TREES & SHRUBS

Many gardeners enjoy the art and science of starting new plants. Although some gardeners are willing to try growing annuals from seeds and perennials from seeds, cuttings or divisions, they may be unsure how to go about propagating their own trees and shrubs. Yet many woody plants can be propagated with ease, allowing the gardener to buy a single specimen and then clone it, rather than buying additional plants.

Do-it-yourself propagating does more than cut costs. It can become an enjoyable part of gardening and an interesting hobby in itself. As well, it allows gardeners to add to their landscapes species that may be hard to find at nurseries.

A number of methods can be used to propagate trees and shrubs. Many species can be started from seed; this can be a long, slow process, but some gardeners enjoy the variable and sometimes unusual results. Simpler techniques include cuttings, ground layering and mound layering.

CUTTINGS

Cut segments of stems can be encouraged to develop their own roots and form new plants. Taking cuttings is a more difficult method for starting your own plants than layering, but the basic principles are useful to know nonetheless.

Cuttings are treated differently depending on the maturity of the growth. Those taken in spring or early summer from new growth are called **greenwood** or **softwood** cuttings. These can actually be the most difficult cuttings to start because they require warm, humid conditions that are as likely to cause the cuttings to rot as to root.

Cuttings taken in fall from mature, woody growth are called **hardwood** or **ripe** cuttings. In order to take root, these cuttings require a coarse, gritty, moist soil mix and cold, but not freezing, temperatures. They may take all winter to root. These special conditions make it difficult to start hardwood cuttings unless you have a cold frame, heated greenhouse or propagator.

The easiest cuttings to start are those taken in late summer or early fall from new, but mature, growth that has not yet become completely woody. These are called **semi-ripe, semi-mature** or **semi-hardwood** cuttings.

Follow these basic steps to take and plant semi-ripe cuttings:

1) Take cuttings about 2–4" long from the tip of a stem, cutting just below a leaf node (the node is the place where the leaf meets the stem). There should be at least two nodes on the cutting. The tip of each cutting will be soft, but the base will be starting to harden.

2) Remove the leaves from the lower half of the cutting. Moisten the stripped end and dust it lightly with rooting hormone powder. Consult your local garden center to find an appropriate rooting hormone for your cutting.

3) Plant cuttings directly in the garden, in a cold frame or in pots. The soil mix should be well drained but moist. Firm the cuttings into the soil to ensure there are no air spaces that will dry out roots as they emerge.

4) Keep the cuttings out of direct sunlight and keep the soil moist.

Plants should root by the time winter begins. Make sure roots are well established before transplanting. Protect the new plants from extreme cold for the first winter. Plants in pots should be kept in a cold but frost-free location.

Butterfly bush

Nootka false cypress

PLANTS FOR SEMI-RIPE CUTTINGS

Beautyberry
Butterfly bush
Caryopteris
Deutzia
Euonymus
Forsythia
Hydrangea
Kerria
Ninebark
Potentilla
Willow

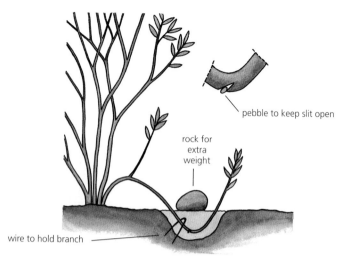

pebble to keep slit open

rock for
extra
weight

wire to hold branch

Ground layering

GROUND LAYERING

Layering, and particularly ground layering, is the easiest propagation method and the one most likely to produce successful results. Layering allows future cuttings to form their own roots before being detached from the parent plant. In ground layering, a section of a flexible branch is buried until it produces roots. The method is quite simple.

1) Choose a branch or shoot growing low enough on the plant to reach the ground. Remove the leaves from the section that will be underground. At least four nodes should be buried, and at least another four should protrude above ground.

2) Twist this section of the branch or make a small cut on the underside near a leaf node. This damage will stimulate root growth. A toothpick or small pebble can be used to hold the cut open.

3) Bend the branch down to see where it will touch the ground, and dig a shallow trench about 4" deep in this position. The end of the trench nearest the shrub can slope gradually upwards, but the end where the branch tip will be should be vertical to force the tip upwards.

4) Use a peg or bent wire to hold the branch in place. Fill the soil back into the trench, and water well. A rock or brick on top of the soil will help keep the branch in place.

5) Keep the soil moist but not soggy. Roots may take a year or more to develop. Once roots are well established, the new plant can be severed from the parent and planted in a permanent location.

The best shrubs for layering have low, flexible branches. Spring and fall are the best times to start the layer, and many species respond better in one season or the other. Some, such as rhododendron, respond equally well in spring and fall.

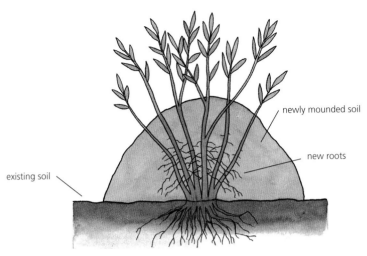

existing soil

newly mounded soil

new roots

Mound layering

MOUND LAYERING

Mound layering is a simple way to propagate low, shrubby plants. With this technique, the shrub is partially buried in a mound of well-drained soil mix. The buried stems will then sprout roots along their lengths. This method can provide quite a few new plants with little effort.

Mound layering should be initiated in spring, once the new shoots begin to grow. Make a mound from a mixture of sand, peat moss and soil over half or more of the plant. Leave the branch tips exposed. More soil can be mounded up over the course of the summer. Keep the mound moist but not soggy.

At the end of the summer, gently wash the mound away and detach the rooted branches. You can plant them directly where you want them or in a protected, temporary spot if you want to shelter them for the first winter.

PLANTS TO LAYER IN SPRING

Daphne
Dogwood
Lilac
Magnolia
Smokebush
Virginia creeper
Witchhazel

PLANTS TO LAYER IN FALL

Arborvitae
Euonymus
Fothergilla
Hazel
Kalmia
Pieris
Viburnum

PLANTS TO MOUND LAYER

Cotoneaster
Dogwood
Euonymus
Forsythia
Heather
Lilac
Potentilla

PROBLEMS & PESTS

Tree and shrub plantings can be both assets and liabilities when it comes to pests and diseases. Many insects and diseases attack only one plant species. Mixed plantings can make it difficult for pests and diseases to find their preferred hosts and establish a population. At the same time, because woody plants are in the same spot for many years, the problems can become permanent. The advantage is that beneficial birds, insects and other pest-devouring organisms can also develop permanent populations.

For many years pest control meant spraying or dusting, with the goal to eliminate every pest in the landscape. A more moderate approach advocated by many authorities today is known as IPM (Integrated Pest Management or Integrated Plant Management). The goal of IPM is to reduce pest problems to levels at which only negligible damage is done. Of course, you, the gardener, must determine what degree of damage is acceptable to you. Consider whether a pest's damage is localized or covers the entire plant. Will the damage being done kill the plant or is it affecting only the outward appearance? Are there methods of controlling the pest without chemicals?

IPM is an interactive system in which observation and identification are the primary tools. Observing your plants on a regular basis will give you the chance to uncover problems when they are just beginning. Seeing an insect does not mean you have a problem. Most insects do no harm at all, and many are beneficial to your garden as pollinators or predators. Beyond a few well-known garden pests you may already be familiar with, it is best to wait until you have identified an insect as harmful before attempting to control it. You may even find that the insect you are concerned about is actually eating the ones you really don't want. Catching problems early makes them easier to control with minimal effort.

Chemicals should always be the last resort. They can endanger gardeners and their families and pets, and they kill as many good organisms as bad ones, leaving the whole garden vulnerable to even worse attacks.

A good IPM program includes learning about the following aspects of your plants: the conditions they need for healthy growth; what pests might affect your particular plants; where and when to look for those pests; and how and when to best control them. Keep records of pest damage because your observations can reveal patterns useful in spotting recurring problems and in planning your maintenance regime.

There are four steps in effective and responsible pest management. Cultural controls are the most important. Physical controls should be attempted next, followed by biological controls. Resort to chemical controls only when the first three possibilities have been exhausted.

Cultural controls are the gardening techniques you use in the day-to-day care of your garden. Perhaps the best defense against pests and diseases is to grow your woody plants in the conditions for which they are adapted. It is also very important to keep your soil healthy, with plenty of organic matter.

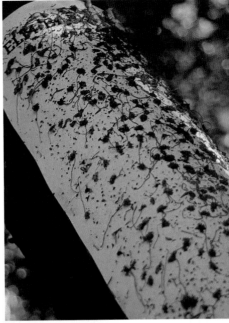

Sticky trap

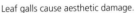

Leaf galls cause aesthetic damage.

Other cultural controls are equally simple and straightforward. Choose resistant varieties of trees and shrubs that are not prone to problems. Space your plants so that they have good air circulation in and around them and are not stressed from competing for light, nutrients and space. Remove

Frogs eat many insect pests.

plants that are decimated by the same pests every year. Dispose of diseased foliage and branches. Prevent the spread of disease by keeping your gardening tools clean and by tidying up dead plant matter at the end of every growing season.

Physical controls are generally used to combat insect and mammal problems. An example of such a control is picking insects off shrubs by hand, which is not as daunting as it may seem if you catch the problem when it is just beginning. Large, slow insects such as Japanese beetles are particularly easy to pick off. Other physical controls include traps, barriers, scarecrows and natural repellents that make a plant taste or smell bad to pests. Garden centers offer a wide array of such devices. Physical control of diseases usually involves removing the infected plant or parts of the plant in order to keep the problem from spreading.

Biological controls make use of populations of predators that like to eat pests. Animals such as birds, snakes, frogs, spiders, ladybird beetles and certain bacteria can play an important role in keeping pest populations manageable. Encourage these creatures to take up permanent residence in your garden. A birdbath and birdfeeder will encourage birds to enjoy your yard and feed on a wide variety of insect pests. Beneficial insects are probably already living in your landscape, and you can encourage them to stay by planting appropriate alternate food sources. Many beneficial insects eat nectar from pollen-producing plants such as yarrow and daisies. In many cases it is the young and not the adult insects that are predatory.

Another form of biological control is the naturally occurring soil bacterium *Bacillus thuringiensis* var. *kurstaki,* or B.t. for short, which breaks down the gut lining of some insect pests. It is commonly available in garden centers.

Chemical controls should rarely be necessary, but if you must use them, many low-toxicity and organic options are available. Organic sprays are no less dangerous than chemical ones, but they will break down into harmless compounds eventually. The main drawback to using chemicals is that they may also kill the beneficial insects you have been trying to attract.

Organic chemicals are available at most garden centers, and you should follow the manufacturer's instructions very carefully. A larger amount or concentration of the insecticide is not going to be any more effective in controlling insect pests than the recommended dosage. Note that if a particular pest is not listed on the package, it will probably not be controlled by that product. It is also important to find out at what stage in an insect's life you will get the best control. Some can be controlled only at certain stages. Proper and early identification of pests is vital for finding a quick solution.

Consumers are demanding effective pest products that do not harm the environment, and less toxic, more precisely targeted pesticides are becoming available. As well, alternatives to commercial chemical pesticides are available or can be made easily at home. Horticultural oils and insecticidal soaps, for example (see p. 71),

are effective and safe to use for pest control. These products are essentially nontoxic to people and animals.

Cultural, physical, biological and chemical controls are all possible defenses against insects, but many diseases can be controlled only culturally. It is most often weakened plants that succumb to diseases, although some diseases can infect plants regardless of their level of health. Some diseases, such as powdery mildew, are largely a cosmetic concern, but they may weaken a plant enough to make it susceptible to other pests and diseases. Prevention is often the only hope: once a plant has been infected, it should generally be destroyed in order to prevent the disease from spreading.

GLOSSARY OF PESTS & DISEASES

ANTHRACNOSE

Fungus. Yellow or brown spots on leaves; sunken lesions and blisters on stems; can kill plant.

What to Do. Choose resistant varieties and cultivars; keep soil well drained; thin out stems to improve air circulation; avoid handling wet foliage. Remove and destroy infected plant parts; clean up and destroy debris from infected plants at end of growing season. Applying liquid copper can minimize damage.

APHIDS

Tiny, pear-shaped insects, wingless or winged; green, black, brown, red or gray. Cluster along stems, on buds and on leaves. Example: woolly adelgids. Suck sap from plants and

cause distorted or stunted growth. Sticky honeydew forms on surfaces, encouraging sooty mold growth.

What to Do. Squish small colonies by hand; dislodge with brisk water spray from hose. Predatory insects and birds feed on them. Spray serious infestations with insecticidal soap or neem oil according to directions.

Aphids

Japanese beetles

BEETLES

Many types and sizes; usually rounded in shape with hard, shell-like outer wings covering membranous inner wings. Some are beneficial; e.g., ladybird beetles ('ladybugs'). Others are not; e.g., Japanese beetles, leaf skeletonizers, bark beetles and weevils. Larvae: see Borers, Grubs. Leave wide range of chewing damage: make small or large holes in or around margins of leaves; consume entire leaves or areas between leaf veins ('skeletonize'); may also chew holes in flowers. Some bark beetles carry deadly plant diseases.

What to Do. For shrubs, pick beetles off at night and drop them in an old coffee can half filled with soapy water (soap prevents them from floating and climbing out); spread an old sheet under small trees and shrubs and shake off beetles to collect and dispose of them; use a broom to reach tall branches. The Hot Pepper Wax brand of insect repellent will help discourage beetles and is also known to repel rabbits and deer.

BLIGHT

Fungal or bacterial diseases, many types; e.g., leaf blight, needle blight, twig blight, petal blight, snow blight. Leaves, stems and flowers blacken, rot, die. See also Fire Blight, Gray Mold.

What to Do. Thin out stems to improve air circulation; keep mulch away from base of plant; remove debris from garden at end of growing season. Remove and destroy infected plant parts. Sterilize equipment after each cut to avoid re-infecting plant and spreading fungus.

BORERS

Larvae of some moths, wasps and beetles; among the most damaging of plant pests. Burrow into plant stems, leaves and/or roots, destroying their conducting tissue and structural strength. Worm-like; vary in size and get bigger as they bore under bark and sometimes into heartwood. Tunnels left by borers create sites where infection and decomposition can begin; some borers carry infection.

What to Do. Keeping tree or shrub as healthy as possible with proper fertilizing and watering prevents some borer damage; may be able to squish borers within leaves. Remove and destroy bored parts; may need to remove entire plant.

BUGS (TRUE BUGS)

Small insects, up to $1/2$" long; green, brown, black or brightly colored and patterned. Many beneficial; a few pests, such as lace bugs, pierce plants to suck out sap. Toxins may be injected that deform plants; sunken areas left where tissue pierced; leaves rip as they grow; leaves, buds and new growth may be dwarfed and deformed.

What to Do. Remove debris and weeds from around plants in fall to destroy overwintering sites. Spray plants with insecticidal soap or neem oil according to package directions.

CANKER

Swollen or sunken lesions on stems or branches, surrounded by living tissue. Caused by many different bacterial and fungal diseases. Most canker-causing diseases enter through wounded wood. Woodpeckers may unwittingly infect plants when they drill for insects.

What to Do. Maintain vigor of plants; avoid wounding or injuring trees (e.g., string trimmer damage), especially in spring when canker-causing organisms most active; control borers and other bark-dwelling insects. Prune out and destroy any infected material. Sterilize pruning tools before, during and after use on infected plants.

CASE BEARERS

see Caterpillars

CATERPILLARS

Larvae of butterflies, moths, sawflies. Include bagworms, budworms, case bearers, cutworms, leaf rollers, leaf tiers, loopers, webworms. Chew foliage and buds. Can completely defoliate a plant if infestation severe.

What to Do. Removal from plant is best control. Use high-pressure water and soap or pick caterpillars off by hand if plant is small enough.

Caterpillar on bud

Cut off and burn large tents or webs of larvae. Control biologically using B.t. (see p. 62). Horticultural oil can be applied in spring. Tree trunks can be wrapped or banded to prevent caterpillars from climbing tree to access leaves.

DIEBACK

Plants slowly wilt, brown and die, starting at branch tips. Can be caused by wide range of disease organisms, cultural problems and nutrient deficiencies.

What to Do. Keep plants healthy by providing them with optimum growing conditions. Cut off dead tips below the dead sections.

FIRE BLIGHT

Highly destructive bacterial disease of the rose family, whose members also include apple, plum, pear, cotoneaster, hawthorn, cherry and firethorn. Infected areas appear to have been burned. Look for bent twigs, branches that retain leaves over winter and cankers forming on lower parts of plant.

What to Do. Choose resistant plant varieties. Remove and burn

Fuzzy oak galls

infected parts, making cuts at least 24" below infected areas. Sterilize tools after each cut on infected plant. Re-infection is possible because fire blight is often carried by pollinating birds and insects and enters plant through flowers. If whole plant is infected it must be removed and burned. Use of fish emulsion as foliar spray on infected trees may prevent re-infection.

GALLS

Unusual swellings of plant tissues caused by insects or diseases. Can affect leaves, buds, stems, flowers, fruit or trunks. Often a specific gall affects a single genus or species.

What to Do. Cut galls out of plant and destroy them. Galls caused by insects usually contain the insect's eggs and juvenile forms. Prevent these galls by controlling insect before it lays eggs; otherwise, try to remove and destroy infected tissue before young insects emerge. Generally insect galls more unsightly than damaging to plant. Galls caused by diseases often require destruction of plant. Avoid

placing other plants susceptible to same disease in that location.

GRAY MOLD (BOTRYTIS BLIGHT)

Fungal disease. Gray fuzz coats affected surfaces. Leaves, flowers or fruits may blacken, rot and die. Common on dead plant matter and on damaged or stressed plants in cool, damp, poorly ventilated areas.

What to Do. Thin stems for better air circulation; keep mulch away from base of plant, particularly in spring when plant starts to sprout; remove debris from garden at end of growing season; do not overwater. Remove and destroy any infected plant parts.

GRUBS

Larvae of different beetles, commonly found below soil level; usually curled in C-shape. Body white or gray; head may be white, gray, brown or reddish. Problematic in lawns; may feed on roots of shallow-rooted trees and shrubs. Plant wilts despite regular watering; may pull easily out of ground in severe cases.

What to Do. Throw any grubs found while digging onto a stone path or patio for birds to devour; apply parasitic nematodes or milky disease spore to infested soil (ask at your local garden center).

LEAFHOPPERS & TREEHOPPERS

Small, wedge-shaped insects; can be green, brown, gray, multi-colored. Jump around frantically when disturbed. Suck juice from plant leaves. Cause distorted growth. Carry diseases such as aster yellows. Treehoppers also damage tree bark when they slit it to lay eggs.

What to Do. Encourage predators by planting nectar-producing species such as yarrow. Wash insects off with strong spray of water; spray insecticidal soap or neem oil according to package directions.

LEAF MINERS

Tiny, stubby larvae of some butterflies and moths; may be yellow or green. Tunnel within leaves leaving winding trails; tunneled areas lighter in color than rest of leaf. Unsightly rather than health risk to plant.

Leaf miner damage

What to Do. Remove debris from area in fall to destroy overwintering sites; attract parasitic wasps with nectar plants such as yarrow. Remove and destroy infected foliage.

LEAF ROLLERS

see Caterpillars

LEAF SCORCH

Yellowing or browning of leaves beginning at tips or edges. Most often caused by drought or heat stress.

What to Do. Water susceptible plants during droughts, and avoid planting them where excessive heat reflects from pavement or buildings.

LEAF SPOT

Two common types. *Bacterial:* small speckled spots grow to encompass entire leaves; brown or purple in color; leaves may drop. *Fungal:* black, brown or yellow spots; leaves wither; e.g., scab, tar spot.

What to Do. Bacterial infection more severe; must remove entire plant. For fungal infection, remove and destroy infected plant parts. Sterilize removal tools; avoid wetting foliage or touching wet foliage; remove and destroy debris at end of growing season. Spray compost tea (see p. 71) on leaves.

MEALYBUGS

Tiny crawling insects related to aphids; appear to be covered with white fuzz or flour. Sucking damage stunts and stresses plant. Mealybugs excrete honeydew that promotes growth of sooty mold.

What to Do. Remove by hand on smaller plants; wash plant with soap and water; wipe with alcohol-soaked swabs; remove heavily infested leaves; encourage or introduce natural predators such as mealybug destroyer beetle and parasitic wasps; spray with insecticidal soap or horticultural oil. Keep in mind larvae of mealybug destroyer beetles look like very large mealybugs.

MILDEW

Two types, both caused by fungus, but with slightly different symptoms. *Downy mildew:* yellow spots on upper

Powdery mildew

sides of leaves and downy fuzz on undersides; fuzz may be yellow, white or gray. *Powdery mildew:* white or gray powdery coating on leaf surfaces that doesn't brush off.

What to Do. Choose resistant cultivars; space plants well; thin stems to encourage air circulation; tidy any debris in fall. Remove and destroy infected leaves or other parts. For powdery mildew, spray foliage with compost tea or very dilute fish emulsion (1 tsp. per qt. of water). For downy mildew, spray foliage with mixture of 5 tbsp. horticultural oil, 2 tsp. baking soda and 1 gal. water. Apply once a week for three weeks.

MITES

Tiny, eight-legged relatives of spiders; do not eat insects, but may spin webs. Almost invisible to naked eye; red, yellow or green; usually found on undersides of plant leaves. Examples: bud mites, spider mites, spruce mites. Suck juice out of leaves. May see fine webbing on leaves and stems; may see mites moving under leaves. Leaves become discolored, speckled; then turn brown and shrivel up.

What to Do. Wash off with strong spray of water daily until all signs of infestation are gone; predatory mites available through garden centers; spray plants with insecticidal soap or with horticultural oil at a rate of 5 tbsp. to 1 gal. of water. Another application may be needed after one month or so.

MOSAIC

see Viruses

NEEDLE CAST

Fungal disease causing premature needle drop. Spotty yellow areas turn brown; infected needles drop up to a year later.

What to Do. Ensure good air circulation. Clean up and destroy fallen needles. Prune off damaged growth. To prevent recurrence the following year, treat plants with Bordeaux mix twice, two weeks apart, as candles elongate the next spring.

NEMATODES

Tiny worms that give plants disease symptoms. One type infects foliage and stems; the other type infects roots. *Foliar:* yellow spots that turn brown on leaves; leaves shrivel and wither; problem starts on lowest leaves and works up plant. *Root-knot:* plant is stunted; may wilt; yellow spots on leaves; roots have tiny bumps or knots.

What to Do. Mulch soil, mix in organic matter, clear garden debris in fall. Avoid wetting the leaves, and don't touch wet foliage of infected plants. Can add parasitic nematodes to soil. Remove infected plants in extreme cases.

PSYLLIDS
Treat as for aphids (see Aphids).

ROT
Several different fungi that affect different parts of the plant and can kill plant. *Crown rot:* affects base of plant; stems blacken and fall over, and leaves yellow and wilt. *Heart rot (wood rot):* decay of the heartwood of a tree. Damage often evident only after high winds cause branches or whole tree to fall. *Root rot:* leaves yellow and plant wilts; digging up plant will show roots rotted away. **What to Do.** Keep soil well drained; don't damage plant if you are digging or working around it; keep mulches away from plant base. Destroy infected plant if whole plant affected. Replant area with only rot-resistant species or cultivars and not the same species of plant that died.

RUST
Fungi. Pale spots on upper leaf surfaces; orange, fuzzy or dusty spots on leaf undersides. Examples: blister rust, cedar-apple rust, cone rust. **What to Do.** Choose varieties and cultivars resistant to rust; avoid handling wet leaves; provide plant with good air circulation; clear up garden debris at end of season. Remove and destroy infected plant parts. A late-winter application of lime-sulfur can delay infection the following year.

SAWFLIES
see Caterpillars

SCAB
see Leaf Spot

SCALE INSECTS
Tiny, shelled insects that suck sap, weakening and possibly killing plant or making it vulnerable to other problems. Once female scale insect has pierced plant with mouthpart, it is there for life. Juvenile scale insects are called crawlers. **What to Do.** Wipe plant off with alcohol-soaked swabs; spray plant with water to dislodge crawlers; prune out heavily infested branches; encourage natural predators and parasites; spray dormant oil in spring before bud break.

SKELETONIZERS
see Beetles

SLUGS & SNAILS
Both are mollusks; slugs lack shells whereas snails have spiral shells. Slimy, smooth skin; can be up to 8" long, though many are smaller; gray, green, black, beige, yellow or spotted. Leave large, ragged holes in leaves and silvery slime trails on and around plants. **What to Do.** Attach strips of copper to wood around raised beds or to smaller boards inserted around susceptible groups of plants; slugs and snails will get shocked if they touch copper surfaces. Pick off by hand in the evening and squish with boot or drop in can of soapy water. Spread wood ash or diatomaceous earth (available in garden centers) around plants; it will pierce mollusks' soft bodies and cause them to dehydrate. **Do not** use diatomaceous earth intended for swimming pool filters.

Slug control is possible with various nontoxic methods.

THRIPS

Difficult to see; may be visible if you disturb them by blowing gently on an infested flower. Yellow, black or brown; tiny, slender; narrow, fringed wings. Suck juice out of plant cells, particularly in flowers and buds, resulting in mottled petals and leaves, dying buds and distorted and stunted growth.

What to Do. Remove and destroy infected plant parts; encourage native predatory insects with nectar plants such as yarrow; spray severe infestations with insecticidal soap or neem oil according to package directions. Use blue sticky cards to prevent re-infection. Horticultural oil will control adult thrips.

Beer in a shallow dish may be effective. Slug baits containing iron phosphate (also available at garden centers) are not harmful to humans or animals and control slugs when used according to package directions. If slugs damaged garden late in season, begin controls in spring as soon as green shoots appear.

SOOTY MOLD

Fungus. Thin black film forms on leaf surfaces and reduces amount of light getting to leaves.

What to Do. Wipe mold off leaf surfaces; control aphids, mealybugs, whiteflies (honeydew they deposit on leaves encourages sooty mold).

SPIDER MITES

see Mites

TAR SPOT

see Leaf Spot

VIRUSES

Plant may be stunted and leaves and flowers distorted, streaked or discolored. Viral diseases in plants can't be treated. Examples: mosaic virus, ringspot virus.

What to Do. Control insects, such as aphids, leafhoppers and whiteflies, that spread disease. Destroy infected plants.

WEEVILS

see Beetles

WHITEFLIES

Tiny flying insects that flutter up into the air when plant is disturbed. Tiny, moth-like, white; live on undersides of plant leaves. Suck juice out of leaves, causing yellowed leaves and weakened plants; leave behind sticky honeydew on foliage, encouraging sooty mold growth.

What to Do. Destroy weeds that may be home to insects. Attract native predatory beetles and parasitic wasps with nectar plants such as yarrow and sweet alyssum; spray severe cases with insecticidal soap. Can make a sticky flypaper-like trap by mounting tin can on stake; wrap can with yellow paper and cover with clear plastic bag smeared with petroleum jelly; replace bag when full of flies. Apply horticultural oil.

WILT

If watering hasn't helped a wilted plant, one of two wilt fungi may be at fault. *Fusarium wilt:* plant wilts, leaves turn yellow then die; symptoms generally appear first on one part of plant before spreading elsewhere on plant.

Verticillium wilt: plant wilts; leaves curl up at edges; leaves turn yellow then drop off; plant may die.

What to Do. Both wilts difficult to control. Choose resistant plant varieties and cultivars; clean up debris at end of growing season. Destroy infected plants; solarize (sterilize) soil before replanting (this may help if you've lost an entire bed of plants to these fungi)—contact local garden center for assistance.

WOOLLY ADELGIDS

see Aphids

WORMS

see Caterpillars, Nematodes

RECIPES

COMPOST 'TEA'

Mix 1–2 lb. compost in 5 gal. of water. Let sit for four to seven days. Dilute the mix until it resembles weak tea. Use during normal watering or apply as a foliar spray to prevent or treat fungal diseases.

HORTICULTURAL OIL

Mix 5 tbsp. horticultural oil in 1 gal. of water and apply as a spray for a variety of insect and fungal problems. If purchased, follow package directions.

INSECTICIDAL SOAP

Mix 1 tsp. of mild dish detergent or pure soap (biodegradable options are available) with 1 qt. of water in a clean spray bottle. Spray surfaces of insect-infested plants, and rinse well within an hour of spraying to avoid foliage discoloration.

ABOUT THIS GUIDE

The trees and shrubs in this book are organized alphabetically by common name. Alternative common names and scientific names are given beneath the main headings and in the index. The illustrated **Trees & Shrubs at a Glance** allows you to become familiar with the different plants quickly, and it will help you find a tree or shrub if you aren't sure what it's called.

Clearly displayed at the beginning of each entry are the special features of the woody plant; height and spread ranges; preferred planting forms (bare-root, balled-and-burlapped or container); planting seasons; and hardiness zones (see map, p. 15).

Our favorite species, hybrids and cultivars are listed in each entry's 'Recommended' section. There are often many more types available; check with your local garden center. Note that all cultivar names not enclosed by quotation marks are actually trade names registered by particular companies. In these cases, the cultivar name proper follows the trade name in parentheses. The trade

name is often more commonly used in garden centers.

Where plant height and spread ranges and hardiness zones are not indicated in the 'Recommended' section, refer to the information at the beginning of the entry. In other cases, the ranges at the beginning of the entry encompass the measurements for all species and cultivars listed.

Common pests and problems, if any, are also noted for each entry. Consult the 'Problems & Pests' section of the introduction (pp. 60–71) for information on how to address these problems.

The **Quick Reference Chart** at the back of the book (pp. 334–339) is a handy guide to planning for a diversity of features, forms, foliage types and blooming times in your garden.

Because Michigan is climatically diverse, we can refer to seasons only in a general sense. Keep in mind the timing and duration of seasons in your area when planning your garden. Hardiness zones, too, can vary locally; consult a horticulturalist or garden center in your area.

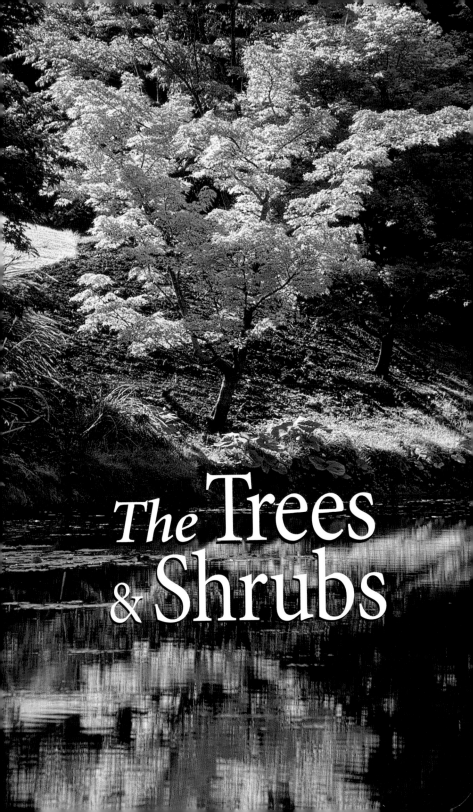

The Trees
& Shrubs

Aralia
Aralia

Features: foliage, flowers, fruit, stems **Habit:** deciduous small tree or large shrub
Height: 10–30' **Spread:** 10–20' **Planting:** container, bare-root; early spring to
early winter **Zones:** 4–8

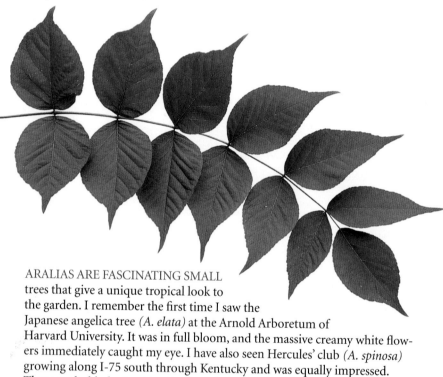

ARALIAS ARE FASCINATING SMALL
trees that give a unique tropical look to
the garden. I remember the first time I saw the
Japanese angelica tree *(A. elata)* at the Arnold Arboretum of
Harvard University. It was in full bloom, and the massive creamy white flowers immediately caught my eye. I have also seen Hercules' club *(A. spinosa)*
growing along I-75 south through Kentucky and was equally impressed.
These are bold plants, attractive both in leaf and in bloom. The variegated
forms are particularly striking.

Growing
Aralias prefer **full sun** or **light shade**. They grow best in **fertile, moist, well-
drained** soil but tolerate dry, clay or rocky soil. Provide **shelter** from strong
winds, which can dry out the foliage.

These shrubs rarely require pruning, which is fortunate considering their
plentiful prickles. You will, however, have to spend some time controlling
these suckering plants. Barriers such as buildings and driveways can help
prevent spread, but you may still want to pull some or all of the suckers. If
you get the suckers while they are small, they are easier to remove and the
prickles are a bit softer.

Tough gloves are an absolute requirement when handling aralias. I have found thick rubber gloves useful when pulling up suckers. They allow a good grip and will stretch rather than puncture when prickles are encountered.

Tips

These shrubs are best suited to an informal garden. They can be included in a border at the edge of a wooded area and should be used where their spread can be controlled and where you won't inadvertently brush against the thorny stems.

The berries should not be eaten; they are thought to be poisonous. The berries rarely last long because they are quickly eaten by birds.

Recommended

A. elata (Japanese angelica tree) is the larger of the two recommended species, usually growing 20' tall, but potentially reaching 30'. It bears clusters of creamy flowers in late summer, followed by berries that ripen to dark purple. The foliage turns purple, orange or yellow in fall. This species doesn't sucker quite as vigorously as *A. spinosa* and is not quite as spiny. '**Aureo-variegata**' has leaves variegated yellow and green. '**Variegata**' has leaves with creamy white margins. Suckers sometimes have solid green rather than variegated leaves.

A. spinosa (Hercules' club, devil's walking stick) usually grows 10–15' tall. What it lacks in height, compared with *A. elata*, it makes up for by spreading vigorously. Unless you can provide this plant with lots of

A. spinosa (above)

A. elata 'Variegata'

room to grow, be prepared to wade in with thick gloves at least once a year to pull up suckers. This species bears large clusters of white flowers in late summer, followed by black berries.

Problems & Pests

Problems are rare, limited to occasional trouble with fungal leaf spot, aphids or mealybugs.

Arborvitae
Cedar
Thuja

Features: foliage, bark, form **Habit:** small to large, evergreen shrub or tree
Height: 18"–50' **Spread:** 18"–12' **Planting:** B & B, container; spring, fall
Zones: 2–9

THE EASTERN ARBORVITAE IS ONE OF THE MOST FUNCTIONAL
evergreens in home landscaping. Easy to grow and tough, it provides unique
architecture and winter interest. Many superior cultivars of this common
native have been selected for gardeners to enjoy. The cultivars are diverse in
form and color, offering everything from pyramidal forms, which make great
specimen plants and narrow privacy hedges, to yellow cultivars that add
diversity to the summer and winter landscape. Dwarf and globe-shaped
selections make wonderful additions to the mixed border, rock garden or
entrance garden.

Growing

Arborvitae prefer **full sun**. The soil should be of **average fertility, moist** and **well drained**. These plants enjoy humidity and in the wild are often found growing near marshy areas. Arborvitae will perform best in a location with some **shelter** from wind, especially in winter, when the foliage can easily dry out and give the entire plant a rather brown, drab appearance.

T. occidentalis 'Danica' (both photos)

These plants take very well to pruning and are often grown as hedges. Though they may be kept formally shaped, they are also attractive if just clipped to maintain a loose but compact shape and size.

T. occidentalis was grown in Europe as early as 1536. It was named arborvitae (Latin for 'tree of life') because a vitamin C–rich tea made from its foliage and bark saved Jacques Cartier's crew from scurvy.

T. occidentalis 'Sunkist'
T. plicata 'Zebrina'

Tips

Large varieties of arborvitae make excellent specimen trees, and smaller cultivars can be used in foundation plantings, shrub borders and formal or informal hedges.

Deer enjoy eating the foliage of eastern arborvitae. If deer or other ungulates are a problem in your area, you may wish to avoid using this plant. Alternatively, consider using western arborvitae, which is relatively resistant to deer browsing.

Recommended

T. occidentalis (eastern arborvitae, American arborvitae) is native in much of eastern and central North America. In the wild this tree can grow to about 60' tall and 10–15' wide. In cultivation it grows about half this size or smaller. '**Danica**' is a dwarf globe form growing to about 18" tall and wide, featuring emerald green foliage. '**Emerald**' ('Smaragd') can grow 10–15' tall, spreading about 4'. This cultivar is small and very cold hardy; the foliage does not lose color in winter. '**Hetz Midget**' is a dwarf, rounded cultivar. It grows to 2–4' tall and wide but can be kept smaller with pruning. '**Nigra**' ('Nigra Dark Green') has a neat pyramidal habit and keeps its dark green foliage color in winter. It reaches 20–30' tall and 8' wide. '**Sunkist**' is a low, slow-growing, pyramidal cultivar with bright yellow foliage. It grows 5–10' tall and 5–8' wide. '**Techny**' is a very hardy cultivar with a broad pyramidal form. It grows 10–20' tall and 5–8' wide and keeps its bluish green color all winter. '**Woodwardii**' is a globe form that grows 3–5' tall and wide. (Zones 2–7; cultivars may be less cold hardy)

T. plicata (western arborvitae, western redcedar) can grow up to 200' tall in its native Pacific Northwest but usually stays under 50' in Michigan. This narrowly pyramidal evergreen grows quickly, resists deer browsing and maintains good foliage color all winter. '**Atrovirens**' is popular for its dark green, glossy foliage. It grows 15–20' tall and 5–10' wide. **Spring Grove** ('Grovepli') is a very narrow, hardy cultivar with bright green foliage. It grows about 20' tall and up to 10' wide. '**Zebrina**' has foliage variegated yellow and green. This pyramidal cultivar can grow more than 30' tall and 12' wide. (Zones 5–9)

Problems & Pests

Bagworm, heart rot, leaf miners, scale insects, blight, canker and red spider mites are possible, though not frequent, problems. The most likely problem is winter browning, which usually occurs in cold, windy areas where foliage easily loses moisture. Leaf miner damage may resemble winter browning—hold branch tips up to the light and look for tiny caterpillars feeding inside. Trim and destroy infested foliage before June.

Crush some foliage between your fingers to enjoy the wonderful aroma. Be cautious, though, if you have sensitive skin; the pungent oils may irritate.

T. plicata Spring Grove

An eastern arborvitae in Michigan has made the record books with a height of 113' and spread of 43'.

T. occidentalis 'Nigra'

Aronia
Chokeberry
Aronia

Features: flowers, fruit, fall foliage **Habit:** suckering, deciduous shrub
Height: 3–6' **Spread:** 3–10' **Planting:** container, bare-root; spring or fall
Zones: 3–8

WHAT A SHAME ARONIAS ARE OFTEN CALLED 'CHOKEBERRY.'
These shrubs are too good to be saddled with such a nasty common name.
I like aronias because they offer something for all seasons. In spring they are
adorned with small but abundant, white, apple-like blossoms. In summer
the blooms are replaced with showy black or red fruit, depending upon the
species. And in fall the leaves turn wonderful hues of orange and red.

Aronia fruit is high in vitamins, especially vitamin C.
It was used as an easily available alternative to citrus
in eastern Europe during the Cold War.

Growing
Aronias grow well in **full sun** or **partial shade,** but the best flowering and
fruiting occurs in full sun. The soil should be of **average fertility** and **well
drained,** but the plants adapt to most soils and tolerate wet, dry or poor soil.
Up to one-third of the stems, preferably the older ones, can be pruned out
annually once flowering is finished.

Tips

These plants are useful in a shrub or mixed border. They also make interesting, low-maintenance specimens. Left to their own devices, they will colonize a fairly large area.

Recommended

A. arbutifolia (*Photinia floribunda;* aronia, red chokeberry) is an upright shrub that grows 3–6' tall. White flowers are borne in late spring, followed by bright red waxy fruit in fall. **'Brilliantissima'** has brilliant red fall foliage.

A. melanocarpa (*A. prunifolia, Photinia melanocarpa;* aronia, black chokeberry) is an upright, suckering shrub that is native to Michigan and the eastern U.S. It grows 3–6' tall and can spread to about 10'. It bears white flowers in late spring and early summer, followed by dark fruit that ripens in fall and persists through winter. The foliage turns bright red to purplish red in fall. **'Autumn Magic'** has red to purple fall foliage. **Iroquois Beauty** ('Morton') is a compact cultivar that grows only 3–4' tall. **'Viking'** has glossy dark green foliage that turns dark red in fall. It grows 3–5' tall. The persistent large, dark fruit is edible, but bitter.

Problems & Pests

Aronias rarely suffer from any major problems, though some fungal leaf spot or rust is possible.

The fruit of these plants persists all winter because it is so bitter, even birds aren't interested in eating it until it is well fermented.

A. melanocarpa Iroquois Beauty (above)

A. melanocarpa 'Autumn Magic' (center & below)

Barberry
Berberis

Features: foliage, flowers, fruit **Habit:** deciduous shrub **Height:** 18"–5'
Spread: 2–6' **Planting:** container; spring or fall **Zones:** 4–8

BARBERRY IS A TOUGH, EASY-TO-GROW SHRUB. TYPICALLY THE leaves are green, but many ornamental selections have eye-catching purple, red or yellow leaves. Most often gardeners prefer using the dwarf, mounding cultivars, which can be placed in the front of the border as an edger, massed to form a groundcover or simply mixed into the perennial garden. The taller selections are less common but make excellent medium-sized hedges. Barberry is thorny, so be careful where you plant it. In urban areas it is often planted under windows to deter crime. A burglar would definitely think twice before climbing through barberry.

Growing

Barberry develops the best fall color when grown in **full sun,** but it tolerates partial shade. Any **well-drained** soil is suitable. This plant tolerates drought and urban conditions but suffers in poorly drained, wet soil.

Barberry is flexible when it comes to pruning. It can take heavy pruning well and is often grown as a hedge. A plant in an informal border can be left alone or can be lightly pruned. Remove old or dead wood and unwanted suckers.

Tips

Large barberry plants make excellent hedges with formidable prickles. Barberry can also be included in shrub and mixed borders. Small cultivars can be grown in rock gardens, in raised beds and along rock walls.

Recommended

B. thunbergii (Japanese barberry) is a dense shrub with a broad, rounded habit. It grows 3–5' tall and spreads 4–6'. The foliage is bright green and turns variable shades of orange, red or purple in fall. Yellow spring flowers are followed by glossy red fruit later in summer. **'Aurea'** (golden barberry) grows up to 5' tall, with an equal spread. It has bright yellow new growth. **'Concorde'** is a dwarf cultivar with purple foliage. It grows about 18" tall. **'Crimson Pygmy'** ('Atropurpurea Nana') is a dwarf cultivar with reddish purple foliage. It grows 18–24" tall and spreads up to 36". **'Helmond Pillar'** is a narrow, upright form with reddish purple leaves that turn bright red in fall. It grows up to 5' tall and spreads about 24". **'Rose Glow'** has purple foliage variegated with white and pink splotches. It grows 5–6' tall.

'Rose Glow' (center), 'Helmond Pillar' (below)

Problems & Pests

Healthy barberry rarely suffers from problems, but stressed plants can be affected by leaf spot, spider mites, aphids, weevils, root rot, wilt, mosaic or scale insects.

Extracts from the rhizomes of Berberis *have been used to treat rheumatic and other inflammatory disorders and the common cold.*

Bearberry
Kinnikinnick
Arctostaphylos

Features: late-spring flowers, fruit, foliage **Habit:** low-growing, mat-forming, evergreen shrub **Height:** 4–6" **Spread:** 8"–4' **Planting:** container; spring, fall **Zones:** 2–7

BEARBERRY IS AN ATTRACTIVE MAT-FORMING EVERGREEN THAT thrives in well-drained, acidic soils of low fertility. At first glance you might mistake this native for a cotoneaster, but bearberry hugs the ground very closely and has small, urn-shaped flowers. Once established, it makes a wonderful ground-cover. Like the cotoneasters, it looks fantastic creeping over rocks and boulders.

Growing

Bearberry grows well in **full sun** or **partial shade**. The soil should be of **poor to average fertility, well drained, acidic** and **moist**. Bearberry will adapt to alkaline soils. Generally no pruning is required.

Tips

Bearberry can be used as a ground-cover or can be included in a rock garden. Once established, it is a vigorous, wide-spreading grower, but it can be slow to get started. Use mulch to keep the weeds down while the plant is becoming established.

Recommended

A. uva-ursi is a low-growing native shrub that grows 4–6" tall and spreads 8–20". White flowers appear in late spring, followed by berries that ripen to bright red. The cultivars share the white flowers and red fruit but also have leaves that turn bright red in winter. **'Vancouver Jade'** is a low-growing plant with arching stems. It grows 6" high and spreads 18". This cultivar is resistant to the leaf spot that can afflict bearberry. **'Wood's Compact'** spreads about 3–4'.

Problems & Pests

Possible problems include bud and leaf galls as well as fungal diseases of the leaves, stems and fruit.

'Vancouver Jade'

This plant's alternative common name, kinnikinnick, is said to be an Algonquian term meaning 'smoking mixture,' reflecting that traditional use for the leaves.

A. uva-ursi

Beautyberry
Callicarpa

Features: late-summer and fall fruit **Habit:** bushy deciduous shrub with arching stems **Height:** 3–10' **Spread:** 3–6' **Planting:** container; spring or fall **Zones:** 5–10

WHETHER YOU LIKE TO ARRANGE FLOWERS OR JUST ENJOY THE occasional bouquet in a vase, consider growing one of the beautyberries. Their flowers are less striking than their sprays of wonderful light purple fruit that follow in autumn. These shrubs are easy to grow, although in Michigan they behave like perennials and die back each winter. Simply cut them back close to the ground each spring. By fall you'll be enjoying a fantastic display of branches laden with brightly colored fruit, great for cutting.

Growing

Beautyberries grow well in **full sun** or **light shade**. The soil should be **well drained** and of **average fertility**.

These plants will probably die back completely each winter. This isn't a problem because the flowers and fruit are formed on the current year's growth.

Cut the dead stems back completely in spring. New growth will sprout from ground level.

Tips

Beautyberries can be used in naturalistic gardens and in shrub and mixed borders. The fruit-covered branches are often cut for fresh and dried arrangements. The colorful fruit persists on the branches when they are cut and dried.

C. dichotoma 'Early Amethyst' (above)

Recommended

C. dichotoma (purple beautyberry) grows about 3–4' tall, with an equal or slightly greater spread. The purple fruit is borne in dense clusters that surround the arching branches at the base of each leaf. '**Early Amethyst**' bears lots of fruit earlier in the season than the species. '**Issai**' is a compact cultivar that bears plentiful fruit.

C. japonica (Japanese beautyberry) is a large, open shrub with arching branches and decorative purple fruit. This shrub can grow to 10' tall and spread 4–6', but it is unlikely to grow more than 4' tall when it dies back each winter. '**Leucocarpa**' is an attractive white-fruited cultivar.

C. japonica 'Leucocarpa'
C. dichotoma 'Issai'

Problems & Pests

Scale insects, leaf spot and mildew are possible problems, but they are not serious and do not occur frequently.

To encourage vigorous new growth, fertilize beautyberry plants that suffer winter dieback.

Beauty Bush
Kolkwitzia

Features: late-spring flowers **Habit:** suckering, deciduous shrub with arching branches **Height:** 6–15' **Spread:** 5–11' **Planting:** B & B; spring or fall **Zones:** 4–8

BEAUTY BUSH PUTS ON A GARDEN MAGIC SHOW. AT A WELL-TIMED moment in early June, when few other shrubs or trees are in flower, this plant bursts into bloom. Every square inch is draped in blossoms. Its name is certainly well deserved, but the beauty is fleeting. When the blooms fall, beauty bush disappears—now you see it, now you don't. Some may dismiss it as a one-season plant, but it certainly does shine in its season. If you have the room to spare, let beauty bush work its magic in your garden.

Beauty bush is resistant to most pests and diseases.

Growing

Beauty bush flowers most profusely in **full sun**. The soil should be **fertile** and **well drained**. This shrub adapts to soils of various pH levels.

Prune out one-third of the old wood each year. Old, overgrown plants can be cut right back to the ground if they need rejuvenation. Start new plants by removing rooted suckers from the base of the plant in spring.

Tips

Beauty bush can be included in a shrub border or placed at the back of a mixed border. It can also be grown as a specimen, but it isn't exceptionally attractive when not in flower.

Recommended

K. amabilis is a large shrub with arching canes. Clusters of bell-shaped pink flowers are borne in late spring or early summer. '**Pink Cloud**' is a popular cultivar with deep pink flowers.

K. amabilis (above)

'Pink Cloud' (center & below)

Beech

Fagus

Features: foliage, bark, habit, fall color **Habit:** large, oval, deciduous shade tree
Height: 30–80' **Spread:** 10–65' **Planting:** B & B, container; spring **Zones:** 4–9

FEW TREES IN THE WORLD ARE AS MAJESTIC OR STATELY AS BEECH.
The native American beech is a common sight in Michigan. American beech
trees are easily identified by their tall, straight, smooth, silvery trunks, standing like giant elephant legs in the forest. The European beech is just as lovely
and is a more adaptable and tolerant landscape tree. This imported species is
also more refined in habit and texture and has provided us with many interesting cultivars. Unfortunately, there are, as yet, no cultivated selections of
American beech.

*The leaves and bark of American beech
have been used to make an ointment
for soothing burns and sores.*

Growing

Beeches grow equally well in **full sun** or **partial shade**. The soil should be of **average fertility, loamy** and **well drained,** though almost all well-drained soils are tolerated.

American beech doesn't like having its roots disturbed and should be transplanted only when very young. European beech transplants easily and is more tolerant of varied soil conditions than American beech.

Very little pruning is required. Remove dead or damaged branches in spring or at any time after the damage occurs. European beech is a popular hedging species and responds well to severe pruning.

F. sylvatica 'Tricolor'

Beeches retain their very smooth and elastic bark long into maturity.

F. sylvatica 'Pendula'

F. sylvatica 'Pendula'
F. sylvatica 'Tricolor'

Tips

Beeches make excellent specimens. They are also used as street trees, as shade trees and in woodland gardens. These trees need a lot of space, but the European beech's adaptability to pruning makes it a reasonable choice in a small garden.

The nuts are edible when roasted.

Recommended

F. grandifolia (American beech) is a broad-canopied tree that can grow 50–80' tall and often almost as wide. This species is native to most of eastern North America.

F. sylvatica (European beech) is a spectacular tree that can grow 60' tall and wide or even larger. Too massive for most settings, the species is best used as a hedge in smaller gardens. You can find a number of interesting cultivars of this tree, and several are small enough to use in the home garden. **'Fastigiata'** ('Dawyck') is a narrow, upright tree. It can grow to 80' but spreads only about 10'. Yellow- or purple-leaved forms are available. **'Pendula'** (weeping beech) is a dramatic tree whose pendulous branches reach down to the ground. It varies in form; some spread widely, resulting in a cascade effect, while other specimens may be rather upright with branches drooping from the central trunk. This cultivar can grow as tall as the species,

Young lovers' initials carved into a beech will remain visible for the life of the tree—an effect that outlasts many young relationships.

but a specimen with the branches drooping from the central trunk may be narrow enough for a home garden. **'Purpurea'** is a purple-leaved form with the same habit as the species. Purple-leaved weeping forms are also available. **'Tricolor'** ('Roseo-Marginata') has striking foliage with pink and white variegation that develops best in partial shade. This slow-growing tree matures to about 30'. It can be grown as a smaller tree if constrained to a large planter.

Problems & Pests

Canker, powdery mildew, leaf spot, bark disease, borers, scale insects and aphids can afflict beech trees. None of these pests causes serious problems.

F. grandifolia

Beech nuts provide food for a wide variety of animals, including squirrels and birds, and they were once a favorite food of the passenger pigeon, now extinct.

F. grandifolia

Birch

Betula

Features: foliage, fall color, habit, bark, winter and early-spring catkins **Habit:** open, deciduous tree **Height:** 25–90' **Spread:** 10–60' **Planting:** B & B, container; spring, fall **Zones:** 3–9

THERE'S NO DOUBT THAT BIRCHES are beautiful trees. Not only is the bark highly attractive, but most species boast a graceful habit as well. Unfortunately, many of the species with lovely white bark are also susceptible to bronze birch borer, which can be devastating. Don't let this problem discourage you from growing birch. If you choose the right species and take pains to water the tree during droughts, you will be rewarded with years of pleasure.

Some people make birch syrup from the sap of cherry birch. The heavy flow of sap in spring is tapped and the sap is boiled down, the same way maple syrup is made.

Growing

Birches grow well in **full sun, partial shade** or **light shade**. The soil should be of **average to rich fertility, moist** and fairly **well drained.** Many birch species naturally grow in wet areas, such as along streams. They don't, however, like to grow in places that remain wet for prolonged periods. Provide supplemental water during periods of extended drought.

B. platyphylla

Minimal pruning is required. Remove any dead, damaged, diseased or awkward branches as needed.

Any pruning of live wood should be done in late summer or fall to prevent the excessive bleeding of sap that occurs if branches are cut in spring.

The bark of B. papyrifera *(paper birch) has been used to make canoes, shelters, utensils and—as the Latin and common names imply—paper.*

B. nigra

Tips

Birch trees are generally grown for their attractive, often white and peeling bark. The bark contrasts nicely with the dark green leaves in summer and with the glossy red or chestnut-colored younger branches and twigs in winter.

Often used as specimen trees, birches' small leaves and open canopy provide light shade that allows perennials, annuals or lawns to flourish beneath. Birch trees are also attractive when grown in groups near natural or artificial water features. They do need quite a bit of room to grow and are not the best choice in gardens with limited space.

The common and popular European white birch *(B. pendula)* and its weeping cultivars are poor choices for gardens because of their susceptibility to pests and diseases, particularly the fatal bronze birch borer. If you plan to grow or already have one of these trees, consult a local gardening center or tree specialist to begin a preventive program.

Recommended

B. lenta (cherry birch) has glossy, serrated leaves and brown-black bark. The fall color is a delicate gold. This birch is excellent for naturalizing. It will grow 25–50' tall and 20–45' wide. (Zones 3–7)

B. nigra (river birch, black birch) has shaggy, cinnamon brown bark that flakes off in sheets when it is young but thickens and becomes ridged as it matures. This fast-growing tree attains a height of 60–90' and a spread of 40–60'. The bright green leaves are silvery white on the undersides. River birch is one of the most disease-resistant species. It also resists bronze birch borer. **Heritage** ('Cully') is an excellent cultivar. It is a vigorous grower and resistant to leaf spot and heat stress. The leaves are larger and glossier than those of the species. The bark begins peeling when the tree is quite young, to show off white or pink areas that mature to salmon brown as the tree ages. (Zones 3–9)

B. platyphylla (Asian white birch) is rarely grown, but several varieties and cultivars are quite common. **'Crimson Frost'** is a purple-leaved cultivar developed from a cross

B. lenta (above), *B. nigra* Heritage (below)

between *B. platyphylla* var. *szechuanica* and *B. pendula* 'Purpurea.' It grows 25–30' tall and about 10' wide. Selected for its resistance to bronze birch borer, **var. *japonica* 'Whitespire'** is similar in appearance to European white birch. It has white bark that doesn't exfoliate. Be sure you buy plants raised from cuttings rather than seeds because seedlings may not resist borers. 'Whitespire' has an upright habit, growing about 40' tall, with a spread of 15–20'. (Zones 4–8)

Problems & Pests

Aphids are fond of birch trees, and the sticky honeydew these insects secrete may drip off the leaves. Avoid planting birch where drips can fall onto parked cars, patios or decks. Other potential problems include leaf miners, birch skeletonizer and tent caterpillars. The bronze birch borer can be fatal; plant a resistant species or cultivar.

B. platyphylla var. *japonica* 'Whitespire'

Birch trees were once a common part of spring fertility rituals in Europe. The maypole, for example, was often a skinned birch.

B. nigra

B. lenta

Black Jetbead
White Kerria
Rhodotypos

Features: habit, flowers, fruit **Habit:** arching, deciduous shrub **Height:** 3–6'
Spread: 3–8' **Planting:** container; any time **Zones:** 4–8

FEW PLANTS BLOOM IN THE SHADE, AND EVEN FEWER PLANTS
bloom and thrive in *dry* shade, but black jetbead is capable of this and more.
Unlike most members of the rose family, it is relatively trouble free and easy
to grow. Its pure white flowers are beautiful in their simplicity, contrasting
wonderfully with the rich green leaves. The jet black berries are lovely but
poisonous, so this shrub shouldn't be planted where its fruit might tempt
children.

Growing

Black jetbead prefers **full sun** but tolerates shade well. The soil should preferably be of **average fertility, moist** and **well drained,** but this plant adapts to
most well-drained soil conditions and tolerates pollution.

Little pruning should be needed, but one-third of the older growth can be
removed each year to keep the shrub vigorous.

Tips

This tough and adaptable plant is useful in difficult garden situations and poor soil locations. It makes an attractive addition to a natural woodland garden or to a shrub or mixed border, where the foliage creates a good backdrop for brightly colored flowers. The black berries persist and add winter interest.

The berries are poisonous.

Recommended

R. scandens is a mound-forming shrub with arching branches. It grows 3–6' tall, with an equal or greater spread. A flush of white flowers is produced in late spring, with sporadic blooms appearing over the summer. Hard, black, round fruits follow the flowers and often persist on the branches over the winter. The foliage emerges early in spring and persists long into fall.

Black jetbead rarely suffers from any pest or disease problems.

Boxwood
Box
Buxus

Features: foliage, habit **Habit:** dense, rounded, evergreen shrub **Height:** 2–20'
Spread: equal to height **Planting:** B & B, container; spring **Zones:** 4–9

IT DOESN'T MATTER IF YOU LIKE TO SHEAR YOUR SHRUBS INTO
meatballs, or if you take an informal and naturalistic approach to shrub gardening; either way, you'll love the boxwoods. They're easy to grow, easily
sheared and shaped, and rich in texture and color. I like to shape my boxwoods in early spring and let them grow feathery for the rest of the year. In
their unpruned form, they become dense and rounded, creating attractive
mounds in the landscape.

Growing

Boxwoods prefer **partial shade** but adapt to full shade or to full sun if kept well watered. The soil should be **fertile** and **well drained**. Once established, boxwoods are drought tolerant.

Many formal gardens include boxwoods because they can be pruned to form neat hedges, geometric shapes or fanciful creatures. The dense growth and small leaves form an even green surface, which, along with the slow rate of growth, makes this plant one of the most popular for creating topiary. When left unpruned, a boxwood shrub forms an attractive, rounded mound.

Boxwoods will sprout new growth from old wood. A plant that has been neglected or is growing in a lopsided manner can be cut back hard in spring. By the end of summer the exposed areas will have filled in with new green growth.

'Green Velvet'

B. sempervirens

A good mulch will benefit these shrubs because their roots grow very close to the surface. For the same reason it is best not to disturb the earth around a boxwood once the shrub is established.

Tips

These shrubs make excellent background plants in a mixed border. Brightly colored flowers show up well against the even, dark green surface of the boxwood. Dwarf cultivars can be trimmed into small hedges for edging garden beds or walkways. An interesting topiary piece can create a formal or whimsical focal point in any garden. Larger species and cultivars are often used to form dense evergreen hedges.

Boxwood foliage contains toxic compounds that, when ingested, can cause severe digestive upset.

Recommended

B. microphylla (littleleaf boxwood) grows about 4' in height and spread. This species is quite pest resistant. It is hardy in Zones 6–9. The foliage tends to lose its green in winter, turning shades of bronze,

'Wintergreen'

The wood of Buxus, *particularly the wood of the root, is very dense and fine-grained, making it valuable for carving. It has been used to make ornate boxes, hence the common name.*

'Green Velvet'

yellow or brown. **Var.** *koreana* is far more cold resistant than the species; it is hardy to Zone 4. **Var.** *koreana* **'Wintergreen'** has foliage that keeps its light green color through the winter. It is hardy to Zone 4.

B. sempervirens (common boxwood) is a much larger species. If left unpruned it can grow to 20' in height and width. It has a low tolerance to extremes of heat and cold and should be grown in a sheltered spot. The foliage stays green in winter. Many cultivars are available with interesting features, such as compact or dwarf growth, variegated foliage and pendulous branches. **'Vardar Valley'** is a wide, mounding cultivar, with dark bluish green foliage. It grows up to 36" tall and spreads about 5'. It is prone to winter damage in Zone 5. (Zones 5–8)

Several cultivars have been developed from crosses between *B. m.* var. *koreana* and *B. sempervirens*. Some of these have inherited the best attributes of each parent—hardiness and pest resistance on the one hand and attractive foliage year-round on the other. **Chicagoland Green** ('Glencoe') boasts a neat, rounded habit, and

it grows quickly to a mature height of 24–36".
'**Green Gem**' becomes a rounded 24" mound.
The deep green foliage stays green all winter.
'**Green Mountain**' forms a large upright shrub
5' tall, with dark green foliage. '**Green Velvet**' is
a hardy cultivar developed in Canada. It has
glossy foliage and a rounded habit, growing up
to 36" in height and spread. (Zones 4–8)

Problems & Pests

Leaf miners, psyllids, scale insects, mites, powdery mildew, root rot and leaf spot are all possible
problems affecting boxwoods.

*Boxwoods are steeped in legend and lore. The
foliage was a main ingredient in an old mad-
dog bite remedy, and boxwood hedges were
traditionally planted around graves to keep
the spirits from wandering.*

B. sempervirens

B. microphylla with *Acer palmatum* cultivar

Bush Honeysuckle
Diervilla

Features: habit, flowers, foliage, adaptability **Habit:** low, thicket-forming deciduous shrub **Height:** 3–5' **Spread:** 3–5' or more **Planting:** container; spring through fall **Zones:** 3–8

BUSH HONEYSUCKLES ARE IN THE SAME BOTANICAL FAMILY AS the true honeysuckles (genus *Lonicera*). The *Diervilla* species are easy-to-grow workhorse shrubs. I have seen the native *D. lonicera* in the Upper Peninsula, growing in difficult shady, dry conditions, and it looked great. Although not spectacular in bloom, the small yellow flowers are attractive, and the foliage is always clean and healthy. These shrubs have excellent resistance to drought and shade and for this reason are highly prized by professional landscapers.

Growing

Bush honeysuckles grow best in **full sun** or **partial shade** but tolerate full shade. Any **well-drained** soil will do. These shrubs will tolerate even dry, rocky soil. Pruning is rarely required, but the plants can be cut back to within 6–12" of the ground in early spring, when the buds begin to swell.

Tips

The bush honeysuckles are hard to beat for low-maintenance or difficult locations. They can be used to stabilize banks or to fill in hot, dry flowerbeds close to the house. They can also be added to mixed or shrub borders or to woodland gardens.

Recommended

D. lonicera (bush honeysuckle, northern bush honeysuckle) is a low, suckering shrub. It grows about 36" tall and spreads 3–5' or more. Small yellow flowers are borne in mid-summer. This is the hardiest species, to Zone 3.

D. sessifolia (southern bush honeysuckle) spreads by suckers to form a dense thicket. It grows 3–5' tall, with an equal or greater spread. The yellow flowers are produced over a long period, from May through July. 'Butterfly' is a cultivar with neater, more compact growth. It flowers over the same long period as the species. (Zones 4–8)

Problems & Pests

These easy-care shrubs rarely suffer any problems, though powdery mildew can occur in locations with poor air circulation.

D. lonicera in fall color

These species used to be grouped with Weigela *but recently have been given their own genus.*

D. sessifolia 'Butterfly'

Butterfly Bush
Summer Lilac
Buddleia (Buddleja)

Features: flowers, habit, foliage **Habit:** large deciduous shrub with arching branches
Height: 4–12' **Spread:** 4–10' **Planting:** container; spring, summer **Zones:** 5–9

IF YOU HAVE KIDS, AND EVEN IF YOU DON'T, you'll definitely want to grow a butterfly bush. It's the one shrub in my yard that actually gets my kids excited. Fast growth and big, fragrant blooms in many different colors are great features, but it's the butterflies these shrubs attract that make them so much fun. Summer wouldn't be the same without the excitement of butterfly bush.

The genus name Buddleia *honors Adam Buddle (1665–1715), a rector from Essex, England, and the author of* English Flora *(1708). Like many clergymen of the time, he also studied botany, believing that doing so helped people understand God's world and brought them closer to the innocence of Eden.*

Growing

Butterfly bushes prefer to grow in **full sun**. Plants grown in shady conditions will produce few, if any, flowers. The soil should be **average to fertile** and **well drained**. These shrubs are quite drought tolerant once established.

Flowers form on the current year's growth. Early each spring cut your shrub back to within 6–12" of the ground to encourage new growth and plenty of flowers. Deadheading will encourage new shoots, extend the blooming period and prevent self-seeding.

Tips

These plants make beautiful additions to shrub and mixed borders. The graceful, arching branches make butterfly bushes excellent specimen plants as well. The dwarf forms that stay under 5' are suitable for small gardens.

B. x weyeriana 'Honeycomb'

Butterfly bushes are among the best shrubs for attracting butterflies and bees to your garden. Don't spray your plant for pests—you will harm the beautiful and beneficial insects that make their homes there.

B. davidii

B. davidii 'Pink Delight'

B. davidii cultivar

Recommended

B. davidii (orange-eye butterfly bush, summer lilac) is the most commonly grown species. It grows 4–10' tall, with an equal spread. This plant has a long blooming period, bearing flowers in bright and pastel shades of purple, white, pink or blue from mid-summer to fall. Popular cultivars include '**Black Knight**,' with dark purple flowers; '**Dubonnet**,' with large spikes of pinkish purple flowers; '**Ellen's Blue**,' with dark blue blooms; '**Harlequin**,' with purple-red flowers and cream and green variegated leaves; '**Orchid Beauty**,' with long spikes of lavender purple flowers; '**Pink Delight**,' with pink flowers; '**Potters Purple**,' with large spikes of dark purple flowers; '**Royal Red**,' with purple-red flowers; '**Summer Beauty**,' with deep pink flowers; '**Summer Rose**,' with purplish pink, yellow-centered flowers; and '**White Ball**' and '**White Bouquet**,' both with white flowers. (Zones 5–9)

B. x *weyeriana* is a wide-spreading shrub with arching stems. It grows 6–12' tall, spreads 5–10' and bears purple or yellow flowers from mid-summer through fall. '**Honeycomb**' bears clusters of attractive yellow flowers. (Zones 6–9)

Problems & Pests

Many insects are attracted to butterfly bushes, but most come just for the pollen and any others aren't likely to be a big problem. Spider mites can be troublesome occasionally. Good air circulation helps keep spider mites at bay and helps prevent the fungal problems that might otherwise afflict these plants.

B. davidii 'White Ball'

These lovely shrubs have a habit of self-seeding, and you may find tiny bushes popping up in unlikely places in the garden. The seedlings are easily pulled up from places they aren't wanted.

B. davidii

Caryopteris
Bluebeard, Blue Spirea
Caryopteris

Features: flowers, foliage, scent **Habit:** rounded, spreading, deciduous shrub
Height: 2–4' **Spread:** 2–5' **Planting:** container; spring, fall **Zones:** 5–9

BLUE FLOWERS ARE ALWAYS WELCOME IN MY GARDEN, AND
caryopteris has a permanent spot on the guest list. This is a great shrub for deliv-
ering a big splash of cool blue flowers in late summer, when few other plants are
blooming. It's easy to grow, it's drought tolerant and, best of all, it's blue!

*Caryopteris is cultivated for
its aromatic stems, foliage
and flowers. A few cut
stems in a vase will
delicately scent a room.*

Growing

Caryopteris prefers **full sun,** but it tolerates light shade. It does best in soil of **average fertility** that is **light** and **well drained.** Wet and poorly drained soils can kill this plant. Caryopteris is very drought tolerant once it is established.

Pruning this shrub is easy. It flowers in late summer, so each spring cut the plant back to within 5–6" of the ground. Flowers will form on the new growth that emerges. Dead-heading or lightly shearing once the flowers begin to fade may encourage more flowering. This plant can be treated as a herbaceous perennial if it is killed back each winter.

Tips

Include caryopteris in your shrub or mixed border. The bright blue, late-season flowers are welcome when many other plants are past their flowering best.

Recommended

C. x *clandonensis* forms a dense mound up to 36" tall and 3–5' in spread. It bears clusters of blue or purple flowers in late summer and early fall. The cultivars are grown more often than *C.* x *clandonensis.* **'Blue Mist'** has fragrant, light blue flowers. It is a low-growing, mounding plant, rarely exceeding 24" in height. **'First Choice'** is a compact, early-flowering cultivar with dark blue flowers. **Grand Bleu** ('Inoveris') is a compact cultivar that matures to about 30" in both height and spread. It has glossy green foliage and dark violet blue flowers. **'Longwood Blue'** is a large,

'Blue Mist'

mound-forming cultivar that grows to about 4' in height and spread. It has light purple-blue flowers and gray-green foliage. **'Worcester Gold'** has bright yellow-green foliage that contrasts vividly with the violet blue flowers. It grows about 36" tall, with an equal spread. This cultivar is often treated as a herbaceous perennial because it may die back in winter. New growth will sprout from the base in spring.

'Worcester Gold'

Cherry
Plum, Almond
Prunus

Features: spring to early-summer flowers, fruit, bark, fall foliage
Habit: upright, rounded, spreading or weeping, deciduous tree or shrub
Height: 3–75'
Spread: 3–50'
Planting: bare-root, B & B, container; spring
Zones: 2–9

CHERRY TREES AND OTHER *Prunus* species have a reputation for being short-lived. It's true that they have their problems, but when I see them blooming each spring, I'm convinced they're worth growing. We who are trained in horticulture feel compelled to share our knowledge. In doing so, unfortunately, we often scare people away from beautiful plants. The world is a better place because people continue to grow ornamental cherries, flowering almonds and their kin in spite of our well-intentioned warnings.

Cut cherry stems in February, mash the ends with a hammer and arrange the stems in a vase indoors for an early burst of fragrant blooms.

Growing

These flowering fruit trees prefer **full sun**. The soil should be of **average fertility, moist** and **well drained**. Plant on mounds when possible to encourage drainage. Shallow roots will come up from the ground if the tree isn't getting enough water.

Pruning should be done after flowering. See the 'Recommended' section for specific pruning requirements for each species.

Tips

Prunus species are beautiful as specimens, and many are small enough to be included in almost any garden. Small species and cultivars can also be included in borders or grouped to form informal hedges or barriers. Pissard plum, Fuji cherry and purple-leaf sand cherry can be trained to form formal hedges.

Because of the pest problems that afflict many cherries, they can be rather short-lived. Choose resistant

P. incisa 'Kojo No Mai'

species, such as Sargent cherry or Higan cherry. If you plant a more susceptible species, such as Japanese flowering cherry, enjoy it while it thrives but be prepared to replace it once the problems surface.

The fruits, but not the pits, of *Prunus* species are edible. Too much of the often sour fruit can cause stomachaches.

P. subhirtella 'Pendula'

Recommended

P. cerasifera 'Atropurpurea' (Pissard plum) is a shrubby, often multi-stemmed tree that grows 20–30' tall, with an equal spread. Light pink flowers that fade to white emerge before the deep purple foliage. The leaves turn dark green as they mature. Pissard plum can be pruned to form a hedge, but plants grown as shrubs or trees need very little pruning. After flowering is finished, remove damaged growth and any awkward branches as required. 'Newport' was bred by crossing 'Atropurpurea' back to the species (*P. cerasifera*). 'Newport' is more commonly available in Michigan because it is more cold hardy and flowers earlier. (Zones 4–8)

P. x *cistena* (purpleleaf sand cherry, purpleleaf dwarf plum) is a dainty, upright shrub that grows 5–10' high, with an equal or lesser spread. The deep purple leaves keep their color all season. The fragrant white or slightly pink flowers open in mid- to late spring after the leaves have developed. The fruits ripen to purple-black in July. This hybrid needs very little pruning if grown as a shrub. It can be trained to form a small tree in space-restricted gardens. Hedges can be trimmed back after flowering is complete. (Zones 3–8)

P. glandulosa (dwarf flowering almond) is a scruffy-looking shrub that grows 4–6' in height and width. The beautiful pink or white, single or double flowers completely cover the stems in early spring, before the leaves emerge. Though very attractive when in flower, this species loses much of its appeal once flowering

P. tomentosa

is finished. Planting it with other trees and shrubs will allow it to fade gracefully into the background as the season wears on. This shrub may spread by suckers; keep an eye open for plants turning up in unexpected and unwanted places. Prune one-third of the old wood to the ground each year, after flowering is complete. '**Rosea Plena**' features pink double flowers. (Zones 4–8)

P. '**Hally Jolivette**' forms a small, bushy tree 15–20' tall, with an equal spread. The light pink double flowers do not open all at once, so the blooming period may last up to three weeks in mid-spring. This cultivar needs little pruning; remove dead or damaged growth as needed and awkward growth in spring, once flowering is complete. (Zones 5–7)

P. incisa (Fuji cherry) is an attractive small tree that grows to about 15' tall and about 10' in spread. It bears white or pink flowers in early spring. Little pruning is needed; remove dead or damaged growth as needed and awkward growth in spring once flowering is finished. Fuji cherry tolerates the heavy pruning needed to form a hedge. '**Kojo No Mai**' is a dwarf cultivar with an interesting zigzagged and layered branching habit. It grows 3–4' tall, with an equal spread. Pink flowers appear in spring, and the leaves turn bright orange in fall. (Zones 4–8)

P. maackii (Amur chokecherry) is a rounded tree that grows 30–45' tall and spreads 25–45'. It tolerates cold winter weather and does well in central and northern parts of Michigan.

P. serrulata

P. glandulosa 'Rosea Plena'

P. x cistena

Fragrant, white mid-spring flowers are followed by red fruits that ripen to black. The glossy, peeling bark is a reddish or golden brown and provides interest in the garden all year. Amur chokecherry needs little or no pruning. Remove damaged growth and wayward branches as required. (Zones 2–6)

P. sargentii (Sargent cherry) is a rounded or spreading tree that grows 20–70' tall, with a spread of 20–50'. Fragrant light pink or white flowers appear in mid- to late spring, and the fruits ripen to a deep red by mid-summer. The orange fall color and glossy, red-brown bark are very attractive. This tree needs little pruning; remove damaged growth and wayward branches as needed. '**Columnaris**' is a narrow, upright cultivar that is suitable for tight spots and small gardens. (Zones 4–9)

P. serrulata (Japanese flowering cherry) is a large tree that grows up to 75' tall, with a spread of up to 50'. It bears white or pink flowers in mid- to late spring. The species is rarely grown in favor of the cultivars. '**Kwanzan**' (Kwanzan cherry) is a popular cultivar with drooping clusters of pink double flowers. It is sometimes grafted onto a single trunk, creating a small, vase-shaped tree. Grown on its own roots it becomes a large spreading tree 30–40' tall, with an equal spread. Because this cultivar has been planted in such large numbers, it has become susceptible to many problems. These problems may shorten the life of the tree, but for 20 to 25 years it can be a beautiful addition to the garden. '**Mount Fuji**' ('Shiro-tae') bears pink buds that open to fragrant white flowers in early spring. It has a spreading habit and grows 15–30' tall, with an equal spread. '**Shirofugan**' is a spreading, vigorous tree that grows 25' tall and 30' wide. Pink flower buds appear in mid-spring and open to fragrant white flowers. The leaves are bronze when young and mature to dark green, turning orange-red in fall. These cultivars need little pruning; remove damaged and wayward branches as needed. (Zones 5–8)

P. Snow Fountain ('Snofozam') is hardier than most flowering cherries, with graceful cascading branches covered in white double flowers. It grows about 25' tall. Little pruning is necessary; remove damaged and wayward branches as needed. (Zones 3–8)

P. incisa 'Kojo No Mai'

Many important fruit and nut crops belong to the genus Prunus, *including apricot* (P. armeniaca), *garden plum* (P. domestica), *peach and nectarine* (*both* P. persica) *and almond* (P. amygdalus).

P. serrulata 'Kwanzan'

P. serrulata 'Shirofugan'
P. serrulata 'Kwanzan'

P. subhirtella (Higan cherry) is a rounded or spreading tree that grows 20–40' tall and spreads 15–25'. The light pink or white flowers appear in early to mid-spring. The cultivars are grown more frequently than the species. 'Autumnalis' (autumn flowering cherry) bears light pink flowers sporadically in fall and prolifically in mid-spring. It grows up to 25' tall, with an equal spread. 'Pendula' (weeping Higan cherry) has flowers in many shades of pink, appearing before the leaves in mid-spring. The weeping branches make this tree a cascade of pink when in flower. It rarely needs pruning; remove damaged and wayward branches as needed. It is sometimes grafted onto a standard trunk, creating a small weeping tree about 7' tall. (Zones 4–8)

P. tomentosa (Nanking cherry, Manchu cherry) is a hardy shrub cherry that is popular for its tart,

edible fruit. Fragrant white flowers appear in mid-spring from pink buds, followed by fruit that ripens by the middle of summer. The shiny, exfoliating, reddish bark is an attractive winter feature. This species grows 6–10' tall and spreads up to 15'. Little pruning is required. Remove awkward or damaged branches as needed to keep the plant tidy. Pruning out some of the lower branches will make the interesting bark easier to see. (Zones 2–7)

Problems & Pests
The many possible problems include aphids, borers, caterpillars, leafhoppers, mites, nematodes, scale insects, canker, crown gall, fire blight, powdery mildew and viruses. Root rot can occur in poorly drained soils. Stress-free plants are less likely to have problems.

P. tomentosa

Although most cherries and plums have edible flesh, the pits, bark and leaves contain hydrocyanic acid. Almonds contain this toxin as well, but in harmless amounts.

P. subhirtella 'Pendula'

Cotoneaster

Cotoneaster

Features: foliage, early-summer flowers, persistent fruit, variety of forms **Habit:** evergreen or deciduous groundcover, shrub or small tree **Height:** 4"–15' **Spread:** 3–12' **Planting:** container; spring, fall **Zones:** 4–9

THERE IS NOTHING BETTER THAN A CREEPING cotoneaster to soften the edges of a cement walk or stone retaining wall. Any place you have too much hardscape, a cotoneaster is a natural, but don't stop there. Cotoneasters come in many shapes and sizes. Attractive flowers, showy fruit, glossy leaves and interesting, graceful forms combine to create a group of first-class garden plants.

Growing

Cotoneasters grow well in **full sun** or in **partial shade**. The soil should be of **average fertility** and **well drained**.

Though pruning is rarely required, these plants tolerate even hard pruning. Pruning cotoneaster hedges in mid- to late summer will let you see how much you can trim off while still leaving some of the ornamental fruit in place. Hard pruning encourages new growth and can rejuvenate plants that are looking worn out.

The name is pronounced cuh-TONE-ee-aster rather than cotton-easter. It means 'quince-like,' possibly referring to the shape of the leaves.

Tips

Cotoneasters can be included in shrub or mixed borders. The low spreaders work well as ground-covers, and shrubby species can be used to form hedges. Larger species are grown as small specimen trees, and some low growers are grafted onto standards and grown as small weeping trees.

Although cotoneaster berries are not poisonous, they can cause stomach upset if eaten in large quantities. The foliage may be toxic.

Recommended

C. adpressus (creeping cotoneaster) is a low-growing deciduous species that is used as a groundcover. It grows only 12" high but spreads up to 7'. The foliage turns reddish purple in fall. (Zones 4–6)

C. apiculatus (cranberry cotoneaster) is a deciduous species that forms a mound of arching, tangled branches. It grows about 36"

C. dammeri

Try a mix of low-growing cotoneasters as a bank planting, or use a shrubby type as a foundation plant.

C. dammeri 'Mooncreeper'

C. apiculatus
C. salicifolius 'Scarlet Leader'

high and spreads up to 7'. The bright red fruits persist into winter. This species is sometimes available in a tree form. (Zones 4–7)

C. dammeri (bearberry cotoneaster) is evergreen. Its low-growing, arching stems gradually stack up on top of one another as the plant matures. This species grows to 18" in height and spreads to 7'. Small white flowers blanket the stems in early summer and are followed by bright red fruits in fall. **'Coral Beauty'** is a groundcover that grows up to 36" in height and spreads 7'. The abundant fruits are bright orange to red. **'Mooncreeper'** is a low-growing cultivar with large white flowers. (Zones 4–8)

C. x **'Hessei'** is a tidy, low-growing deciduous cultivar with an irregular branching habit. It grows about 18" tall and spreads about 6'. The dark pink, late-spring flowers are followed

by fruits that ripen to bright red. The leaves turn burgundy in fall. This cultivar is resistant to spider mites and fire blight. (Zones 4–7)

C. horizontalis (rockspray cotoneaster) is a low-growing deciduous species with a distinctive, attractive herringbone branching pattern. It grows 24–36" tall and spreads 5–8'. The leaves turn bright red in fall. Light pink, early-summer flowers are followed by red fall fruits. (Zones 5–9)

C. salicifolius (willowleaf cotoneaster) is an upright evergreen shrub. It can grow up to about 15' tall and spreads about 12'. The clusters of small, white, late-spring flowers are often hidden by the leaves. The bright red fruits often persist through the winter. '**Scarlet Leader**' is a low, mounding groundcover. It grows 4–24" tall and spreads 6–8'. This cultivar grows quickly and produces plentiful red fruits. (Zones 5–8)

C. horizontalis

Problems & Pests
These plants are generally problem free, but occasional attacks of rust, canker, powdery mildew, fire blight, scale insects, lace bugs, slugs, snails and spider mites are possible.

C. x 'Hessei'

Crabapple
Malus

Features: spring flowers, late-season and winter fruit, fall foliage, habit, bark
Habit: rounded, mounded or spreading, small to medium, deciduous tree
Height: 5–30' **Spread:** 8–30' **Planting:** B & B, container; spring, fall
Zones: 4–8

LIVING IN MICHIGAN, WE'RE BLESSED TO HAVE MANY CRABAPPLE trees in our neighborhoods. My friends from the South and even those from Europe express envy when they see our colorful crabs. These small trees bring us so much joy. In spring they're draped in showy blooms, and in fall and winter we are treated to a display of attractive, edible fruit. Enjoy!

Growing

Crabapples prefer **full sun** but tolerate **partial shade.** The soil should be of **average to rich fertility, moist** and **well drained.** These trees tolerate damp soil.

One of the best ways to prevent the spread of crabapple pests and diseases is to clean up all the leaves and fruit that fall off the tree. Many pests overwinter in the fruit, leaves or soil at the base of the tree. Clearing away their winter shelter helps keep pest populations under control.

Crabapples require very little pruning but adapt to aggressive pruning. Remove damaged or wayward branches and suckers when necessary. Branches that shoot straight up should be removed because they won't flower as much as horizontal branches. The next year's flower buds form in early summer, so any pruning done to shape the tree should be done by late spring, or as soon as the current year's flowering is finished.

Tips

Crabapples make excellent specimen plants. Many varieties are quite small, so there is one to suit almost any size of garden. Some forms are even small enough to grow in large containers. Crabapples' flexible young branches make them a good choice for creating espalier specimens along walls or fences.

M. 'Snowdrift'

Recommended

The following are just a few suggestions from among the hundreds of crabapples available. When choosing a species, variety or cultivar, look for disease resistance. Even the most beautiful plant will never look good if it is ravaged by pests or diseases. Ask for information about new, resistant cultivars at your local nursery or garden center.

M. 'Adirondack' resists all diseases. It is an upright oval tree that grows about 10' tall and spreads about 6'. Red buds open to red-tinged white flowers. The fruit is red or orange. (Zones 4–8)

M. 'Centurion' is highly resistant to all diseases. It is an upright tree that becomes rounded as it matures. It grows to 25' in height, with a spread of 20'. Dark pink flowers appear in late spring. The bright red fruit persists for a long time. (Zones 5–8)

M. 'Christmas Holly' is a bit susceptible to scab but resists other diseases. This small, upright tree grows up to 15' tall. The bright red buds open to white flowers, and the bright red fruit persists into early winter. (Zones 4–8)

M. 'Donald Wyman' is resistant to all diseases except powdery mildew, which can be prevented by pruning out enough growth to allow good air circulation. This cultivar has an open, rounded habit and grows to 20' tall and 25' in spread. Dark pink buds open to white flowers in mid-spring; flowering tends to be heavier in alternating years. The persistent fruit is bright red. (Zones 5–8)

M. floribunda (Japanese flowering crabapple, showy crabapple) is a medium-sized, densely crowned, spreading tree. It grows up to 30' in both height and width. This species is fairly resistant to crabapple problems. Pink buds open to pale pink flowers in mid- to late spring. The apples are small and yellow. (Zones 4–8)

M. 'Ormiston Roy' is fairly disease resistant. This tree grows about 20' tall and develops an open, spreading habit to 25' wide as it matures. The dark pink buds fade as they open to white flowers. The yellowy orange fruit persists. (Zones 4–8)

Though crabapples are usually grown as trees, their excellent response to training makes them good candidates for bonsai and espalier.

An espalier specimen

Opening flowers (below)

M. **'Prairie Fire'** ('Prairifire') is very disease resistant. This rounded tree grows about 20' tall, with an equal spread. New leaves have a reddish tinge but mature to dark green. The red buds and flowers are followed by persistent dark red fruit. (Zones 4–8)

M. **'Professor Sprenger'** is also very disease resistant. This is a bushy, upright tree that can grow 15–20' tall. The pink buds and white flowers are followed by dark orange fruit that persists into early winter. (Zones 4–8)

M. **'Red Swan'** has an attractive weeping habit and grows to about 10' tall. It bears pale pink flowers that mature to white, followed by bright red fruit. (Zones 4–8)

M. sargentii (Sargent crabapple) is a small, mounding tree that is fairly resistant to disease. It grows 6–10' tall and spreads 8–15'. In late spring, red buds open to white flowers. The dark red fruit is long lasting. **'Tina'** is almost identical to the species, except that it grows only 5' tall and spreads up to 10'. With a bit of pruning to control the spread, this cultivar makes an interesting specimen for a large container on a balcony or patio. (Zones 4–8)

M. **'Sinai Fire'** is very disease resistant. This tree has a broad, weeping habit, growing about 12' tall. The red buds and white flowers are followed by persistent orangy red fruit. (Zones 4–8)

M. **'Snowdrift'** is a dense, quick-growing, rounded tree that is resistant to apple scab diseases. It grows 15–20' tall, with an equal spread. Red buds open to white flowers in late spring or early summer. The foliage is dark green and the fruit is bright orange. (Zones 5–8)

Some gardeners use crabapple fruit to make preserves, cider or even wine.

M. **'Sugar Thyme'** ('Sugar Tyme') is very disease resistant. This upright tree grows about 18' tall and spreads about 15'. The buds are pale pink and the flowers are white. The bright red fruit persists through the winter. (Zones 4–8)

M. **'White Angel'** is quite disease resistant and is admired for the masses of white flowers and red fruit that it bears. The habit is rounded, but the branches often bend down with the weight of the fruit. This cultivar grows about 20' tall, with an equal spread. (Zones 4–8)

M. **'White Cascade'** is fairly disease resistant. As the name implies, this tree has a weeping habit that gives the impression of water tumbling over rocks. It grows 10–15' tall and bears dark pink buds that open to white flowers. The apples are small and yellow. (Zones 4–8)

M. 'Sugar Thyme'

Problems & Pests

Aphids, tent caterpillars, leaf rollers, leaf skeletonizers and scale insects are insect pests to watch for, though the damage they cause is largely cosmetic. Leaf drop caused by apple scab is the most common problem with susceptible cultivars. Fire blight, cedar-apple rust, leaf spot and powdery mildew can also be problematic, depending on the weather.

The apple blossom (M. coronaria) is Michigan's official state flower.

Daphne

Daphne

Features: foliage, fragrant spring flowers **Habit:** upright, rounded or low-growing, evergreen, semi-evergreen or deciduous shrub **Height:** 6"–5' **Spread:** 3–5' **Planting:** container; early spring, early fall **Zones:** 4–7

DAPHNES ARE WONDERFUL PLANTS NOTABLE FOR ATTRACTIVE foliage and sweetly fragrant flowers. Once you experience a daphne in full bloom, you will never forget it, and you will want to own one or more. But a word of caution to beginner gardeners: daphnes can be temperamental. They require exacting cultural conditions, and even the best gardeners may lose one. Ah, but it is better to have loved and lost than never to have loved at all.

Growing

Daphnes prefer **full sun** or **partial shade**. The soil should be **moist, well drained** and of **average fertility**. A layer of mulch will keep the shallow roots cool. Avoid over-fertilizing and overwatering.

These plants have neat, dense growth that needs very little pruning. Remove damaged or diseased branches. Flowerheads can be removed if desired, once flowering is finished. Cut flowering stems back to where they join main branches in order to preserve the natural growth habit of the shrub.

Tips

Daphnes can be included in shrub or mixed borders. Rose daphne also makes an attractive groundcover in rock gardens or woodland gardens. Plant daphnes near paths, doors, windows or other places where the wonderful scent can be enjoyed.

D. x *burkwoodii* 'Brigg's Moonlight'

Daphnes have wonderfully fragrant flowers and attractive, often evergreen foliage, making these shrubs appealing all year round.

D. x *burkwoodii* 'Carol Mackie'

Though daphnes are usually said to be hardy to Zone 4, they often thrive as smaller plants in even colder climates. These plants do, however, have a strange habit of dying suddenly. Experts have various theories about why this happens and how to avoid it, but the best advice seems to be to plant daphnes in well-drained soil and then leave them alone. Any disturbance that could stress them should be avoided. Don't move daphnes after they are planted.

All parts of these plants are toxic if eaten, and the sap may cause skin irritations. Avoid planting daphnes where children may be tempted to sample the berries.

Recommended

D. x *burkwoodii* (Burkwood daphne) is a semi-evergreen, upright shrub that grows 3–5' in height and spread. It bears fragrant white or light pink flowers in late spring and sometimes again in fall. **'Brigg's Moonlight'** has yellow foliage with

D. x *burkwoodii* 'Somerset'
D. caucasica

green margins and bears clusters of fragrant pink flowers. 'Carol Mackie' is a common cultivar; its dark green leaves have creamy margins. 'Somerset' has darker pink flowers than *D*. x *burkwoodii*.

D. caucasica (Caucasian daphne) is a rounded, upright, deciduous shrub 4–5' tall, with an equal spread. It bears clusters of fragrant white flowers in a main flush in late spring and sporadically all summer.

D. cneorum (rose daphne, garland flower) is a low-growing evergreen shrub. It grows 6–12" tall and can spread to 4'. The fragrant pale to deep pink or white flowers are borne in late spring. 'Alba' has white flowers. 'Ruby Glow' (sometimes attributed to *D. mezereum*) has reddish pink flowers.

Problems & Pests
Viruses, leaf spot, crown or root rot, aphids, scale insects and twig blight affect daphnes. Poor growing conditions can result in greater susceptibility to these problems. A plant may wilt and die suddenly if diseased.

In late winter cut a few stems and arrange them in a vase indoors— they should come into bloom in a warm, bright room. Enjoy both the sweet scent and the delicately beautiful flowers.

D. cneorum cultivar

Dawn Redwood

Metasequoia

Features: foliage, bark, cones, buttressed trunk **Habit:** narrow, conical, deciduous conifer **Height:** 70–125' **Spread:** 15–25' **Planting:** bare-root, B & B, container; spring, fall **Zones:** 4–8

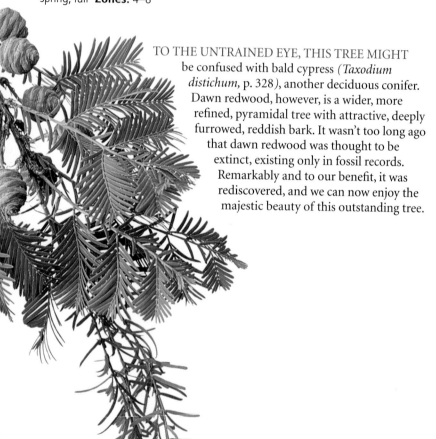

TO THE UNTRAINED EYE, THIS TREE MIGHT be confused with bald cypress (*Taxodium distichum*, p. 328), another deciduous conifer. Dawn redwood, however, is a wider, more refined, pyramidal tree with attractive, deeply furrowed, reddish bark. It wasn't too long ago that dawn redwood was thought to be extinct, existing only in fossil records. Remarkably and to our benefit, it was rediscovered, and we can now enjoy the majestic beauty of this outstanding tree.

Growing

Dawn redwood grows well in **full sun** or **light shade**. The cultivar 'Gold Rush' prefers **partial shade**. The soil should be **humus rich, slightly acidic, moist** and **well drained**. Most types tolerate wet or dry soils, though the rate of growth will be reduced in dry conditions. This tree likes humid conditions and should be mulched and watered regularly until it is established.

Pruning is not necessary. The lower branches must be left in place in order for the buttressing to develop. Buttressed trunks are flared and grooved, and the branches appear to be growing from deep inside the grooves.

Tips

These large trees need plenty of room to grow. Larger gardens and parks can best accommodate them. As single specimens or in group plantings, these trees are attractive and impressive. The cones may not develop in many Michigan gardens because the tree matures very slowly in cold-winter climates.

Recommended

M. glyptostroboides has a pyramidal, sometimes spire-like form. The needles turn gold or orange in fall before dropping. The cultivars do not differ significantly from the species. **'Gold Rush'** has attractive yellow-green foliage. It needs a moist soil. This cultivar grows more slowly than the species and doesn't grow quite as large. **'National'** is narrower than the species. It has not been in cultivation long enough to have reached its mature height, but it is expected to be as tall as the species.

Problems & Pests

Dawn redwood is not generally prone to pest problems, although it can be killed by canker infections.

Don't worry when this tree drops its needles each fall: it's a deciduous conifer.

'Gold Rush'

M. glyptostroboides

Deutzia
Deutzia

Features: early-summer flowers **Habit:** bushy, deciduous shrub **Height:** 2–8'
Spread: 3–8' or more **Planting:** container; spring to fall **Zones:** 4–9

DEUTZIAS MAY BE OLD-FASHIONED, BUT NOSTALGIA IS BACK IN
style, and these shrubs have come a long way since Grandma first used the
large, cumbersome, white-flowered varieties. Nowadays, nurseries are offering new, low-growing cultivars that reach only 12" in height, as well as spectacular selections with colorful pink or lavender blooms. Nostalgia is back,
with style.

Growing
Deutzias grow best in **full sun**. They tolerate light shade but will not bear as
many flowers. The soil should be of **average to high fertility, moist** and **well
drained**.

These shrubs bloom on the previous year's growth. When flowering ceases,
cut flowering stems back to strong buds, main stems or basal growth as
required to shape the plant. Remove one-third of the old
growth on established plants at ground level to encourage new growth.

Tips

Include deutzias in shrub or mixed borders or in rock gardens; you can also use them as specimen plants.

Deutzias are quite frost hardy. If you live in a colder area than is generally recommended for these plants, try growing them in a sheltered spot where they will be protected from the worst extremes of weather.

D. x hybrida 'Magician'

Recommended

D. x elegantissima (elegant deutzia) is an upright shrub with a rounded habit. It grows 4–6' tall, spreads about 5' and bears clusters of pinkish white flowers in early summer. **'Rosealind'** ('Rosalind') bears darker pink flowers. (Zones 5–8)

D. gracilis (slender deutzia) is a low-growing, mounding species hardy in Zones 5–8. It grows 2–4' high, with a spread of 3–7'. In late spring the plant is completely covered with white flowers. **'Nikko'** has white double flowers, and its foliage turns purple in fall. It is hardier than the species, to Zone 4.

D. x hybrida **'Magician'** is a large, arching shrub hardy to Zone 5. It grows 6–8' tall, with an equal or greater spread. The pink-and-white-streaked flowers are borne in loose clusters in early to mid-summer.

D. x lemoinei is a dense, rounded, upright hybrid 5–7' tall, with an equal spread. The early-summer blooms are white. **'Compacta'** ('Boule de Neige') has denser, more compact growth than *D. x lemoinei*. It has large clusters of white flowers. (Zones 5–9)

Problems & Pests

Problems are rare, though these plants can have trouble with fungal leaf spot, aphids and leaf miners.

D. x lemoinei 'Compacta'

Dogwood
Cornus

Features: late-spring to early-summer flowers, fall foliage, fruit, habit
Habit: deciduous large shrub or small tree **Height:** 5–30' **Spread:** 5–30'
Planting: B & B, container; spring to summer **Zones:** 2–9

I LOVE ALL THE MANY DOGWOODS. THE TREE-SIZED FLOWERING
dogwoods—our native, gorgeous *C. florida* and *C. alternifolia* and the exotic
C. kousa—have large, showy blooms and are all worthy of a prominent place
in my garden. The shrub dogwoods *(C. alba, C. sericea)* are easy-growing,
colorful plants that can lift Michiganders out of a winter funk. Choose from
varieties with red, yellow, orange or purple stems, and try planting some of
each. In mid-winter, when they achieve their best color, I like to cut the stems
and display them in a vase or in an urn near the front door.

*The showy parts of
flowering dogwood blooms
are actually bracts, not
petals; the true flowers are
small and clustered in the
center of the four bracts.*

Growing

Flowering dogwoods grow well in **light shade** or **partial shade**. Shrub dogwoods prefer **full sun** or **partial shade**. The best stem colors develop in full sun. For all dogwoods, the soil should be of **average to high fertility,** rich in **organic matter, neutral or slightly acidic** and **well drained.** Shrub dogwoods adapt to most soils but prefer moist soil. *C. sericea* tolerates wet soil.

Flowering dogwoods require very little pruning. Simply removing damaged, dead or awkward branches in early spring is sufficient.

C. alba and *C. sericea,* which are grown for the colorful stems that are so striking in winter, need ongoing rejuvenation pruning because the color is best on young growth. There are two ways to encourage new growth. A drastic, but effective, method is to cut back all stems to within a couple of buds of the ground, in early spring. To make up for the loss of top growth, feed the plant once it starts growing. The second, less drastic, method is to cut back about one-third of the old

C. sericea cultivars

growth to within a couple of buds of the ground, in early spring. This procedure leaves most of the growth in place, and branches can be removed as they age and lose their color.

Tips

The tree species make wonderful specimen plants and are small enough to include in most gardens. Use them along the edge of a woodland garden, in a shrub or mixed border, alongside a house, or near a pond, water feature or patio. Shrub dogwoods can be included in a shrub or mixed border. They look best in groups rather than as single specimens.

C. florida in fall color

Recommended

C. alba (red-twig dogwood, Tartarian dogwood) is a shrub dogwood grown for its bright red winter stems. The stems are green all summer, turning red as winter approaches. This species can grow 5–10' tall, with an equal spread. It prefers cool climates and can develop leaf scorch and canker problems in hot weather. 'Argenteo-marginata' ('Elegantissima') has gray-green leaves with creamy margins. 'Sibirica' (Siberian dogwood) has pinkish red to bright red winter stems. (Zones 2–7)

C. alternifolia (pagoda dogwood) is a native dogwood that can be grown as a large, multi-stemmed shrub or a small, single-stemmed tree. It grows 15–25' tall and spreads 10–25'. The branches have an attractive layered look. Clusters of small white flowers appear in early summer. This species prefers light shade. **Golden Shadows** ('W. Stackman') has leaves variegated yellow and green. (Zones 3–8)

C. 'Constellation' is an upright to somewhat spreading flowering dogwood that grows 15–25' tall and spreads 15–20'. This hybrid was developed from crosses between *C. kousa* and *C. florida*. It is fast growing and resistant to anthracnose and borers. The white blossoms are borne in late spring and early summer, and the leaves become reddish in fall. (Zones 5–9)

C. florida (flowering dogwood) is native to eastern North America. It is usually grown as a small tree 20–30' tall, with an equal or greater spread. It features horizontally layered branches and showy pink or white blossoms that appear in late spring. 'Apple Blossom' has light pink bracts with white at the bases. 'Cherokee Chief' has dark pink bracts. 'Cloud Nine' has large white bracts. Var. *rubra* has light pink bracts. 'Spring Song' has rose pink bracts. This species and its cultivars are susceptible to blight. (Zones 5–9)

C. sericea 'Silver & Gold'

C. kousa (Kousa dogwood) is grown for its flowers, fruit, fall color and interesting bark. This flowering dogwood grows 20–30' tall and spreads 15–30'. It is more resistant to leaf blight and other problems than *C. florida*. The white-bracted, early-summer flowers are followed by bright red fruit. The foliage turns red and purple in fall. **Var.** *chinensis* (Chinese dogwood) grows more vigorously and has larger flowers. '**Gold Star**' has green leaves with a central band of yellow. The stems are reddish. '**Lustgarten Weeping**' has trailing branches and is grafted to a trunk to form a small weeping tree. '**Temple Jewel**' is a compact cultivar that grows about 10–20' tall and 6–15' in spread. It has dark and light green variegated leaves. '**Wolf Eyes**' has white-margined leaves that turn pink or red in fall. (Zones 5–9)

C. sericea (*C. stolonifera*; red-osier dogwood) is a widespread, vigorous native shrub with bright red stems. It grows about 6' tall, spreads up to 12' and bears clusters of small white flowers in early summer. The fall color is red or orange. '**Bud's Yellow**' has bright yellow stems and is disease resistant. '**Cardinal**' has pinkish red stems that become bright red

C. kousa

in winter. '**Flaviramea**' has bright yellow-green stems. '**Silver and Gold**' has excellent white and green variegated leaves and yellow-green stems. '**Winter Flame**' ('Midwinter Fire') has yellow, orange and red stems. (Zones 2–8)

C. '**Stellar Pink**' is a flowering dogwood with an attractive rounded habit. It grows 15–25' tall, with an equal spread. The late-spring or early-summer flowers have pale pink bracts with darker pink veins. The leaves become pinkish to red in fall. This cultivar resists borers and anthracnose. (Zones 5–8)

Problems & Pests

The many possible problems include blight, canker, leaf spot, powdery mildew, root rot, borers, aphids, leafhoppers, scale insects, weevils, nematodes and thrips.

C. florida

Elderberry
Elder
Sambucus

Features: early-summer flowers, fruit, foliage **Habit:** large, bushy, deciduous shrub
Height: 30"–15' **Spread:** 30"–15' **Planting:** bare-root, container; spring, fall
Zones: 3–9

AMERICANS ARE JUST STARTING TO DISCOVER WHAT EUROPEANS
have known for some time: elderberries are great garden plants. In recent
years many new cultivars have become available. Some of the most exciting
have colorful leaves ranging from yellow to dark purple. Several very nice
variegated forms are available as well. I particularly like the cut-leaved selections, which look much like Japanese maple but are hardier and easier to
grow. Elderberries are versatile shrubs that can be treated as perennials.
You can cut back them hard each year or train them
into a small tree form.

Growing

Elderberries grow well in **full sun** or **partial shade**. Cultivars grown for burgundy or black leaf color develop the best color in full sun; cultivars with yellow leaf color develop the best color in light or partial shade. The soil should be of **average fertility, moist** and **well drained**. These plants tolerate dry soil once established.

Though elderberries do not require pruning, they can become scraggly and untidy if ignored. These shrubs will tolerate even severe pruning. Plants can be cut back to within a couple of buds of the ground in early spring. This treatment controls the spread of these vigorous growers and encourages the best foliage color on specimens grown for this purpose.

Plants cut right back to the ground will not flower or produce fruit that season. If you desire flowers and fruit as well as good foliage color, remove only one-third to one-half of the growth in early spring. Fertilize or apply a layer of compost after pruning to encourage strong new growth.

S. nigra Black Beauty (both photos)

S. nigra 'Pulverulenta'

Elderberry fruit attracts birds to the garden and can be used to make wine or jelly.

S. nigra 'Madonna'

Tips

Elderberries can be used in a shrub or mixed border, in a natural woodland garden or next to a pond or other water feature. Plants with interesting or colorful foliage can be used as specimen plants or to create focal points in the garden.

Both the flowers and the fruit can be used to make wine. The berries are popular for pies and jelly. The raw berries are marginally edible but not palatable and can cause stomach upset, particularly in children. Cooking the berries before eating them is recommended. Try them in place of blueberries in pies, scones or muffins.

All other parts of elderberries are toxic.

Recommended

S. canadensis (*S. nigra* subsp.
canadensis; American elderberry) is
a shrub about 12' tall, with an equal
spread. White mid-summer flowers
are followed by dark purple berries.
Native to much of the central and
eastern U.S., this species is generally
found growing in damp ditches and
alongside rivers and streams. **'Aurea'**
has yellow foliage and red fruit.
(Zones 4–9)

S. canadensis 'Aurea'

S. nigra (*S. nigra* subsp. *nigra;* European elderberry, black elderberry) is
a large shrub that can grow 15' tall
and wide. The early-summer flowers
are followed by purple-black fruit.
Black Beauty ('Gerda') has dark
foliage that gets blacker as the season
progresses. It grows 8–12' tall, with
an equal spread. **'Laciniata'** has
deeply dissected leaflets that give the
shrub a feathery appearance. It grows
up to 10' tall. **'Madonna'** has dark
green foliage with wide, irregular,
yellow margins. **'Pulverulenta'** has
unusually dark green and white mottled foliage. It grows slower than
other cultivars but reaches 10'.
(Zones 4–8)

S. racemosa (red elderberry, European red elderberry) grows 8–12'
tall, with an equal spread. This shrub
bears pyramidal clusters of white
flowers in spring, followed by bright
red fruit. **'Goldenlocks'** is a dwarf
cultivar with finely cut yellow leaves.
It grows up to 30" tall, with an equal
spread. **'Sutherland Gold'** has deeply
cut, yellow-green foliage. It grows
5–10' tall. (Zones 3–7)

Problems & Pests

Powdery mildew, borers, dieback,
canker and leaf spot may occasionally affect elderberries.

S. racemosa 'Goldenlocks'

English Ivy

Hedera

Features: foliage, habit **Habit:** evergreen or semi-evergreen, climbing vine or groundcover **Height:** indefinite **Spread:** indefinite **Planting:** container; spring to fall **Zones:** 5–9; some cultivars to Zone 4

ENGLISH IVY IS A BEAUTIFUL, VERSATILE vine. The dark, glossy evergreen leaves create a wonderful groundcover for those difficult shady sites where it's impossible to grow grass. Ivy is easy to grow and fills in quickly to shade out weeds. While it can be very attractive when grown on trees and buildings, it can also create maintenance headaches when it grows across windows, into gutters and over nearby shrubs. Keep your shears handy, and enjoy ivy's reliable, easy-care growth.

Growing

English ivy prefers **light or partial shade** but will adapt to any light conditions from full shade to full sun. The foliage can become damaged or dried out in winter if the plant is growing in a sunny or windy, exposed site. The soil should be **average to fertile, moist** and **well drained**. The richer the soil, the better this vine will grow.

Once established, English ivy can be pruned as much as necessary, at any time of the year, to keep this strong grower where you want it.

Tips

English ivy is grown as a trailing groundcover or as a climbing vine. It clings tenaciously to house walls, tree trunks and many other rough-textured surfaces. Ivy rootlets can damage walls and fences. This vine can also become invasive, but our cold Michigan winters prevent the rampant growth that makes English ivy a noxious weed in the Pacific Northwest.

Many varieties of English ivy are grown as houseplants.

Recommended

H. helix is a vigorous vine that can grow as high as 100', though it is usually pruned to keep it well below its potential size. As a groundcover, it may spread indefinitely but grows about 12" high. Many cultivars have been developed. Some, such as 'Baltica' and 'Thorndale,' are popular for their increased cold hardiness. In a sheltered spot these cultivars are hardy to Zone 4. Others, such as

'Gold Heart,' have interesting foliage but are not exceptionally hardy. This variegated cultivar has leaves with yellow centers.

Problems & Pests

English ivy has very few serious problems. Keep an eye open for infestations of spider mites or bacterial leaf spot. Plants exposed to winter wind may suffer desiccation of the foliage.

Euonymus

Euonymus

Features: foliage, corky stems *(E. alatus)*, habit **Habit:** deciduous or evergreen shrub, small tree, groundcover or climber **Height:** 18"–20' **Spread:** 18"–20' **Planting:** B & B, container; spring, fall **Zones:** 3–9

JUST AS FORSYTHIAS ARE DEAR TO US BECAUSE THEY FORETELL the coming of spring, burning bush *(E. alatus)* is our dependable, much-loved autumn messenger. It is one of the most popular shrubs in Michigan and across the Midwest. Everyone loves its near-fluorescent, pinkish red to scarlet fall color. Furthermore, burning bush is easy to grow, adaptable and willing to be sheared into hedges, balls and other odd and interesting shapes.

Another euonymus can help if you're one of those Midwestern gardeners who pines for the lavish but tender broad-leaved evergreens growable where the weather is less extreme. Wintercreeper euonymus *(E. fortunei)* is a wonderful broad-leaved evergreen we can grow right here in Michigan, and it has plenty of fantastic cultivars.

The name Euonymus *translates as 'of good name'—rather ironically, given that all parts of these plants are poisonous and can cause severe stomach upset.*

Growing

Euonymus prefer **full sun** but tolerate light or partial shade. Soil of **average to rich fertility** is preferable, but any **moist, well-drained** soil will do.

E. alatus requires very little pruning except to remove dead, damaged or awkward growth. It tolerates severe pruning and can be used to form hedges. *E. fortunei* is a vigorous, spreading plant that can be trimmed as required to keep it within the desired growing area; it too tolerates severe pruning. It is also easy to propagate. Bend a branch to the ground, bury the middle section under a bit of soil and hold it down with a rock. Cut this branch off once roots have formed and plant it where you wish.

Tips

E. alatus adds season-long color in a shrub or mixed border, as a specimen, in a naturalistic garden or as a hedge. Dwarf cultivars can be used to create informal hedges. *E. fortunei* can be grown as a shrub in borders

E. fortunei Blondy

or as a hedge. It is an excellent substitute for boxwood. Its trailing habit also makes it suitable as a groundcover or climber.

Recommended

E. alatus (burning bush, winged euonymus) is an attractive, open, mounding, deciduous shrub. It grows 15–20' tall, with an equal or greater spread. The foliage turns a vivid red in fall. The small, red fall berries are somewhat obscured by the bright foliage. Winter interest is

E. alatus Fireball

E. fortunei 'Emerald Gaiety'

provided by the corky ridges, or wings, that grow on the stems and branches. This plant is often pruned to form a neat, rounded shrub, but if left to grow naturally it becomes an attractive, wide-spreading, open shrub. '**Compactus**' (dwarf burning bush) is a popular cultivar. It has more dense, compact growth, reaching up to 10' tall and wide, and has less prominently corky ridges on the branches. It may suffer winter damage during unusually cold winters. **Fire Ball** ('Select') is a hardier selection of 'Compactus' that grows up to 7' tall. It has brilliant red fall color and suffers no winter damage. '**Rudy Haag**' is a dwarf plant with consistent bright red fall color. It grows 3–5' tall. (Zones 3–8)

E. alatus achieves the best fall color when grown in full sun.

E. fortunei (wintercreeper euonymus) as a species is rarely grown in favor of the wide and attractive variety of cultivars. These can be

E. alatus

prostrate, climbing or mounding evergreens, often with attractive, variegated foliage. **Blondy** ('Interbolwji') has yellow foliage with narrow, irregular dark green margins. It grows 18–24" tall. **'Coloratus'** (purple leaf wintercreeper) is a popular cultivar, usually grown as a groundcover. The foliage turns red or purple over the winter. **'Emerald Gaiety'** is a vigorous, shrubby cultivar that grows about 5' tall, with an equal or greater spread. It sends out long shoots that will attempt to scale any nearby wall. This rambling habit can be encouraged, or the long shoots can be trimmed back to maintain the plant as a shrub. The foliage is bright green with irregular, creamy margins that turn pink in winter. **'Vegetus'** grows up to 5' in height and width. This cultivar has large, dark green leaves, and it can

E. alatus

be trained up a trellis as a climber or trimmed back to form a shrub. (Zones 5–9)

Problems & Pests
The two worst problems are crown gall and scale insects, both of which can prove fatal to the infected plant. Other possible problems include leaf spot, aphids, powdery mildew, tent caterpillars and leaf miners.

E. fortunei 'Vegetus'

False Cypress
Chamaecyparis

Features: foliage, habit, cones **Habit:** narrow, pyramidal, evergreen tree or shrub
Height: 10"–100' **Spread:** 1–55' **Planting:** B & B, container; spring, fall
Zones: 4–8

FROM TOWERING 100' GIANTS TO MINUTE 10" DWARFS, THE MYRIAD
species and cultivars of false cypress are as diverse and beautiful as the
landscapes of North America. There is room in every garden for at
least one selection. The attractive evergreen foliage ranges in color
from loud yellow to steel blue to the most elegant emerald
green. With proper placement and careful selection, false
cypresses will add texture, color and form unrivaled by
any other plant.

Chamaecyparis *comes from the
Greek and means 'low cypress,'
even though many species are
very tall trees.*

Growing

False cypresses prefer **full sun**. The soil should be **fertile, moist, neutral to acidic** and **well drained**. Alkaline soils are tolerated. In shaded areas, growth may be sparse or thin.

No pruning is required on tree specimens. Plants grown as hedges can be trimmed any time during the growing season. Avoid severe pruning because new growth will not sprout from old wood. To tidy shrubs, pull dry, brown leaves from the base by hand.

Tips

Tree varieties are used as specimen plants and for hedging. The dwarf and slow-growing cultivars are used in shrub or mixed borders, in rock gardens and as bonsai. False cypress shrubs can be grown near the house.

As with the related arborvitae, oils in the foliage of false cypresses may be irritating to sensitive skin.

Recommended

C. nootkatensis (yellow-cedar, Nootka false cypress) grows 30–100' tall, with a spread of about 25'. The species is rarely grown in favor of the cultivar. **'Pendula'** has a very open habit and even more pendulous foliage than the species. (Zones 4–8)

C. obtusa (Hinoki false cypress), a native of Japan, has foliage arranged in fan-like sprays. It grows about 70' tall, with a spread of 20'. **'Minima'** is a very dwarf, mounding cultivar. It grows about 10" tall and spreads 16". **'Nana Aurea'** grows 3–6' in height and spread. The foliage is

C. obtusa 'Nana Aurea'
C. nootkatensis 'Pendula'

C. *pisifera* cultivar

C. *nootkatensis*

gold-tipped, becoming greener in the shade and bronzy in winter. **'Nana Gracilis'** (dwarf Hinoki false cypress) is a slow-growing cultivar that reaches 24–36" in height, with a slightly greater spread. (Zones 4–7)

C. pisifera (Japanese false cypress, Swara cypress) is another Japanese native. It grows 70–100' tall and spreads 15–25'. The cultivars are more commonly grown than the species. **'Filifera Aurea'** (golden thread-leaf false cypress) is a slow-growing cultivar with golden yellow, thread-like foliage. It grows about 40' tall. **'Nana'** (dwarf false cypress) is a dwarf cultivar with feathery foliage similar to that of the species. It grows into a mound about 12" in

height and width. **'Plumosa'** (plume false cypress) has very feathery foliage. It grows about 20–25' tall, with an equal or greater spread. **'Squarrosa'** (moss false cypress) has less pendulous foliage than the other cultivars. Young plants grow very densely, looking like fuzzy stuffed animals. The growth becomes more relaxed and open with maturity. This cultivar grows about 65' tall, with a spread of about 55'. **'Vintage Gold'** is a dwarf culti-var with bright yellow, feathery foliage that resists fading in summer and winter. It grows 18–30" tall. (Zones 4–8)

Problems & Pests

False cypresses are not prone to problems but can occasionally be affected by spruce mites, root rot, gall or blight.

C. obtusa 'Nana Gracilis'

In the wild, C. nootkatensis *can grow as tall as 165' and as old as 1800 years.*

C. pisifera 'Vintage Gold'

False Spirea
Ural False Spirea
Sorbaria

Features: summer flowers, foliage **Habit:** large, suckering, deciduous shrub
Height: 5–10' **Spread:** 10' or more **Planting:** container; any time **Zones:** 2–8

ADD A TROPICAL LOOK TO YOUR LANDSCAPE WITH THIS FANTASTIC, fast-growing, summer-flowering shrub. To me, false spirea looks more like a monster astilbe or goat's beard than a spirea. Its large, fleecy, white, 8–10" flower clusters combine with foot-long leaves to make a bold statement. But be careful where you plant it. This suckering shrub thrives in rich garden soils and will outpace slower-growing species. Grow it in a location where its suckers are confined, and you'll be pleased with the results.

Growing

False spirea grows equally well in **full sun, partial shade** or **light shade.** The soil should be of **average fertility, moist, well drained** and high in **organic matter.** This plant tolerates hot, dry conditions.

Pruning this suckering shrub is both easy and important. Use a barrier in the soil to help prevent excessive spread, and remove any suckers whenever they appear in undesirable places. As well, yearly after flowering, remove about one-third of the oldest growth. When needed, rejuvenation pruning can be done in spring as the buds begin to swell. To rejuvenate, cut the entire plant back to within a few buds of the ground.

The faded brown seedheads can be removed if you like.

Tips

Use false spirea in large shrub borders, as barrier plants, in naturalized gardens and in lightly shaded wood-land gardens. This plant can be aggressive, but its spread will be most troublesome in smaller gardens.

Recommended

S. sorbifolia is a large, many-stemmed, suckering shrub. Clusters of many tiny, fluffy, white or cream flowers are produced in mid- or late summer. This shrub is native to Asia and is very cold hardy.

Problems & Pests

False spirea has no serious problems but can fall victim to fire blight in stressful conditions.

Fir
Abies

Features: foliage, cones **Habit:** narrow, pyramidal or columnar, evergreen tree or shrub **Height:** 2–70' **Spread:** 3–25' **Planting:** B & B, container; spring **Zones:** 3–7

MANY PEOPLE ARE FAMILIAR WITH THESE LOVELY, SOFT-NEEDLED evergreens as cut Christmas trees. Unfortunately, the species sold as Christmas trees don't do well as ornamentals in Michigan. Most firs are far too exacting in their soil and moisture requirements to be used horticulturally. Even balsam fir *(A. balsamea)*, a common native evergreen in the cool, moist lowlands of northern Michigan, suffers under most landscape situations. Fortunately for fir lovers, white fir *(A. concolor)* and Korean fir *(A. koreana)* are exceptions that can be grown successfully in the right conditions.

Fir and spruce resemble each other, but fir needles are flat and spruce needles are sharply pointed.

Growing

Firs usually prefer **full sun** but tolerate partial shade. The soil should be **rich, cool, moist, neutral to acidic** and **well drained**. These trees prefer a **sheltered** site and generally don't tolerate extreme heat or polluted, urban conditions. *A. concolor* is far more tolerant of such conditions than other *Abies* species.

No pruning is required. Remove dead or damaged growth as needed.

Tips

Firs make impressive specimen trees in large areas. The species tend to be too large for the average home garden. Several compact or dwarf cultivars can be included in shrub borders or used as specimens.

Recommended

A. concolor (white fir, silver fir) is an impressive specimen that grows 40–70' tall in garden conditions but can grow up to 130' in unrestricted natural conditions. It spreads 15–25'. The needles have a whitish coating, giving the tree a hazy blue appearance. **'Candicans'** is a narrow, upright tree with silvery blue needles. **'Compacta'** is a dwarf cultivar. It has whiter needles than the species and grows to 10' in height and spread. This cultivar makes an attractive specimen tree. (Zones 3–7)

A. koreana (Korean fir) is slow growing and small, by evergreen standards. It grows 15–30' tall and spreads 10–20'. The unusual, attractive purple-blue cones are produced while the tree is still young. **'Horstmann's Silberlocke'** ('Silberlocke') has unusual, twisted needles,

A. concolor

which show off the silvery stripes on their undersides. **'Prostrata'** ('Prostrate Beauty') is a low-growing cultivar with bright green needles. It reaches about 24" in height and spreads 3–6'. (Zones 5–7)

Problems & Pests

Firs are susceptible to aphids, bark beetles, spruce budworm, bagworm, rust, root rot and needle blight.

A. koreana 'Horstmann's Silberlocke'

Firethorn

Pyracantha

Features: foliage, early-summer flowers, late-summer and fall fruit **Habit:** dense, thorny, evergreen or semi-evergreen shrub **Height:** 3–18' **Spread:** equal to or greater than height **Planting:** container; spring through summer **Zones:** 5–9

FIRETHORN IS UNRIVALED WHEN IT COMES TO ATTRACTIVE FRUIT displays. A planting of this shrub loaded with masses of bright red, berry-like fruit in late summer or autumn is nothing less than spectacular. Hardiness issues and fire blight have made many a Midwesterner gun-shy when it comes to firethorn. Fortunately, horticulturists have identified the hardiest and healthiest cultivars, so give it a second look. It makes a great, impenetrable hedge, and it's fantastic as a walled espalier.

Firethorn obeys the version of Murphy's Law that states that the more prickly a plant is, the more pruning it will need.

Growing

Firethorn prefers **full sun** and tolerates partial shade, but it doesn't fruit as heavily in partial shade. The soil should preferably be **rich, moist** and **well drained,** but this shrub is fairly adaptable to any well-drained soil, and well-established plants tolerate dry soil. **Shelter** plants from strong winds. Firethorn resents being moved once established, and you will resent having to move this prickly plant.

Some pruning is required to keep this shrub looking neat. In a naturalized setting, it can be left much to its own devices. Remove any damaged growth or wayward branches, and trim back new growth to better show off the fruit.

If using firethorn in a shrub or mixed border, you will have to prune more severely to prevent it from overgrowing its neighbors. Trim hedges in early summer to mid-summer. Trim espalier and other wall-trained specimens in mid-summer. To extend the framework of the specimen, tie growth in place as needed.

Tips

Despite its potential for rampant growth, firethorn has a wide variety of uses. Its prickles make it useful for formal or informal hedges and barriers. It can be grown as a large informal shrub in naturalized gardens and borders. It can also be used as a climber if tied to a trellis or other support. Firethorn's responsiveness to pruning and its dense growth make it an ideal espalier specimen.

Recommended

P. coccinea is a large, spiny shrub 6–18' tall and wide. White flowers cover the plant in early summer, followed by scarlet fruit in fall and winter. 'Aurea' bears distinctive yellow fruit. 'Chadwick' is a compact, spreading plant with abundant red-orange fruit. It is one of the most hardy cultivars, to Zone 5. 'Kasan' ('Kazan') is a hardy cultivar (to Zone 5) from Russia. It has a spreading habit, up to 10' wide, and bears orange-red fruit. 'Red Cushion' grows 3–4' tall and wide. It has a compact habit, bears bright red fruit and resists fire blight. (Zones 6–9)

Problems & Pests

The worst problems are fire blight and scab. Fire blight can kill the plant, and scab disfigures the fruit, turning it a sooty brown. Grow cultivars that are resistant to blight. A few less serious or less frequent problems are root rot, aphids, spider mites, scale insects and lace bugs.

Flowering Quince
Chaenomeles

Features: spring flowers, fruit, spines **Habit:** spreading, deciduous shrub with spiny branches **Height:** 2–10' **Spread:** 2–15' **Planting:** B & B, container; spring, fall **Zones:** 5–9

THEY MAY BE CONSIDERED OLD-FASHIONED by some, but flowering quinces are simply magnificent in bloom. The clear, brightly colored flowers are rich and velvety. In my opinion, the trick to getting the most out of a flowering quince is to plant it against a brick or stone wall. Training it up the wall better exposes its elegant early-spring flowers, which are normally hidden within the framework of the shrub. This espalier technique also highlights the interesting branching and glossy leaves.

Growing

Flowering quinces grow well in **full sun** or **partial shade** but bear fewer flowers and fruit in shade. The soil should be of **average fertility, moist** and **well drained,** and **slightly acidic** soil is preferred. These shrubs tolerate pollution.

On established plants prune back about one-third of the old growth right to the ground every year or so. Tidy plants by cutting back flowering shoots to a strong branch after flowering is finished.

The fruits of flowering quinces are edible when cooked.

Tips

Flowering quinces can be included in a shrub or mixed border. They are very attractive grown against a wall. The spiny habit also makes them useful for barriers. Use them along the edge of a woodland or in a naturalistic garden. The dark bark stands out well in winter.

Leaf drop in mid- to late summer is usually caused by leaf spot. Try drawing attention away from the plant with later-flowering perennials.

C. speciosa 'Toyo-Nishiki'

Recommended

C. japonica (Japanese flowering quince) is a spreading shrub that grows 24–36" tall and spreads up to 6'. Orange or red flowers appear in early to mid-spring, followed by small, fragrant, greenish yellow fruit. This species is not as commonly grown as *C. speciosa* and its cultivars. (Zones 5–9)

C. speciosa (common flowering quince) is a large, tangled, spreading shrub. It grows 6–10' tall and spreads 6–15'. Red flowers emerge in spring and are followed by fragrant, greenish yellow fruit. Many

cultivars are available. **'Cameo'** has large, peach pink double flowers. **'Crimson and Gold'** has a low, spreading habit and bears crimson flowers. It grows 24–36" tall, with an equal or slightly greater spread. **'Texas Scarlet'** bears many red flowers over a fairly long period on plants about half the size of the species. **'Toyo-Nishiki'** is more upright than the species, with white, pink and red flowers that all appear on the same plant. (Zones 5–8)

Problems & Pests

In addition to leaf spot (see above), possible but not often serious problems include aphids, canker, fire blight, mites, rust and viruses.

C. speciosa 'Texas Scarlet'

Forsythia

Forsythia

Features: early- to mid-spring flowers
Habit: spreading, deciduous shrub with upright or
arching branches **Height:** 2–10' **Spread:** 5–12'
Planting: B & B or container in spring or fall; bare-root
in spring **Zones:** 4–9

MANY GARDENERS HAVE A LOVE-HATE
relationship with forsythias. We love them because
they greet us cheerfully with their bright golden
flowers after a long Michigan winter. We hate them
because they grow so darn big, in excess of 10' tall,
and they do little for the garden once the blooms
are finished. The good news is that several new
dwarf and low, mounding forms are available
and fit better into today's smaller residential
landscape. You no longer have to fight the
beast back each year in order to see out
of your windows.

Growing

Most forsythias grow best in **full sun**
but tolerate light shade. *F. viridissima*
var. *koreana* 'Suwan Gold' prefers **partial
shade.** The soil should be of **average
fertility, moist** and **well drained.**

Correct pruning is essential to keep forsythias attractive. Flowers are produced on
growth that is usually at least two years
old. Prune after flowering is finished.
On mature plants, one-third of the oldest
growth can be cut right back to the ground.

Some gardeners trim these shrubs into formal
hedges, but this practice often results in uneven
flowering. An informal hedge allows the plants
to grow more naturally. Size can be restricted by
cutting shoots back to a strong junction.

Tips

These shrubs are gorgeous while in flower, but they aren't very exciting the rest of the year. Include one in a shrub or mixed border where other flowering plants will take over once the forsythia's early-season glory has passed.

The cold-hardiness designation for forsythias can be somewhat misleading. The plants themselves are very cold hardy, surviving in Zone 3 quite happily. The flowers, however, are not as tolerant because the buds form in summer and are then vulnerable to winter cold. Hardiness zones listed here apply to bud and flower hardiness.

In the coldest areas, snow cover is often the deciding factor in flower bud survival. A tall shrub may flower only on the lower half—the part that was buried in and protected by snow. Don't despair, therefore, if your garden is outside the recommended zonal region. If you

F. x intermedia 'Fiesta'

Forsythias can be used as hedging plants, but they look most attractive when grown informally.

F. x intermedia Gold Tide

F. viridissima var. koreana 'Kumson'

For an early touch of spring indoors, cut forsythia for forcing. Simply cut the dormant branches, smash the stem ends with a hammer and place in warm water. Change the water daily and you should have blooms in about a week.

have a good snowfall every year and choose a hardy cultivar, pile some salt-free snow over the plant and you should be able to enjoy forsythia flowers each spring.

Recommended

F. x *intermedia* is a large shrub with upright stems that arch as they mature. It grows 5–10' tall and spreads 5–12'. Yellow flowers emerge in early to mid-spring before the leaves. Many cultivars have been developed from this hybrid. **'Fiesta'** has bright yellow and green variegated foliage and red young stems. **Golden Peep** ('Courdijau') is a dwarf cultivar that grows up to 36" tall. The bright yellow flowers are borne on wood that is only one year old. **Goldilocks** ('Courtacour') is a dwarf cultivar that grows to 4' tall. The flowers are densely clustered along the stems. **Gold Tide** ('Courtasol') is a unique low, spreading

F. ovata 'Northern Gold'

cultivar that grows only 24–30" tall. **'Lynwood'** ('Lynwood Gold') grows to 10' in both height and width. The light yellow flowers open widely and are distributed evenly along the branches. (Zones 6–9)

F. ovata (early forsythia) is an upright, spreading shrub that grows up to 6' tall. This species has the hardiest buds, and its flowers open in early spring. It has been crossed with other species to create more attractive, floriferous, hardy hybrids. **'New Hampshire Gold'** is an attractive compact cultivar with very hardy buds. This reliable bloomer grows up to 6' tall and has the added attraction of developing red-purple fall color. **'Northern Gold'** is a hardy, upright shrub that develops a more arching habit as it matures. It grows 5–8' tall and spreads up to 10'. The bright yellow flowers are very cold hardy. (Zones 4–7)

F. viridissima (greenstem forsythia) is an upright plant with shoots that stay green for several years. It grows 6–10' tall, with an equal spread. Bright yellow flowers appear in early and mid-spring. **Var. *koreana* 'Kumson'** has silvery veins on the green leaves. It grows 4–6' tall. **Var. *koreana* 'Suwan Gold'** has bright yellow foliage and grows 3–4' tall. (Zones 5–8)

Problems & Pests
Most problems are not serious but may include root-knot nematodes, stem gall and leaf spot.

F. x intermedia

Forsythia was named after Scotsman William Forsyth (1737–1804), who served as superintendent of the Royal Gardens at Kensington Palace.

F. x intermedia Goldilocks

Fothergilla

Fothergilla

Features: spring flowers, scent, fall foliage **Habit:** dense, rounded or bushy, deciduous shrub **Height:** 2–10' **Spread:** 2–10' **Planting:** B & B, container; spring, fall **Zones:** 4–9

ALTHOUGH FOTHERGILLAS AREN'T FLASHY, THESE ELEGANT, beautiful shrubs boast multi-season garden interest. In spring they are adorned with lightly fragrant, white, bottlebrush-like flowers. In summer the clean, attractive foliage adds interest and contrast. And in autumn the foliage shines with colors ranging from yellow to orange to scarlet.

The name honors British physician John Fothergill (1712–80), who studied the cultivation of American plants.

Growing

Fothergillas grow well in **full sun** or **partial shade**. In full sun they bear the most flowers and have the best fall color. The soil should be of **average fertility, acidic, humus rich, moist** and **well drained.**

These plants require little pruning. Remove wayward and dead branches as needed.

Tips

Fothergillas are attractive and useful in shrub or mixed borders, in woodland gardens and in combination with evergreen groundcovers.

Recommended

F. gardenii (dwarf fothergilla) is a bushy shrub that grows 24–36" tall, with an equal spread. In mid- to late spring it bears fragrant white flowers. The foliage turns yellow, orange and red in fall. 'Blue Mist' is similar to the species, but the summer foliage is blue-green rather than dark green. This weak-growing cultivar requires rich soil, even moisture and a bit of good luck to grow well.

F. gardenii 'Blue Mist' (both photos)

F. major (large fothergilla) is a rounded shrub that grows 6–10' tall, with an equal spread. The fall colors are yellow, orange and scarlet. 'Mount Airy' is a more compact cultivar, growing 5–6' in height and width. It bears lots of flowers and has more consistent fall color than the species.

The bottlebrush-shaped flowers of fothergillas have a delicate honey scent. Use these generally problem-free plants with rhododendrons and azaleas.

Fringe Tree
Chionanthus

Features: early-summer flowers, fall and winter fruit, bark, habit **Habit:** rounded or spreading, deciduous large shrub or small tree **Height:** 10–25'
Spread: 10–25' **Planting:** B & B, container; spring **Zones:** 4–9

IF I COULD CHOOSE ONLY ONE SMALL FLOWERING TREE FOR MY garden, it would definitely be a fringe tree. The truth is that I have two fringe trees in my garden: a white fringe tree, noted for its abundant flowers and big, glossy leaves; and a Chinese fringe tree, with attractive peeling bark and clouds of lacy white flowers. Both were a challenge to find, but they were well worth the patience and effort needed to get them.

Growing

Fringe trees prefer **full sun**. They do best in soil that is **fertile, acidic, moist** and **well drained** but will adapt to most soil conditions. In the wild they are often found growing alongside streams.

Little pruning is required on mature fringe trees. Thin the stems of young plants to encourage an attractive habit. Prune after flowering, or in spring for young plants that aren't yet flowering.

Tips

Fringe trees work well as specimen plants, in borders or beside water features. Plants begin flowering at a very early age.

These trees may not produce fruit because not all trees of a given species bear both female and male flowers. Male and female trees must be growing near each other for the female to bear fruit. When fruit is produced it attracts birds.

Fringe trees can be difficult to find in nurseries, so you may want to propagate them at home. Seeds planted outdoors in early or mid-summer will germinate after about two years. Semi-ripe cuttings or layerings can be started from Chinese fringe tree in mid- or late summer. White fringe tree does not root well from cuttings.

Recommended

C. retusus (Chinese fringe tree) is a rounded, spreading shrub or small tree. It grows 15–25' tall, with an equal spread. In early summer it bears erect, fragrant white flowers followed in late summer by dark blue fruit. The bark is deeply furrowed and peeling. (Zones 5–9)

C. virginicus (white fringe tree) is a spreading small tree or large shrub that is native to the eastern U.S., excluding Michigan. It grows 10–20' tall, with an equal or greater spread. In early summer it bears drooping, fragrant white flowers, followed only occasionally by dark blue fruit. (Zones 4–9)

Problems & Pests

Fringe trees rarely have any serious problems but can be affected by borers, leaf spot, powdery mildew or canker.

C. virginicus

These small, pollution-tolerant trees are good choices for city gardens.

C. retusus

Ginkgo
Ginko, Maidenhair Tree
Ginkgo

Features: summer and fall foliage, habit, fruit, bark **Habit:** conical in youth, variable with age; deciduous tree **Height:** 40–100' **Spread:** 10–100'
Planting: B & B, bare-root, container; spring, fall **Zones:** 3–9

EVERYTHING ABOUT GINKGO IS UNIQUE AND ADMIRABLE. THIS ancient tree, which has survived ice ages and outlived the dinosaurs, can no longer be found in the wild. Thankfully, people have long cultivated ginkgo for its fruit, medicinal properties and shade. It is an excellent urban shade tree revered for its pest resistance and clear yellow autumn coloration. Remarkably, and as if on cue, it sheds nearly all of its golden leaves within a single day. Raking has never been so easy.

Growing
Ginkgo prefers **full sun**. The soil should be **fertile, sandy** and **well drained,** but this tree adapts to most soils. It also tolerates urban conditions and cold weather. Little or no pruning is necessary.

Tips

Though its growth is very slow, ginkgo eventually becomes a large tree that is best suited as a specimen in parks and large gardens. It can also be used as a street tree. If you buy an unnamed plant, be sure it has been propagated from cuttings. Seed-grown trees may prove to be female, and the stinky fruit is not something you want littering your lawn, driveway or sidewalk.

Recommended

G. biloba is variable in habit. It grows 50–100' tall, with an equal or greater spread. The leaves can turn an attractive shade of yellow in fall, after a few cool nights. Female plants are generally avoided because the fruit has a very unpleasant odor. Several cultivars are available. **'Autumn Gold'** is a broadly conical male cultivar. It grows 50' tall and spreads 30'. Fall color is bright golden yellow. **'Princeton Sentry'** is a narrow, upright male cultivar 40–80' tall and 10–25' in spread.

G. biloba (both photos)

Problems & Pests

This tree seems to have outlived most of the pests that might have afflicted it. A leaf spot may affect ginkgo, but it doesn't cause any real trouble.

The unique leaves of ginkgo resemble those of maidenhair fern (inset).

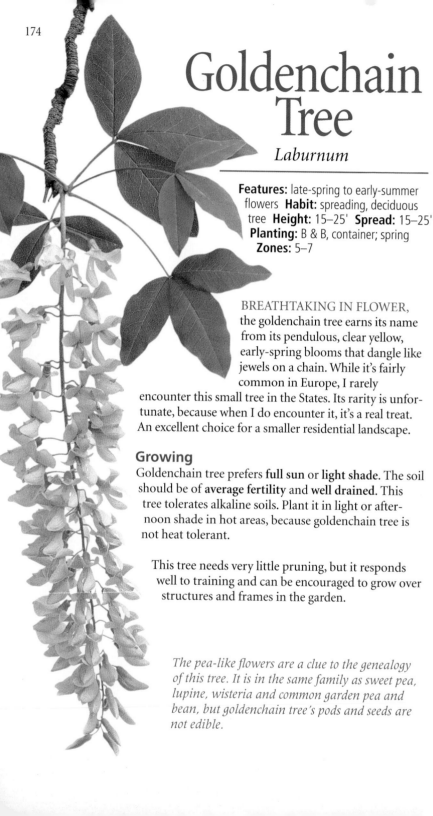

Goldenchain Tree

Laburnum

Features: late-spring to early-summer flowers **Habit:** spreading, deciduous tree **Height:** 15–25' **Spread:** 15–25' **Planting:** B & B, container; spring **Zones:** 5–7

BREATHTAKING IN FLOWER, the goldenchain tree earns its name from its pendulous, clear yellow, early-spring blooms that dangle like jewels on a chain. While it's fairly common in Europe, I rarely encounter this small tree in the States. Its rarity is unfortunate, because when I do encounter it, it's a real treat. An excellent choice for a smaller residential landscape.

Growing

Goldenchain tree prefers **full sun** or **light shade.** The soil should be of **average fertility** and **well drained.** This tree tolerates alkaline soils. Plant it in light or afternoon shade in hot areas, because goldenchain tree is not heat tolerant.

This tree needs very little pruning, but it responds well to training and can be encouraged to grow over structures and frames in the garden.

The pea-like flowers are a clue to the genealogy of this tree. It is in the same family as sweet pea, lupine, wisteria and common garden pea and bean, but goldenchain tree's pods and seeds are not edible.

Tips

Goldenchain tree can be used as a specimen tree in small gardens. This plant is not very attractive when not in flower. Plant an annual or perennial vine like a morning glory or clematis at the foot of your goldenchain tree, and let the vines climb up to provide summer flowers once the golden chains have faded.

All parts of this tree, but especially the seeds, contain a poisonous alkaloid. Children can be poisoned by eating the seeds, which resemble beans or peas.

Recommended

L. x *watereri* bears bright yellow flowers in pendulous clusters up to 10" long. This plant lives longest in climates with cool summers. **'Vossii'** has a denser growth habit and bears flower clusters up to 24" long. This cultivar can be trained to form an espalier.

Problems & Pests

Goldenchain tree may have occasional difficulties with aphids, canker, laburnum vein mosaic, leaf spot, mealybugs and twig blight.

L. x *watereri*

Goldenchain tree can be trained to grow over an arbor, pergola or other such structure.

'Vossii'

Golden Rain Tree

Koelreuteria

Features: habit, foliage, flowers **Habit:** rounded, spreading, deciduous tree
Height: 30–40' **Spread:** 30–40' or more **Planting:** B & B; spring **Zones:** 5–8

THE GOLDEN RAIN TREE IS UNIQUE IN THAT IT IS ONE OF THE FEW trees with showy mid-summer blooms. Massive sprays of small, bright yellow flowers shine against the blue summer sky. And the seed capsules are as memorable as the flowers. Conspicuous, lime green, bladder-shaped capsules cover the tree later in summer. You may not find this tree at your average neighborhood garden center, but then again this is not your average tree.

Growing

Golden rain tree grows best in **full sun.** The soil should be **average to fertile, moist** and **well drained.** This tree tolerates heat, drought, wind and polluted air. It is also pH adaptable and fast growing.

Little pruning is required, though dead or broken branches can be removed as needed and awkward growth can be removed in late winter.

Tips

Golden rain tree makes an excellent shade or specimen tree for small properties. Its ability to adapt to a wide range of soils makes it useful in many garden situations. The fruit is not messy and will not stain a patio or deck if planted to shade these areas.

Recommended

K. paniculata is an attractive, rounded, spreading tree. It bears long clusters of small yellow flowers in mid-summer, followed by red-tinged, green, capsular fruit. The leaves are attractive and somewhat lacy in appearance. In some years, fall color can be a bright yellow. **'Fastigiata'** is an upright, columnar tree that bears fewer flowers than the species. **'September'** has a spreading habit and bears many flowers in late summer and early fall. This cultivar is hardy only to Zone 6.

K. paniculata (both photos)

Problems & Pests

Rare problems with wilt, leaf spot, canker and root rot can occur.

This Asian species is one of the few trees with yellow flowers and one of the only trees to bloom in mid- or late summer.

Hawthorn

Crataegus

Features: late-spring or early-summer flowers, fruit, foliage, thorny branches
Habit: rounded, deciduous tree, often with a zigzagged, layered branch pattern
Height: 15–40' **Spread:** 12–40'
Planting: B & B, container; early spring
Zones: 3–8

THESE SMALL TO MEDIUM TREES OFFER an interesting variety of showy flowers and attractive fruit. If not for the large thorns, hawthorns would be much more commonly used. While the thorns can be a drawback in many situations, they can be a benefit in others. Spiny varieties of hawthorn are excellent for warding off intruders when planted under or in front of windows. A late-night bout with a hawthorn is reason enough for a burglar to consider a career change.

Growing

Hawthorns grow equally well in **full sun** or **partial shade**. They adapt to any **well-drained** soil and tolerate urban conditions.

The hawthorns are members of the rose family, and their fragrant flowers call to mind the scent of apple blossoms.

When grown as trees, hawthorns need little pruning, though removing lower branches is a good idea to avoid harming unsuspecting pedestrians. Hawthorns grown as hedges can be pruned after flowering or in fall. Remove any dead or diseased growth immediately, to prevent the spread of diseases such as fire blight and rust. It is prudent to wear leather gloves and safety goggles when pruning hawthorns.

Hawthorns can become weedy, with seedlings and suckers popping up unexpectedly. Remove any that you find while they are young, because they become quite tenacious if allowed to get bigger.

Tips
Hawthorns can be grown as specimen plants or hedges in urban sites and exposed locations. They are popular in areas where vandalism is a problem because very few people wish to grapple with plants that bear stiff 2" thorns. As a hedge, hawthorns create an almost impenetrable barrier.

C. laevigata

Hawthorn fruits are edible but dry and seedy. Some people make jelly from them, or ferment them and mix them with brandy.

C. laevigata 'Paul's Scarlet'

C. laevigata (both photos)

The genus name Crataegus *comes from the Greek* kratos, *'strength,' a reference to the hard, fine-grained wood.*

These trees are small enough to include in most gardens. With the long, sharp thorns, however, a hawthorn might not be a good selection if there are children about.

Recommended

C. laevigata (*C. oxyacantha;* English hawthorn) is a low-branching, rounded tree with zigzagged layers of thorny branches. It grows 15–25' tall and spreads 12–25'. White or pink late-spring flowers are followed by bright red fruit in late summer. Many cultivars are available. **'Paul's Scarlet'** ('Paulii,' 'Coccinea Plena') has many showy, deep pink double flowers. This cultivar is very popular but very susceptible to blight. (Zones 4–8)

C. phaenopyrum (*C. cordata;* Washington hawthorn) is an oval to rounded, thorny tree 25–30' tall, with a spread of 20–30'. It bears white flowers from early to

mid-summer and has persistent shiny red fruit in fall. The glossy green foliage turns red and orange in fall. This species is least susceptible to fire blight. (Zones 3–8)

C. viridis (green hawthorn) is a small, rounded tree with a dense habit. It grows 20–40' tall, with an equal or slightly lesser spread. White flowers appear in late spring and bright red fruit in fall. The glossy green leaves can turn red or purple in fall. **'Winter King'** has an attractive rounded to vase-shaped habit. The red fruit is larger and persists longer than that of the species. The foliage is rust resistant though the fruit is somewhat susceptible. (Zones 4–7)

C. laevigata 'Paul's Scarlet'

Problems & Pests

Borers, caterpillars, leaf miners, skeletonizers, scale insects, fire blight, canker, rust, powdery mildew, scab and fungal leaf spot are all possible problems. Stress-free hawthorns will be less susceptible.

C. laevigata

Hazel
Filbert
Corylus

Features: early-spring catkins, nuts, foliage, habit **Habit:** large, dense, deciduous shrub or small tree **Height:** 8–20' **Spread:** 10–15' **Planting:** B & B, container; spring, fall **Zones:** 3–9

MOST OF US KNOW ABOUT HAZELNUTS AS A TASTY SNACK, BUT several species and cultivars of *Corylus* are also popular garden plants. The corkscrew hazel, often known as Harry Lauder's walking stick, is the most popular of the ornamental hazels. Its curious twisted branching is highly attractive both in the winter landscape and in a vase. The less common but beautiful purple giant filbert is also a fine plant, adding rich foliage color to the landscape.

Forked hazel branches have been used as divining rods to find underground water or precious metals.

Growing

Hazels grow equally well in **full sun** or **partial shade**. The soil should be **fertile** and **well drained**.

These plants require very little pruning but tolerate it well. Entire plants can be cut back to within 6" of the ground to encourage new growth in spring. On grafted specimens of corkscrew hazel, suckers that come up from the roots can be cut out. They will be easy to spot because they won't have the twisted habit.

Tips

Use hazels as specimens or in shrub or mixed borders.

Recommended

C. avellana (European hazel, European filbert) grows as a large shrub or small tree. It reaches 12–20' in height and spreads up to 15'. Male plants bear long, dangling catkins in late winter and early spring, and female plants develop edible nuts. Cultivars are more commonly grown than

C. maxima var. *purpurea* (both photos)

the species. '**Aurea**' (golden European filbert, yellow-leaved European filbert) has bright yellow foliage that matures to light green over the summer. '**Contorta**' (corkscrew hazel, Harry Lauder's walking stick) is perhaps the best known cultivar. It grows 8–10' tall. The stems and leaves are twisted and contorted. This is a particularly interesting feature in winter, when the bare stems are most visible. Cut out any growth that is not twisted. Keep your eyes open for a new selection called '**Red Majestic**,' a purple-leaved form of corkscrew hazel. The leaves emerge deep red in spring and mature to purple that lasts through early summer.

C. avellana 'Contorta' (all photos, both pages)

C. avellana is grown for commercial nut production, both for the delicious nuts themselves and for the extracted oil.

C. maxima (giant filbert) is a large shrub or small tree that is rarely seen in cultivation. More common is **var. *purpurea***, the purple giant filbert. It makes a fine addition to the spring garden. This variety adds deep purple leaf color and adapts to many soils. It grows 10–12' tall, with an equal spread. The best leaf color develops in full sun, though the rich color usually fades in the heat of summer to dark green.

Problems & Pests
Powdery mildew, blight, Japanese beetles, canker, fungal leaf spot, rust, bud mites, tent caterpillars and webworm may cause occasional problems.

The alternative name for corkscrew hazel, Harry Lauder's walking stick, comes from the gnarled, twisted cane the famous vaudeville comedian used.

Heather
Spring Heath, Winter Heath
Erica

Features: late-winter to mid-spring flowers, foliage, habit **Habit:** low, spreading, evergreen shrub **Height:** 6–12" **Spread:** 8–24" **Planting:** container; spring **Zones:** 5–7

A COMMON GROUNDCOVERING SHRUB IN THE ENGLISH ROCK garden, heather remains little known in North America. There are hundreds of cultivars to choose from, including selections with yellow, orange or bronze foliage. Flower colors include white, pink, red and purple. The dainty, urn-shaped flowers appear in late winter or early spring. Bees and other pollinators enjoy these blossoms as some of the first they visit each spring.

In Scotland, these flowers were used to flavor the traditional heather ale. Legend has it that the last Pict jumped to his death rather than give the recipe to a Scottish king. Heather ale is now being brewed commercially in Scotland.

Growing

Heather prefers **full sun** but tolerates partial shade. The soil should be of **average fertility, acidic, moist** and **well drained**. Though it prefers acidic conditions and enjoys having peat moss mixed into the soil, this plant will tolerate alkaline soil. Do not overfertilize.

To keep heather plants compact and tidy, shear back new growth to within 1" of the previous year's growth once flowering is finished.

The center of each clump tends to mat down and dry out. Use a claw tool to fluff the soil in the middle of the mound in early spring.

Tips

Heather makes an excellent groundcover or rock garden plant. It can be combined with other acid-loving plants in a shrub or mixed border. If you aren't having a lot of luck with your heather, try a small planting where the soil and conditions can be more easily adjusted to suit heather's preferences.

Recommended

E. carnea bears pinkish purple flowers in late winter. The species and its many cultivars, which are more commonly available, grow up to 12" high and 24" wide. **'Ghost Hill'** has red flowers, **'Springwood Pink'** has light pink flowers and **'Springwood White'** has white flowers.

Problems & Pests

Rare problems with rust, *Verticillium* wilt, root rot or powdery mildew are possible.

E. carnea cultivars (both photos)

Hemlock
Eastern Hemlock
Tsuga

Features: foliage, habit, cones **Habit:** pyramidal or columnar, evergreen tree
Height: 1–80' **Spread:** 4–35' **Planting:** B & B, container; spring, fall
Zones: 3–8

MANY PEOPLE WOULD AGREE THAT EASTERN HEMLOCK IS ONE of the most beautiful, graceful evergreen trees in the world. A common sight in cool, moist Michigan woodlands, this tree also makes an outstanding landscape specimen or privacy screen, so long as it is sited properly. Windy sites and very wet or dry soils should be avoided. Hemlock takes kindly to shearing and can be trained into a lovely, rich green, fluffy-looking hedge.

Growing
Hemlock generally grows well in any light from **full sun to full shade.** The soil should be **humus rich, moist** and **well drained.** This tree is drought sensitive and grows best in cool, moist conditions. It is also sensitive to air pollution and suffers salt damage, so keep it away from roadways.

Hemlock trees need little pruning though they respond well to it. The cultivars can be pruned to control their growth as required. Trim hemlock hedges in summer.

Tips

With its delicate needles, hemlock is among the most beautiful evergreens to use as a specimen tree. It can also be shaped to form a hedge.

The smaller cultivars may be included in a shrub or mixed border. The many dwarf forms are useful in small gardens.

Recommended

T. canadensis is a graceful, narrowly pyramidal tree that grows 40–80' tall and spreads 25–35'. It is native to the eastern U.S. Many cultivars are available, including groundcovers and dwarf forms. **'Cole's Prostrate'** is a low, spreading plant about 12" tall and 4' wide. **'Gentsch White'** is a small, shrubby cultivar that grows 4' tall and wide. The new growth becomes creamy white the first fall and winter, contrasting with the older growth. **'Jeddeloh'** is a rounded, mound-forming, slow-growing cultivar 5' tall and 6' in spread. **'Sargentii'** is a large, spreading, mounding form with long, pendulous branches. It grows 10–15' tall and spreads 20–30'. It can be trimmed to restrict its growth.

Problems & Pests

Stress-free trees have few problems. Possible problems may be caused by gray mold, rust, needle blight, snow blight, weevils, mites, aphids, woolly adelgids or scale insects.

The name Tsuga *(pronounced SOO-gah) comes from a Japanese word meaning 'tree-mother.'*

'Jeddeloh'

Hemlocks of the genus Tsuga *are not poisonous, bearing no relation to the herb that killed Socrates.*

T. canadensis

Holly

Inkberry, Winterberry

Ilex

Features: spiny foliage, fruit, habit **Habit:** erect or spreading, evergreen or deciduous shrub or tree **Height:** 3–50' **Spread:** 3–40' **Planting:** B & B, container; spring, fall **Zones:** 3–9

OUR COLD MICHIGAN WINTERS LIMIT THE NUMBER OF HOLLY species we can grow. Several, however, do quite well in our winter wonderland. Among the most useful are blue holly and its cultivars. These large shrubs have glossy, dark green, evergreen leaves and dark purple stems. Our lovely native winterberry is actually a deciduous holly. It can be found in low, wet areas of the state and is easily recognized in winter, when it is loaded with red or reddish orange fruit. A vase of cut winterberry branches is a wonderful way to brighten up your home during those long, gray winter months.

Growing

These plants prefer **full sun** but tolerate partial shade. The soil should be of **average to rich fertility, humus rich** and **moist. Shelter** from winter wind to help prevent the leaves from drying out. Apply a summer mulch to keep the roots cool and moist.

Hollies grown as shrubs require little pruning. Simply remove damaged growth in spring. Hollies grown as hedges can be trimmed in summer. Dispose of all trimmings carefully to prevent the spiny leaves from puncturing bare feet or paws.

Tips

Hollies can be used in groups, in woodland gardens and in shrub and mixed borders. They can also be shaped into hedges.

Inkberry looks much like boxwood and has similar uses in the land-scape. Use it as a low hedge or in a mass planting. It adapts to regular shearing and forms a fuller, more appealing plant when cut back hard on a regular basis.

All hollies have male and female flowers on separate plants, and both must be present for the females to set fruit. One male plant will adequately pollinate two to three females.

Recommended

I. glabra (inkberry) is a rounded shrub with glossy, deep green, ever-green foliage and dark purple fruit. It grows 6–10' tall and spreads 8–10'. **'Compacta'** is a female culti-var with a dense branching habit.

I. x meserveae

Even with the most hardy selections of blue holly, a sheltered, well-drained site is critical for success.

I. glabra 'Nigra'

I. glabra 'Densa'

The showy, scarlet berries look tempting, especially to children, but are not edible.

I. verticillata Berry Heavy

It grows 3–6' tall. **'Densa'** is an upright cultivar that holds its foliage well right to the plant base. It grows up to 6' tall. **'Nigra'** is a dwarf female cultivar with dark glossy leaves. The foliage develops a purple hue in winter. This shrub grows up to 36" tall, with an equal spread. **'Shamrock'** has bright green foliage and an upright habit. It grows 3–4' tall. (Zones 4–9)

I. x *meserveae* (blue holly) is an erect or spreading, dense, evergreen shrub. It grows 10–15' tall, with an equal spread, and bears glossy red fruit that persists into winter. Tolerant of pruning, it makes a formidable hedge or barrier. Many cultivars have been developed, often available in male and female pairs. The males and females can be mixed and matched. **'Blue Prince'** and **'Blue Princess'** have larger leaves, and 'Blue Princess' bears fruit prolifically. These cultivars grow 10–12' tall, with an equal spread. (Zones 5–8)

I. opaca (American holly) is an excellent evergreen tree holly that grows 40–50' tall and spreads 20–40'. The form is often neatly pyramidal when young, becoming more open at maturity. Leaves and fruits vary among the many cultivars; ask at your local garden center for the types that grow best in your area. (Zones 5–9)

I. verticillata (winterberry, winterberry holly) is a deciduous native species grown for its explosion of red fruit that persists into winter. It is good for naturalizing in moist sites in the garden. It grows 6–8' tall, or taller, with an equal spread. **'Aurantiaca'** (forma *aurantiaca*) bears reddish orange fruit that does not persist as long as that of some other winterberries. **Berry Heavy** ('Spravey') bears abundant bright red fruit. **Berry Nice** ('Spriber') bears vivid red fruit noticeable even at a distance. **'Jim Dandy'** is a compact male cultivar, useful for pollinating. It grows up to 6' tall. **'Red Sprite'** is a dwarf 3–4' tall, with bright red fruit. **'Southern Gentleman'** is a

I. x *meserveae* 'Blue Prince'

popular male pollinator but is not as compact as 'Jim Dandy,' growing up to 9' tall. **'Winter Gold'** bears gold fruit. (Zones 3–9)

Problems & Pests

Aphids may attack young shoots. Scale insects and leaf miners can present problems, as can root rot in poorly drained soils.

I. verticillata 'Red Sprite'

Hornbeam
Carpinus

Features: habit, fall color **Habit:** pyramidal, deciduous tree **Height:** 10–70'
Spread: 10–50' **Planting:** B & B, container; spring **Zones:** 3–9

THOUGH SOMEWHAT UNCOMMON, HORNBEAMS ARE AMONG
the finest small to medium landscape trees available. These are stately trees
with few serious pest problems. European hornbeam is the most common
and adaptable species, and it has many fine
cultivars to choose from. Our native American
hornbeam is better known as ironwood or
musclewood because of its very dense wood
and its fluted, muscle-like, gray trunks.

*These slow-growing understory
trees can be planted underneath
very large older trees to create a
pleasing visual balance.*

Growing
Hornbeams prefer **full sun** but tolerate partial
shade. The soil should be **average to fertile** and
well drained. American hornbeam prefers moist
soil and grows well near ponds and streams.

Pruning is rarely required, though it is tolerated. Remove damaged, diseased and awkward branches as needed; hedges can be trimmed in late summer.

Tips

These small to medium-sized trees can be used as specimens or shade trees in smaller gardens or can be pruned to form hedges. The narrow, upright cultivars are often used to create barriers and windbreaks.

Recommended

C. betulus (European hornbeam) is a pyramidal to rounded tree that tolerates heavy pruning and urban conditions. It grows 40–70' tall and spreads 30–50'. The foliage turns bright yellow or orange in fall. **'Columnaris'** is a narrow, slow-growing cultivar. It grows 30' tall and spreads 20'. **'Fastigiata'** is an upright cultivar that is narrow when young but broadens as it matures. It grows 50' tall and spreads 40'. **'Pendula'** is a mound-forming, prostrate cultivar that is usually grafted to a standard to create a weeping tree. (Zones 4–8)

C. caroliniana (American hornbeam, ironwood, musclewood, bluebeech) is a small, slow-growing tree that is very tolerant of shade. It grows 10–30' tall, with an equal spread. The foliage turns yellow to red or purple in fall. (Zones 3–9)

Problems & Pests

Rare problems with powdery mildew, canker, dieback and rot can occur.

C. caroliniana

Propagating hornbeams can be complicated. It is easier to purchase plants someone else has fussed over.

C. betulus

Horsechestnut
Buckeye
Aesculus

Features: early-summer flowers, foliage, spiny fruit **Habit:** rounded or spreading, deciduous tree **Height:** 8–80' **Spread:** 8–70' **Planting:** B & B, container; spring, fall **Zones:** 3–9

THIS DIVERSE GROUP OF TREES AND SHRUBS FEATURES LARGE, showy clusters of flowers and bold, hand-shaped leaves. Common horse-chestnut is a beautiful large tree that is best suited for spacious landscapes such as parks, golf courses and commercial sites. Bottlebrush buckeye, a robust shrub bearing large white flower spikes in mid-summer, is a good choice for residential settings.

Growing

Horsechestnuts grow well in **full sun** or **partial shade**. The soil should be **fertile, moist** and **well drained**. These trees dislike excessive drought. Little pruning is required. Remove wayward branches in winter or early spring.

Tips

Horsechestnuts are used as specimen and shade trees. They are best suited to large gardens. The roots of horsechestnuts can break up sidewalks and patios if planted too close. These trees give heavy shade, excellent for cooling buildings but difficult to grow grass beneath. Use a shade-loving groundcover instead of grass under a horsechestnut.

All parts of horsechestnuts, especially the seeds in the spiky round capsules, are toxic. People have been poisoned when they confused the seeds with those of edible sweet chestnuts (*Castanea* species).

A. x carnea 'Briotii'

Recommended

A. x carnea (red horsechestnut) is a dense, rounded to spreading tree. It grows 30–70' tall, with a spread of 30–50'. It is smaller than common horsechestnut but needs more regular water in summer. Spikes of dark pink flowers are borne in late spring and early summer. 'Briotii' has large, lobed leaves and stunning red flowers in spring. It grows 25–40' tall, with an equal spread. This cultivar is hardy in Zones 5–9. 'O'Neill' grows slowly to 35' in height and bears bright red flowers. (Zones 4–8)

A. hippocastanum (common horsechestnut) is a large, rounded tree that branches right to the ground if grown in an open setting. It grows 50–80' tall and spreads 40–70'. The flowers, borne in spikes up to 12" long, appear in late spring; they are white with yellow or pink marks. (Zones 3–7)

A. parviflora (bottlebrush buckeye) is a spreading, mound-forming, suckering shrub 8–12' tall and 8–15' wide. The plant is covered with spikes of creamy white flowers in mid-summer. This species is not susceptible to the problems that plague its larger cousins. (Zones 4–9)

Problems & Pests

Horsechestnuts are most susceptible to disease when they are stressed. Canker, leaf scorch, leaf spot, scale insects, anthracnose, rust and powdery mildew can all cause problems.

A. hippocastanum

Hydrangea

Hydrangea

Features: flowers, habit; also fall foliage of some species **Habit:** deciduous
mounding shrub, woody climber or spreading shrub or tree **Height:** 3–80'
Spread: 2–10' **Planting:** container; spring, fall **Zones:** 3–9

DON'T JUDGE ALL HYDRANGEAS BASED ON THE VERY COMMON,
droopy Pee Gee hydrangea. Many outstanding species and new cultivars are
available. Easy to grow and blooming reliably, smooth hydrangea is an essential shrub for Michigan gardeners. Some of its cultivars boast gorgeous lacy
flower clusters. Panicled hydrangea's loads of blooms last from late summer
until frost and often turn a wonderful rich pink in late autumn. Smooth
hydrangea, panicled hydrangea and some cultivars of bigleaf hydrangea form
flowers on the current season's wood, so they bloom every year, even in our
climate. The bold, beautiful, easy-growing oakleaf hydrangea has large,
white, conical summer blooms and unique oak-like leaves that transform to
a rich burgundy in autumn. Climbing hydrangea may take a few years to
mature and flower, but it's well worth the wait. In late June, it will greet you
with loads of frothy-looking white flowers—a remarkable sight to behold.

Growing

Hydrangeas grow well in **full sun** or **partial shade**. Smooth hydrangea tolerates full shade. Shade or partial shade reduces leaf and flower scorch in the hotter regions. The soil should be of **average to high fertility, humus rich, moist** and **well drained**. These plants perform best in cool, moist conditions, although established oakleaf hydrangea will tolerate some drought if the roots are kept well mulched.

Bigleaf hydrangea responds to the level of aluminum ions in the soil, and this level in turn depends on pH. In acidic soil the flowers tend to be blue, while the same plant grown in an alkaline soil will tend to have pink flowers. Most cultivars develop their best color in one or the other soil type.

Pruning requirements vary from species to species. See the 'Recommended' section of this entry for specific suggestions.

H. arborescens White Dome

Tips

Hydrangeas come in many forms and have many uses in the landscape. They can be included in shrub or mixed borders, used as specimens and informal barriers, or planted in groups or containers. Climbing varieties can be trained up trees, walls, fences, pergolas and arbors. They will also grow over rocks and can be used as groundcovers.

Hydrangea flowerheads consist of inconspicuous fertile flowers and showy sterile flowers. Mophead

H. quercifolia 'Snow Queen' in fall color

H. serrata 'Blue Bird'

Mophead flowers can be used in fresh or dried arrangements. For the longest-lasting fresh flowers, water the hydrangea deeply the evening before cutting to help keep the petals from wilting. For drying, wait until the blooms begin to change color in late summer before cutting.

H. quercifolia

flowerheads consist almost entirely of showy sterile flowers clustered to form a globular, snowball-like shape. Lacecap flowerheads consist of a combination of sterile and fertile flowers. The showy flowers form a loose ring around the fertile ones, giving this flatter flowerhead a delicate, lacy appearance. Both types are worth growing.

Traces of cyanide are found in the leaves and buds of some hydrangeas. Wash your hands well after handling these plants, and avoid burning clippings because the smoke produced can be toxic.

Recommended

H. anomala* subsp. *petiolaris
(*H. petiolaris;* climbing hydrangea) is considered by some gardeners to be the most elegant climbing plant available. It grows 50–80' tall, clinging to any rough surface by means of little rootlets that sprout from the stems. Though this plant is shade tolerant, it will produce the best flowers when exposed to some direct sun each day. The leaves are a dark, glossy green and sometimes show yellow fall color. For more than a month in summer, the vine is covered with white lacecap flowers, and the entire plant appears to be veiled in a lacy mist. This hydrangea can be pruned after flowering, if required, to restrict its growth. With careful pruning and some support when young, it can be trained to form a small tree or shrub. (Zones 4–9)

Softwood cuttings of smooth hydrangea are easy to root.

H. arborescens (smooth hydrangea) is native to the eastern U.S., excluding Michigan. It forms a rounded shrub 3–5' tall and wide. It is often grown as a perennial, with new growth forming from the base each year. The plants flower on new stems each year and will look most attractive if cut back to the ground in fall. The flowers of the species are not all that showy, but the cultivars have large, showy blossoms. 'Annabelle' bears large, ball-like clusters of white mophead flowers. A single flowerhead may be up to 12" in diameter. This cultivar is more compact than the species and is useful for brightening up a shady wall or corner of the garden. It's common for this plant to collapse under its own weight, especially after a rain. **Subsp.** *radiata* bears white lacecap flowers and has silvery leaf undersides. **White Dome** ('Darsdom') bears very large lacecap flowers. The bold leaves are dark green and the stems are strong. (Zones 3–9)

H. macrophylla (bigleaf hydrangea) is a rounded or mounding shrub that flowers from mid- to late summer. It grows 3–5' tall and spreads up to 6'. Flower buds form on the previous season's growth, and a severe winter or late-spring frost can kill this species back to the point where no flowering occurs. Prune flowering shoots back to the first strong buds once flowering is finished or early the following spring. On mature, established plants, you can remove one-third of the oldest growth yearly or as needed to encourage vigorous new growth. The many cultivars can have mophead or lacecap flowers in shades of pink, red, blue or purple. **'All Summer Beauty'** bears light blue mophead flowers on the previous

H. macrophylla 'Nikko Blue'

and sometimes the current season's growth, making this cultivar useful where other bigleaf hydrangeas are frequently killed back in winter. 'Alpenglow' bears dark red mophead flowers. 'Endless Summer' bears light blue or pink mophead flowers on the current season's growth. It survives cold winters and late-spring frosts well. 'Nikko Blue' bears many large blue to deep lavender mophead flowers. 'Penny Mac' blooms on the current season's growth and bears blue mophead flowers. 'Variegata' features leaves with creamy white margins and occasionally bears purple lacecap flowers. (Zones 5–9)

H. paniculata (panicled hydrangea) is a spreading to upright large shrub or small tree. It grows 10–22' tall, spreads to 8' and bears white flowers from late summer to early fall. This species requires little pruning. When young it can be pruned to encourage a shrub-like or tree-like habit. The entire shrub can be cut to within 12" of the ground each fall to encourage vigorous new growth and larger flowers. 'Grandiflora' (Pee Gee hydrangea) is a spreading large shrub or small tree 8–15' tall and 6–10' in spread. The mostly sterile flowers are borne in mophead clusters up to 18" long. 'Limelight' bears upright clusters of bright lime green flowers that mature to pink and burgundy in fall. 'Little Lamb' bears smaller flower clusters than the species; its delicate white flowers mature to pink in fall. 'Pink Diamond' bears large lacy-looking clusters of white flowers that turn an attractive deep pink in fall. The Swan ('Barbara') bears large clusters of huge white flowers. 'Unique' bears large upright clusters of white flowers that turn pink in fall. (Zones 4–8)

H. paniculata 'Limelight'

H. quercifolia (oakleaf hydrangea) is a mound-forming shrub that is native to the southeastern U.S. It grows 4–8' tall, with an equal spread, and features attractive, cinnamon brown, exfoliating bark. The large leaves are lobed like those of oak and often turn bronze or bright red in fall. Conical clusters of sterile and fertile flowers last from midsummer to fall. Pruning can be done after flowering. Remove spent flowers and cut out some of the older growth to encourage young replacement growth. **'Pee Wee'** and **'Skye's Dwarf'** are compact dwarf cultivars that grow half the size of the species. **'Snowflake'** bears clusters of double flowers 12–15" long that open white and fade to pink with age. The flowers are so heavy they cause the stems to arch down toward the ground. This cultivar prefers partial shade. **'Snow Queen'** bears large, upright flower clusters. The foliage turns a deep, blood red in fall. (Zones 4–8)

H. serrata (sawtooth hydrangea) has a compact, upright habit. It grows 4–5' tall, with an equal spread. The pink or blue, usually lacecap flowers are produced in summer and fall. **'Blue Bird'** bears blue flowers. The leaves turn coppery red in fall. **'Coerulea Lace'** bears long-lasting, light blue flowers. **'Preziosa'** bears white mophead flowers that fade to pink. (Zones 5–7)

Considered the Cadillac of vines, climbing hydrangea is beautiful, especially when grown up a tall, high-limbed tree.

H. arborescens 'Annabelle'

Problems & Pests

Occasional problems for hydrangeas include gray mold, slugs, powdery mildew, rust, ringspot virus and leaf spot. Hot sun and excessive wind will dry out and brown the petals.

H. anomala subsp. *petiolaris*

Japanese Hydrangea Vine

Schizophragma

Features: habit, foliage, flowers **Habit:** woody, deciduous climbing vine
Height: up to 40' **Spread:** up to 40' **Planting:** container; spring or fall
Zones: 5–8

AT FIRST GLANCE, YOU MIGHT MISTAKE THIS VINE FOR CLIMBING hydrangea, but look closely and you'll see it's not a hydrangea at all. Compared with hydrangeas, it grows faster and begins flowering at a younger age. Just like climbing hydrangea, however, this vine is at its best scaling a tall brick wall or the trunk of a high-limbed tree. In mid-summer, the large white blooms shine with bold distinction. Japanese hydrangea vine may not be easy to track down, but it will certainly reward those who make the effort.

Growing

Japanese hydrangea vine grows well in **full sun** or **partial shade**. The soil should be **average to fertile, humus rich, moist** and **well drained**.

Little pruning is required. Trim the vine's branches back to keep the plant within the desired space and to keep it looking neat and attractive.

Although this plant develops clinging rootlets, it's best to secure it in place until it is established. A rough surface is easiest for it to cling to. Over time, if the surface is too smooth, you may have to continue to secure the vine to the wall or other structure.

Tips

This vine will cling to any rough surface and looks attractive climbing a wall, fence, tree or arbor. It can also be used as a groundcover on a bank or allowed to grow up or over a rock wall.

Recommended

S. hydrangeoides is an attractive climbing vine similar in appearance to climbing hydrangea. It can grow up to 40' tall, clinging to the climbing surface with aerial rootlets. Lacy clusters of white flowers appear in mid-summer. '**Moonlight**' has silvery blue foliage. '**Roseum**' bears clusters of pink flowers.

Japanese Pagoda-Tree
Sophora

Features: fall foliage, fragrant summer flowers, habit **Habit:** dense, rounded, wide-spreading, deciduous tree **Height:** 10–50' **Spread:** 10–50'
Planting: B & B, container; spring, fall **Zones:** 5–7

JAPANESE PAGODA-TREE IS ONE OF MY FAVORITE LARGE TREES.
I clearly remember seeing a planting of pagoda-trees lining a Boston street in the middle of July. The magnificent trees were loaded with countless creamy yellow-white blooms, and it was a breathtaking sight. In a world with few flowering street trees, this one provides welcome color and fragrance.

Growing
Japanese pagoda-tree grows best in **full sun**. The soil should be of **average fertility** and **well drained**. Plant in a **sheltered** location and provide some protection to young trees, which can be quite tender until they are established. Once established, this species tolerates most conditions, even polluted urban settings. Pruning is rarely required.

Tips

Use Japanese pagoda-tree as a specimen tree or a shade tree. The cultivar 'Pendula' can be used in borders.

The seeds are poisonous and can even be fatal if eaten.

Recommended

S. japonica can reach heights of 100' in the wild, but it usually grows to about 50' in garden settings. It rises quickly to about 20', and then growth is much slower. It bears fragrant white flowers in summer, and the foliage may turn yellow in fall. **'Pendula'** has long, drooping branches that are usually grafted to a standard, creating a small, dramatic, weeping tree. The size depends on the height of the standard, usually 10–25', with an equal or greater spread. This cultivar rarely flowers.

Problems & Pests

Possible problems can be caused by twig blight, *Verticillium* wilt, canker, rust, powdery mildew and leafhoppers.

S. japonica (both photos)

This tree might be considered messy when the flowers drop, but the blanket of delicate petals on the ground is really quite attractive.

Juniper

Juniperus

Features: foliage, variety of color, size and habit **Habit:** evergreen; conical or columnar tree, rounded or spreading shrub, or prostrate groundcover
Height: 4"–70' **Spread:** 1–25' **Planting:** B & B, container; spring, fall
Zones: 3–9

IT'S SOMETIMES EASY TO DISLIKE A PLANT SIMPLY BECAUSE IT HAS been overused. That is the way I felt about junipers before I had a change of heart. No longer do we need to see the big, ugly Pfitzer junipers that once inhabited our parents' gardens. Junipers have seen tremendous improvements, and we are now offered a tempting array of compact, colorful evergreens that are easy to grow and look great too.

Junipers come in all shapes and sizes and can suit almost any garden. Grow them in the sun to avoid open, straggly growth.

Growing

Junipers prefer **full sun** but tolerate light shade. Ideally the soil should be of **average fertility** and **well drained,** but these plants tolerate most conditions.

Though these evergreens rarely need pruning, they tolerate it well. They can be used for topiary and can be trimmed in summer as required to maintain their shape or limit their size.

Tips

With the wide variety of junipers available, there are endless uses for them in the garden. They make prickly barriers and hedges, and they can be used in borders, as specimens or in groups. The larger junipers can be used to form windbreaks, while the low-growing species can be used in rock gardens and as groundcovers.

The prickly foliage gives some gardeners a rash. It is a good idea to wear long sleeves and gloves when handling junipers. Juniper 'berries' are poisonous if eaten in large quantities.

J. conferta 'Emerald Sea'

Recommended

J. chinensis (Chinese juniper) is a conical tree or spreading shrub. It grows 50–70' tall and spreads 15–20'. Many cultivars have been developed from this species. **'Fruitlandii'** is a vigorous spreader with bright green, densely held foliage. It grows about 36" tall and 6' in spread. **'Hetzii Columnaris'** forms an attractive, narrow pyramid about 20' tall. **'Pfitzeriana Compacta'** is a dwarf form that grows about 4' tall, with an equal or greater spread. **Var.** *sargentii* (Sargent juniper) is a low-growing, spreading variety. It grows only 12–24" tall but can spread to 10'. **'Saybrook Gold'** is a low, spreading

J. sabina 'Buffalo'

cultivar with bright gold needles that take on a bronze hue in winter. It grows 24–36" tall, with a spread of about 6'. (Zones 3–9)

J. conferta (shore juniper) is a stellar groundcover for dry, sandy soils. It grows 12–18" tall and spreads 6–9'. **'Blue Pacific'** has excellent blue-green foliage and compact growth, rarely growing higher than 12". **'Emerald Sea'** is the hardiest cultivar, to Zone 5. It is similar to 'Blue Pacific' but has a looser habit and grows taller. (Zones 6–9)

J. horizontalis (creeping juniper) is a prostrate, creeping groundcover that is native to Michigan and boreal regions across North America. It grows 12–24" tall and spreads up to 8'. This juniper looks attractive cascading down rock walls. The foliage is blue-green, with a purple hue in winter. **'Bar Harbor'** grows 12" tall and spreads 6–10'. The foliage turns a distinct purple in winter. **'Wiltonii'** ('Blue Rug') is very low growing, with trailing branches and silvery blue foliage. It grows 4–6" tall and spreads 6–8'. (Zones 3–9)

J. scopulorum 'Skyrocket' (left), *J. squamata* (below)

J. procumbens (Japanese garden juniper) is a wide-spreading, stiff-branched, low shrub 12–36" tall and 6–15' wide. **'Nana'** is a dwarf, compact, mat-forming shrub. It grows 12–24" tall and spreads 6–12'. (Zones 4–9)

J. sabina (Savin juniper) is a variable, spreading to erect shrub. It grows 4–15' tall and may spread 5–20'. Many popular cultivars are available. **'Broadmoor'** is a low spreader with erect branch-lets. It grows 24–36" tall and spreads up to 10'. **'Buffalo'** has bright green, feathery foliage that holds its color well in winter. It grows 12" tall and spreads about 8'. **'Calgary Carpet'** ('Monna') is a low, spreading plant about 12" tall and 4–5' in spread. (Zones 3–7)

J. horizontalis

The blue 'berries' (actually fleshy cones) are used to season meat dishes and to give gin its distinctive flavor. They also make a nice addition to potpourri.

J. scopulorum (Rocky Mountain juniper) is a rounded or spreading tree or shrub. It grows 30–50' tall and spreads 3–20'. **'Skyrocket'** is a very narrow, columnar tree with gray-green needles. It grows up to 20' tall but spreads only 12–24". **'Tolleson's Weeping'** has arching branches and pendulous, silvery blue, string-like foliage. It grows about 20' tall and spreads 10'. It is some-times grafted to create a small, weeping standard tree. This cultivar can be used in a large planter. (Zones 3–7)

J. chinensis

J. squamata (singleseed juniper) forms a pros-trate or low, spreading shrub or a small, upright tree. It grows up to 30' tall and spreads 3–25'. It is rarely grown in favor of the cultivars. **'Blue Carpet'** forms a low groundcover with blue-gray needles. It grows 8–12" high and spreads 4–5'. **'Blue Star'** is a compact, rounded shrub with sil-very blue needles. It grows 12–36" tall and spreads about 3–4'. (Zones 4–7)

Problems & Pests

Although junipers are tough plants, occasional problems may be caused by aphids, bagworm, bark beetles, canker, caterpillars, cedar-apple rust, leaf miners, mites, scale insects and twig blight.

Kalmia
Mountain Laurel
Kalmia

Features: foliage, late-spring to mid-summer flowers **Habit:** large, dense, bushy, evergreen shrub **Height:** 3–15' **Spread:** 3–15' **Planting:** container; spring, fall **Zones:** 4–9

I'VE HAD THE PLEASURE OF SEEING THIS SHRUB IN ITS NATIVE habitat while hiking in the Blue Ridge Mountains of North Carolina and while driving the back roads of Ohio. Whether in the wild or in the garden, kalmia is unrivaled in bloom, especially when viewed at close range. The intricate flower buds and the clustered flowers vary from pure white to pink to blood red. The glossy, dark green foliage can be attractive all year long. Kalmia's cultural conditions are exacting, but the rewards for growing it are great.

Growing

Kalmia prefers **light or partial shade,** but it tolerates full sun if the soil is consistently moist. The soil should be of **average to high fertility, moist, acidic** and **well drained.** A mulch of leaf mold or pine needles will protect the roots of this drought-sensitive plant from drying out.

Little pruning is required, but spent flowerheads can be removed in summer and awkward shoots removed as needed.

Tips

Use kalmia in a shaded part of a shrub or mixed border, in a woodland garden or combined with other acid- and shade-loving plants, such as rhododendrons.

Do not ingest kalmia foliage or flowers; both are extremely poisonous.

Recommended

K. latifolia grows 7–15' tall, with an equal spread. It has glossy green leaves and pink or white flowers. The cultivars are more commonly

K. latifolia

grown. 'Alpine Pink' has a very dense habit and dark pink buds that open to light pink flowers. 'Elf' is a dwarf cultivar that grows to 36" in height and width. It has pink buds, white flowers and quite small leaves. 'Ostbo Red' is an old cultivar with bright red buds and light pink flowers. 'Silver Dollar' has large white flowers.

Problems & Pests

Kalmia suffers no serious problems, but it can be affected by borers, lace bugs, leaf blight, leaf gall, leaf spot, powdery mildew, scale insects and weevils.

'Ostbo Red'

Katsura-Tree
Cercidiphyllum

Features: summer and fall foliage, habit **Habit:** rounded or spreading, often multi-stemmed, deciduous tree **Height:** 10–70' **Spread:** 10–70' or more **Planting:** B & B, container; spring **Zones:** 4–8

AN UNCOMMON TREE WITH EQUALLY UNCOMMON GRACE AND beauty, katsura-tree is well worth searching out and growing. It is noted for its lovely, clean foliage that emerges reddish purple and changes to a pleasing blue-green in summer. In autumn, the leaves transform to a wonderful yellow to yellow-orange and emit a fragrance that brings to my mind brown sugar. Several spectacular weeping forms are available and are better suited in size for the residential garden.

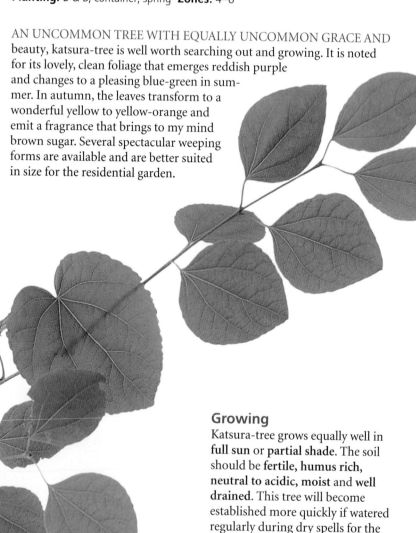

Growing

Katsura-tree grows equally well in **full sun** or **partial shade**. The soil should be **fertile, humus rich, neutral to acidic, moist** and **well drained**. This tree will become established more quickly if watered regularly during dry spells for the first year or two.

Pruning is unnecessary. Damaged branches can be removed as needed.

Tips

Katsura-tree is useful as a specimen or shade tree. The species is quite large and is best used in large landscapes. The cultivar 'Pendula' is wide spreading but can be used in a smaller garden than the species.

This tree is native to eastern Asia, and the delicate foliage blends well into Japanese-style gardens.

Recommended

C. japonicum grows 40–70' tall, with an equal or sometimes greater spread. It is a slow-growing tree that takes a long time to exceed 40'. The heart-shaped, blue-green foliage turns yellow and orange in fall and develops a spicy scent. **'Pendula'** is one of the most elegant weeping trees available. It is usually grafted to a standard and grows 10–25' tall, with an equal or greater spread. Mounding, cascading branches sweep the ground, giving the entire tree the appearance of a waterfall tumbling over rocks.

C. japonicum

Katsura-tree is generally free of pest and disease problems.

'Pendula'

Kerria
Japanese Kerria
Kerria

Features: mid- to late-spring flowers, habit **Habit:** mounding or arching, suckering deciduous shrub **Height:** 3–6' **Spread:** 3–6' **Planting:** B & B, container; spring, fall **Zones:** 4–9

MANY GARDENERS FEEL THAT KERRIA IS ONE OF THE VERY BEST shade-loving, flowering shrubs. Although it can adapt to full shade and full sun, it thrives in partial shade. The early-spring flowers resemble old-fashioned yellow roses, which is no surprise if you know that this shrub is a member of the rose family. When given adequate summer moisture, kerria will bloom again. The kelly green, zigzagged stems are particularly attractive in winter when highlighted with a dusting of snow.

'Picta'

Growing

Kerria prefers **partial shade** but adapts to other light levels. The soil should be of **average fertility** and **well drained**. Fewer flowers will appear on a plant grown in soil that is too fertile.

Prune after flowering. Cut the flowering shoots back to young side shoots or strong buds, or right to the ground. The entire plant can be cut back to the ground after flowering if it becomes overgrown and needs rejuvenating.

Tips

Kerria is useful in group plantings, woodland gardens and shrub or mixed borders.

Most flowers emerge in spring, but some may appear sporadically in summer.

Recommended

K. japonica grows 3–6' tall and spreads 3–6'. It has single yellow blooms. **'Albiflora'** bears light yellow flowers. **'Golden Guinea'** bears large single blooms over a long period.

'Albiflora'

'Picta' has grayish blue-green foliage with creamy margins. **'Pleniflora'** has double flowers; it grows 6' tall, with an equal spread. Its habit is more upright than that of the species.

Problems & Pests

Leaf spot, leaf blight, twig blight, canker and root rot may occur but are not serious.

The distinctive yellow-green to bright green, arching stems of kerria add interest to the winter landscape.

Larch

Larix

Features: summer and fall foliage, cones, habit **Habit:** pyramidal, deciduous conifer **Height:** 30–100' **Spread:** 12–40' **Planting:** B & B, container; early spring **Zones:** 1–7

THE THREE MOST COMMONLY GROWN LARCH species are Japanese larch, European larch and our native eastern larch, often called tamarack. Although larch trees are typically too large for an average residential yard, the low, weeping cultivars are just the right size and are amazingly beautiful. Wavecrest Nursery near Fennville is particularly famous for growing spectacular weeping larch.

Growing

Larches grow best in **full sun**. The soil should be of **average fertility, acidic, moist** and **well drained**. Though tolerant of most conditions, these trees don't like dry or chalky soils. Pruning is rarely required.

Tips

Larches make interesting specimen trees. They are among the few needled trees that lose their foliage each year. In fall the needles turn golden yellow before dropping, and in winter the cones stand out on the bare branches.

Be prepared to reassure your neighbors that your larch is not dying when it loses its needles in fall.

Recommended

L. decidua (European larch) is a large, narrow, pyramidal tree. It grows 70–100' tall and spreads 12–30'. **'Pendula'** has a weeping habit and is usually grafted to a standard. Specimens vary greatly from the bizarre to the elegant. (Zones 3–6)

L. kaempferi (Japanese larch) grows 50–100' tall and spreads 15–40'. It has pendulous branchlets. The summer color of the needles is bluer than that of European larch. Fall color is excellent. (Zones 4–7)

L. laricina (tamarack, eastern larch) is an open, pyramidal tree with drooping branchlets. It is very tolerant of moist soils because it naturally grows in bogs. It grows 30–80' tall and spreads 15–30'. This species is native to Michigan and most of northern North America. (Zones 1–6)

Problems & Pests

Problems may be caused by aphids, case bearers, caterpillars, needle blight, rust and sawflies.

L. laricina

L. decidua 'Pendula'

Lilac

Syringa

Features: mid-spring to early-summer flowers, habit **Habit:** rounded or suckering, deciduous shrub or small tree **Height:** 3–30' **Spread:** 3–25' **Planting:** B & B, container; late winter, early spring **Zones:** 2–8

MOST OF US KNOW AND LOVE LILACS. THE NAME ALONE EVOKES memories of sweet fragrance and romance, yet few of us truly appreciate the diversity of these showy shrubs. Lilacs range from the dwarf Korean lilac, only 36" tall, to the Japanese tree lilac, which reaches 30'. The flowers come in white and many gorgeous shades of pink, purple and blue, and cultivars are available with variegated or otherwise interesting foliage. So don't limit your view of lilacs to that of the common French lilac grown since Grandma's day: you have hundreds of beautiful plants to choose from.

Growing

Lilacs grow best in **full sun**. The soil should be **fertile, humus rich** and **well drained**. These plants tolerate open, windy locations, and the improved air circulation helps keep powdery mildew at bay. Clear up leaves in fall to help discourage overwintering pests.

Most lilacs need little pruning. On established French lilac plants, you can cut one-third to one-half of the growth right back each year after flowering. This treatment will make way for vigorous young growth and prevent the plants from becoming leggy, overgrown and unattractive.

Deadhead lilacs as much as possible to keep plants neat. Remove the flowers as soon as they are finished to give the plant plenty of time to produce next season's flowers.

S. x hyacinthiflora 'Evangeline'

Tips

Include lilacs in a shrub or mixed border or use them to create an informal hedge. Japanese tree lilac can be used as a specimen or small shade tree.

The wonderfully fragrant flowers have inspired the development of some 800–900 cultivars of S. vulgaris.

S. meyeri Tinkerbelle

Recommended

S. x *hyacinthiflora* (hyacinth-flowered lilac) is an upright hybrid that becomes spreading as it matures. It can grow up to 15' tall, with an equal spread. Clusters of fragrant flowers appear in mid- to late spring. The following cultivars are resistant to powdery mildew and bacterial blight. **'Anabel'** is an early-blooming cultivar with pink flowers. It grows 6–9' tall. **'Evangeline'** bears light purple double flowers. This nonsuckering cultivar grows 8–10' tall. **'Excel'** bears lavender flowers and also grows 8–10' tall. **'Pocahontas'** bears very fragrant reddish purple flowers. It grows 10–12' tall. (Zones 3–7)

S. **'Josee'** is a dwarf hybrid that grows 4–6' tall, with an equal spread. It bears clusters of lavender pink blooms in late spring and sporadically until the first frost. (Zones 2–8)

S. meyeri (Meyer lilac, dwarf Korean lilac) is a compact, rounded shrub that grows 3–8' tall and spreads 3–12'. It bears fragrant pink or lavender flowers in late spring and early summer and sometimes again in fall. It does not sucker profusely. **'Palabin'** bears clusters of mauve pink blossoms. **Tinkerbelle** ('Bailbelle') bears fragrant, bright pink flowers. (Zones 3–7)

S. microphylla (littleleaf lilac) is an upright, broad-spreading shrub that grows 6' tall and spreads 9–12'. It bears fragrant, lilac pink flowers in early summer and sometimes again in fall. This is a very neat shrub with small, tidy leaves and attractive, airy clusters of flowers. (Zones 4–8)

S. patula (Manchurian lilac) is a hardy lilac from Korea and northern China. It grows 5–10' tall, spreads 3–8' and bears small clusters of fragrant, lilac-colored flowers. This species produces very few suckers. **'Miss Kim'** is similar to the species in shape and size but is denser in habit. The dark green leaves turn burgundy red in fall. (Zones 3–8)

S. reticulata (Japanese tree lilac) is a rounded large shrub or small tree that grows 20–30' tall and

S. vulgaris 'Sensation'
S. meyeri 'Palabin'

spreads 15–25'. It bears white flowers in early summer and does not produce many suckers. This species and its cultivars are resistant to the troublesome powdery mildew, scale insects and borers. 'Ivory Silk' has a more compact habit and produces more flowers than the species. It grows 10–12' tall and spreads 6'. (Zones 3–7)

S. vulgaris (French lilac, common lilac) is the plant most people think of when they think of lilacs. It grows 8–22' tall, spreads 6–22' and bears fragrant, lilac-colored flowers in late spring and early summer. This suckering, spreading shrub has an irregular habit, but consistent maintenance pruning will keep it neat and in good condition. Many cultivars are available, of which the following are but a few examples. **'Alba'** has white single flowers. **'Belle de Nancy'** has pink double flowers. **'Charles Joly'** has magenta double flowers. **'Krasavitska Moskvy'** ('Pride of Moscow') bears white flowers that open from pink buds. **'Mme. Lemoine'** has large, white double flowers. **'President Lincoln'** has very fragrant, blue single flowers. **'Sensation'** features white-margined, purple flowers. (Zones 3–8)

Problems & Pests
Powdery mildew, leaf spot, stem blight, borers, caterpillars, scale insects and root-knot nematodes are all possible troublemakers for lilacs.

Lilacs are frost-loving shrubs that don't flower at all in the warm southern parts of the U.S.

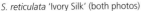

S. reticulata 'Ivory Silk' (both photos)

Linden

Tilia

Features: habit, foliage **Habit:** dense, pyramidal to rounded, deciduous tree
Height: 20–80' **Spread:** 20–45' **Planting:** B & B, bare-root, container;
spring, fall **Zones:** 2–8

THE LINDENS, AND PARTICULARLY THE LITTLELEAF LINDEN, ARE
picturesque shade trees with a signature gumdrop shape. The early-summer
yellowish green flowers are not especially showy, but they're highly fragrant
and add to the trees' charm. Lindens are most desirable shade and street trees
because of their refined habit, moderately fast growth and wide adaptability.
Landscape architects love to use them in allées of single or double rows. The
effect is formal but at the same time comfortable.

Growing

Lindens grow best in **full sun**. The soil should be **average to fertile, moist** and
well drained. These trees adapt to most pH levels but prefer an **alkaline** soil.
T. cordata tolerates pollution and urban conditions better than *T. americana*.

Little pruning is required. Remove dead, damaged, diseased or awkward
growth as needed. On multi-stemmed specimens, all but the strongest stems
should be pruned out.

Tips

Lindens are useful and attractive street trees, shade trees and specimen trees. Their tolerance of pollution and their moderate size make lindens ideal for city gardens.

The blossoms exude a dripping honeydew that will coat anything underneath, so don't plant lindens near a driveway.

Recommended

T. americana (basswood, American linden) is rarely used in gardens. It grows 60–80' tall and spreads about half this wide. This tree is very cold hardy and is native to most of the eastern half of the U.S., including Michigan. The smaller '**Redmond**' is more commonly grown than the species. It becomes a pyramidal tree, more densely branched than the species, and grows about 20–35' tall. (Zones 2–8)

T. cordata (littleleaf linden) is a dense, pyramidal tree that may become rounded with age. It grows 60–70' tall, spreads 30–45' and bears small flowers with narrow yellow-green bracts in summer. '**Greenspire**' is a compact cultivar 40–50' tall and 20–25' in spread. (Zones 3–7)

T. americana (both photos)

Problems & Pests

Occasional problems with anthracnose, aphids, mites, Japanese beetles, canker, powdery mildew, caterpillars, leaf spot, leaf miners and borers can occur.

Given enough space, lindens will branch right to the ground.

Magnolia
Magnolia

Features: flowers, fruit, foliage, habit, bark **Habit:** upright to spreading, deciduous shrub or tree **Height:** 8–30' **Spread:** 8–30' or more **Planting:** B & B, container; winter, early spring **Zones:** 3–9

WHO CAN RESIST SUCH BIG, BEAUTIFUL FLOWERS? I KNOW I CAN'T, so I continue to plant magnolias. In a good spring, these trees rival any plant on the planet. In a bad spring, when an ill-timed frost kills the blooms, you feel sick to your stomach thinking about what might have been. Despite the possibility of losing the flowers to a late frost, magnolia trees are worthy of planting in Michigan. One good spring flower display in three years still makes all other flowering trees seem inadequate.

Growing
Magnolias grow well in **full sun** or **partial shade**. The soil should be **fertile, humus rich, acidic, moist** and **well drained**. A summer mulch will help keep the roots cool and the soil moist. Sweetbay magnolia tolerates wet soils and shaded locations.

Very little pruning is needed. When plants are young, thin out a few branches to encourage an attractive habit. Avoid transplanting; if necessary, transplant in early spring.

Tips

Magnolias are used as specimen trees, and the smaller species can also be used in borders.

Avoid planting magnolias where the morning sun will encourage their blooms to open too early in the season. The blossoms can be damaged by cold, wind and rain.

Recommended

M. x 'Butterflies' is an upright tree that grows about 15' tall and spreads about 11'. In mid-spring, it bears yellow, cup-shaped flowers with red stamens. (Zones 5–9)

M. liliiflora (M. quinquepeta; lily magnolia) forms a large, rounded shrub 8–12' tall, with an equal spread. The outsides of the petals are purple and they open to reveal white insides. Flowers are borne in mid- to late spring. This species can look scruffy by the end of the season and is more famous as one of the parent plants of *M.* x *soulangiana.*

M. liliiflora 'Ann'

Despite their often fuzzy coats, magnolia flower buds are frost sensitive.

M. stellata 'Royal Star'

'Ann' bears purple-red flowers. It is less likely to suffer frost damage because it flowers later than many other magnolias. 'Betty' bears white flowers with many petals that are dark purple on the outsides. 'Susan' bears large, purple-red flowers. (Zones 5–9)

M. x *loebneri* (Loebner magnolia) was developed from a cross between *M. kobus* and *M. stellata*. This rounded, spreading tree grows 15–30' tall, with an equal or greater spread. It is one of the earliest magnolias to bloom, bearing white or pink flowers in early to mid-spring. **'Leonard Messel'** bears white flowers that have a pink or purple stripe down the center and are pink on the undersides. This cultivar doesn't flower as early as the parent hybrid. **'Merrill'** bears abundant white flowers. It is fast growing and cold hardy to Zone 3. (Zones 5–9)

M. liliiflora

M. x *loebneri* 'Merrill'

M. x *soulangiana* (*M.* x *soulangeana;* saucer magnolia) is a rounded, spreading shrub or tree. It grows 20–30' tall, with an equal spread. Pink, purple or white flowers emerge in mid- to late spring. 'Alexandrina' is an upright tree. Its flower petals are pink on the outside and white on the inside. (Zones 5–9)

M. x *soulangiana* (both photos)

M. stellata (star magnolia) is a compact, bushy or spreading shrub or small tree. It grows 10–20' tall and spreads 10–15'. Many-petaled, fragrant white flowers appear in early to mid-spring. '**Centennial**' is a vigorous, upright cultivar that is cold hardy to Zone 3. Its white flowers have 28–32 petals each. '**Royal Star**' is a vigorous cultivar with pink buds that open to white flowers. (Zones 4–9)

M. virginiana (sweetbay magnolia, swamp magnolia) is a spreading, open shrub or small, multi-stemmed tree. It grows 10–20' tall, with an equal spread, and bears very fragrant creamy white flowers in late spring or early summer. (Zones 5–9)

Problems & Pests
Possible problems affecting magnolias include leaf spot, canker, dieback, treehoppers, powdery mildew, scale insects, snails, thrips and weevils.

Maple
Acer

Features: foliage, bark, fruit, fall color, habit, flowers **Habit:** deciduous; multi-stemmed tree or large shrub **Height:** 6–80' **Spread:** 6–70' **Planting:** B & B, container; preferably spring **Zones:** 2–8

MAPLES OFFER A WEALTH OF DIVERSITY AND ORNAMENTAL BEAUTY. These trees or large shrubs are attractive all year long, boasting delicate flowers in spring, attractive foliage and hanging samaras in summer, vibrant leaf color in fall and interesting bark and branch structures in winter. The smaller maples, such as *A. japonicum, A. palmatum* and *A. griseum,* make excellent specimens for residential landscapes. The large maples make outstanding shade trees, especially *A. rubrum* and *A. saccharum* with their remarkable autumn hues. *A. saccharinum,* the silver maple, is one of the few commercially available maples I don't generally recommend. It is a weak-wooded tree, breaking apart at worst and dropping sticks and branches at best. There's really no reason to grow it when the world of maples includes so many excellent alternatives.

Growing

Generally maples do well in **full sun** or **light shade**, though their preference varies from species to species. The soil should be **fertile, moist**, high in **organic matter** and **well drained**.

The amount of pruning needed depends on how much time you have and on what purpose the tree will serve in the garden. Informal and naturalistic gardens will require less pruning, while a formal garden may demand more effort. If maples are allowed to grow naturally, you simply need to remove dead, damaged or diseased branches at any time. These trees respond well to pruning, however, and can even be used to create bonsai specimens. Pruning should take place when maples are fully leafed out, in early to mid-summer.

Tips

Maples can be used as specimen trees, as large elements in shrub or mixed borders or as hedges. Some are useful as understory plants bordering wooded areas; others can be grown in containers on patios or terraces. Few Japanese gardens are without the attractive smaller maples. Almost all maples can be used to create bonsai specimens.

A. palmatum

The sap of A. saccharum *is used to make the famous, and delicious, maple syrup, but other maples can also be tapped for their sweet sap.*

A. rubrum

A. platanoides 'Drummondii'
A. griseum

Recommended

A. campestre (hedge maple) forms a dense, rounded tree 25–35' tall, with an equal spread. Its low-branching habit and tolerance of heavy pruning make it popular as a hedge plant. The foliage is often killed by frost before it turns color, but in a warm fall it may turn an attractive yellow. (Zones 4–8)

A. x *freemanii* and its cultivars were developed from a cross between *A. rubrum* and *A. saccharinum.* They vary in habit and fall coloration. They generally grow 40–50' tall, with a spread of 20–40'. '**Marmo**' has bright red fall color that lasts for several weeks. '**Morgan**' is a fast-growing tree with an open habit and bright orange to red fall color. (Zones 4–7)

A. ginnala (Amur maple) is both attractive and extremely hardy; it can withstand winter temperatures as low as −50° F. It also adapts to many soil types and a wide pH range. This species grows 15–25' tall, with an equal or greater spread. It can be grown as a large, multi-stemmed shrub or pruned to form a small tree. Because it responds well to pruning, it is often used in cold climates in place of the tender *A. palmatum* or *A. japonicum* in Japanese-style gardens. *A. ginnala* has attractive dark green leaves, bright red samaras and smooth bark with distinctive vertical striping. The fall foliage is often a brilliant crimson. The color develops best in full sun, but the tree will also grow well in light shade. This is a popular tree for patios and terraces because it can be grown in a large planter. (Zones 2–8)

A. griseum (paperbark maple) is attractive and adapts to many conditions. It grows very slowly to 20–35' tall, with a width half or equal the height. This maple is popular because of its orange-brown bark that peels and curls away from the trunk in papery strips. Unfortunately, it is difficult to propagate, so it can be expensive and sometimes hard to find. (Zones 5–8)

A. japonicum (fullmoon maple, Japanese maple) is an open, spreading tree or large shrub. It grows 20–30' tall, with an equal or greater spread. This species is more cold hardy than the closely related *A. palmatum*, with a few specimens surviving in very sheltered Zone 3 or 4 gardens. The leaves turn stunning shades of yellow, orange and red in fall. 'Aconitifolium' has deeply lobed leaves that turn deep red in fall. (Zones 5–7)

A. palmatum var. *dissectum* cultivar

A. palmatum (Japanese maple) is considered by many gardeners to be one of the most beautiful and versatile trees available. Though many cultivars and varieties are quite small, the species itself generally grows 15–25' tall, with an equal or greater spread. With enough space it may even reach 50'. Because it leafs out early in spring, this tree can be badly damaged or killed by a late-spring frost. (Zones 5–8)

Maple fruits, called samaras, have wings that act like miniature helicopter rotors and help in seed dispersal.

Two distinct groups of cultivars have been developed from *A. palmatum* and are commonly available. Types without dissected leaves, derived from

A. ginnala samaras

A. platanoides 'Crimson King'

Maple wood is hard and dense and is used for fine furniture construction and for some musical instruments.

A. palmatum var. dissectum

A. p. var. *atropurpureum,* are grown for their purple foliage, though many lose their purple coloring as summer progresses. Two that keep their color are 'Bloodgood' and 'Moonfire,' both of which grow to about 15' tall. Types with dissected leaves, derived from *A. p.* var. *dissectum,* have foliage so deeply lobed and divided that it appears fern-like or even thread-like. The leaves can be green, as in the cultivar 'Waterfall,' or red, as in 'Red Filigree Lace' and 'Crimson Queen.' 'Ornatum' has dissected leaves with silvery variegations. These trees are generally small, growing to 6–10' tall and wide. (Zones 5–8)

A. platanoides (Norway maple) is a rounded or oval tree 40–50' tall or taller, with an equal or slightly lesser spread. It has very dense growth, so grass may not grow well beneath it. Its fall color can be good unless an early frost hits before the color develops. This maple is a tough city tree, but don't use it near natural wooded areas; the seedlings are prolific and can outcompete many native plants when given the opportunity. 'Crimson King' is a very common cultivar with dark purple foliage. This dark tree casts a heavy shade. 'Drummondii' (harlequin maple) has light green foliage with wide creamy margins. Any growth that doesn't develop the variegated foliage should be pruned out. (Zones 4–8)

A. rubrum (red maple) is pyramidal in habit when young and becomes more rounded as it matures. Single- and multi-stemmed specimens are available. It grows 40–70' tall and has a variable spread of 20–70'. The cold tolerance of this maple varies depending on where the plant has been grown. Locally bred trees will adapt best to the local climate. Fall color varies from tree to tree, some developing no fall color and others developing bright yellow, orange or red foliage. Choose named cultivars for the best fall color. 'October Glory' has brilliant fall leaves, starting out orange and gradually turning dark red. The color turns late in fall and an early frost can spoil it. Red Sunset ('Franksred') has deep orange to red fall color and good cold tolerance. (Zones 4–8)

A. saccharum (sugar maple) is considered by many to be the most impressive and majestic of all the maples. It has a rounded pyramidal outline, grows 60–80' tall and spreads 40–50'. Its brilliant fall color ranges from yellow to red. This large species does not tolerate restricted, polluted, urban conditions but makes a spectacular addition to parks, golf courses and large properties. '**Endowment**' is a fast-growing columnar cultivar with scarlet fall color. '**Green Mountain**' has dark green foliage and is tolerant of drought and smaller growing spaces. The fall color may be yellow, orange or scarlet. '**Majesty**' ('Flax Hill Majesty') is a densely branched cultivar with an upright oval habit. The fall color is scarlet. (Zones 3–8)

Problems & Pests

Anthracnose, *Verticillium* wilt, aphids, caterpillars, leafhoppers, borers, leaf spot, scale insects, and canker can affect maples. Chlorosis (leaf yellowing) caused by nutrient deficiency can occur in alkaline soils. Leaf scorch can be prevented by watering young trees during hot, dry spells.

A. japonicum (both photos)

Mock-Orange
Philadelphus

Features: early-summer flowers **Habit:** rounded, deciduous shrub with arching branches **Height:** 18"–12' **Spread:** 18"–12' **Planting:** container; spring, fall **Zones:** 3–8

ONCE CONSIDERED PRIZED POSSESSIONS, MOCK-ORANGES FELL out of favor, only to be rediscovered as worthy garden plants. Sure, they can be one-season wonders, but isn't that true of many popular ornamentals? Grow a mock-orange if only to fill your garden with its exquisite fragrance in early to mid-summer. I'm convinced that gardeners should strive to have something fragrant in bloom all season long. It's a worthy aspiration, and mock-oranges help us achieve it.

Growing
Mock-oranges grow well in **full sun, partial shade** or **light shade.** The soil should be of **average fertility, humus rich, moist** and **well drained.**

On established plants, each year after the bloom, remove one-third of the old wood. Overgrown shrubs can be rejuvenated by cutting them right back to within 6" of the ground. Established mock-oranges transplant readily, although they have a huge mass of woody roots in relation to the amount of top growth.

Tips

Include mock-oranges in shrub or mixed borders or in woodland gardens. Use them in groups to create barriers and screens.

Recommended

P. coronarius (sweet mock-orange) is an upright, broadly rounded shrub with fragrant white flowers in late spring or early summer. It grows 8–12' tall, with an equal width. **'Aureus'** has bright yellow young foliage that matures to yellow-green. It grows 8' tall and spreads 5'. **'Variegatus'** has leaves with creamy white margins. It grows 8' tall and spreads 6'. This cultivar grows best in partial shade. (Zones 4–8)

P. **'Snowbelle'** is a low-growing shrub with graceful, arching branches. It grows 18–36" tall, with a spread of about 18". Fragrant white flowers completely cover the plant in summer. (Zones 4–8)

P. **'Snowdwarf'** is a compact shrub with arching branches. It grows

P. coronarius 'Variegatus'

18–36" tall and spreads 18". The fragrant white flowers appear in summer. (Zones 4–8)

P. x *virginalis* **'Minnesota Snowflake'** is a hardy, dense, upright shrub 8' tall and 8–10' in spread. It bears fragrant, white double flowers in mid-summer. (Zones 3–7)

Problems & Pests

Mock-oranges may be affected by fungal leaf spot, gray mold, powdery mildew, rust and scale insects, but these problems are rarely serious.

P. 'Snowbelle'

Ninebark

Physocarpus

Features: mid-spring or early-summer flowers, fruit, bark, foliage
Habit: upright, sometimes suckering, deciduous shrub **Height:** 4–10'
Spread: 4–15' **Planting:** container; spring, fall **Zones:** 2–8

EVEN THOUGH COMMON NINEBARK IS NATIVE FROM THE SHORES of Lake Superior to the shores of Lake Erie and beyond, it is hardly noticed by many Michiganders. Commanding more attention are the cultivated selections, which now include plants with yellow and purple leaves. When this colorful foliage is combined with white, button-like June blooms, attractive red autumn fruit and peeling winter bark, you have a shrub for all seasons. As a bonus, ninebark is an easy-growing plant that adapts to most garden conditions.

You may not actually find nine layers, but the peeling, flecked bark of ninebark does add interest to the winter landscape.

Growing

Ninebark grows well in **full sun** or **partial shade**. The best leaf coloring develops in a sunny location. The soil should be **fertile, acidic, moist** and **well drained**.

Little pruning is required, but you can remove one-third of the old stems each year after flowering is finished to encourage vigorous new growth.

Tips

Ninebark can be included in a shrub or mixed border, or in a woodland or naturalistic garden.

Recommended

P. opulifolius (common ninebark) is a suckering shrub with long, arching branches and exfoliating bark. It grows 5–10' tall and spreads 6–15'. Light pink flowers in early summer are followed by fruits that ripen to reddish green. **'Dart's Gold'** grows 5' in height and spread. It has bright gold leaves that hold their color well

'Dart's Gold'

in summer. **Diabolo** ('Monlo') has attractive purple foliage and grows 4' in height and spread. **'Nugget'** is a compact plant with bright yellow foliage that matures to lime green over the summer. This cultivar grows 6' tall, with an equal spread.

Problems & Pests

Occasional problems with leaf spot, fire blight and powdery mildew may occur.

'Nugget'

Oak

Quercus

Features: summer and fall foliage, bark, habit, acorns **Habit:** large, rounded, spreading, deciduous tree **Height:** 40–120' **Spread:** 10–100' **Planting:** B & B, container; spring, fall **Zones:** 2–9

WE LIVE IN EXCITING TIMES: NURSERIES ARE NOW GROWING TREES in containers. This simple yet revolutionary change in tree production is opening the door to growing oaks and other trees that were poorly suited to field production and digging. Oaks are stately trees of great diversity, and many species are native to Michigan. We need to use more of them in our landscapes. If chosen carefully, they deliver relatively fast growth and adapt to many soil conditions.

Growing

Oaks grow well in **full sun** or **partial shade**. The soil should be **fertile, moist** and **well drained**. Red oak and pin oak prefer a **moist, acidic** soil.

No pruning is needed. These trees can be difficult to establish. Transplant them only while they are young because oaks don't like having their roots disturbed.

Tips

Oaks are large trees best suited to be grown as specimens or in groves in parks and large gardens. Do not disturb the ground around the base of an oak; these trees are very sensitive to changes in grade.

The acorns are generally not edible. Acorns of certain oak species are edible but usually must be processed first to leach out the bitter tannins.

Recommended

Q. alba (white oak) is a rounded, spreading tree that grows 50–100' tall, with an equal spread. The leaves turn purple-red in fall. This tree is native to Michigan. (Zones 3–9)

Q. palustris

Oaks have been held sacred by many cultures throughout history. The ancient Greeks believed these trees were the first ones to be created, and the Roman poet Virgil said that they gave birth to the human race.

Q. rubra

Q. bicolor

Q. bicolor (swamp white oak) is a broad, spreading tree with peeling bark. It grows 50–70' tall, with an equal or greater spread. The leaves turn orange or red in fall. This species is also native to Michigan. (Zones 3–8)

Q. imbricaria (shingle oak, laurel oak) is a broad, spreading tree with smooth bark. This Michigan native grows 50–70' tall, with an equal spread. It responds well to pruning and is sometimes used as a hedging plant. The leaves turn yellowish brown or sometimes reddish orange in fall. (Zones 4–8)

Q. macrocarpa (bur oak, mossycup oak) is a large, broad tree with furrowed bark. It grows 50–80' tall, with an equal spread, and is native to Michigan. The leaves turn shades of yellow in fall. (Zones 2–8)

Q. palustris (pin oak) is a fast-growing, pyramidal to columnar tree that is native to Michigan. It grows 60–70' tall and spreads 25–40'. The foliage develops a good red to reddish brown color in fall. (Zones 4–8)

Q. imbricaria

Q. prinus (chestnut oak, basket oak) is a dense tree with a rounded habit. It grows 60–70' tall, with an equal spread. The leaves turn yellow-orange to yellow-brown in fall. This tree is a rare native species in Michigan, and the sweet acorns attract wildlife to the garden. (Zones 4–8)

Q. robur (English oak) is a rounded, spreading tree, growing 40–120' tall and spreading 40–80'. The fall color is golden yellow. Narrow, columnar cultivars suitable for a smaller garden are also available. Most of these grow 60' tall but spread only 10–15'. (Zones 3–8)

Q. rubra (red oak) is a rounded, spreading, fast-growing tree that is native to Michigan. It grows 60–75' tall, with an equal spread. The fall color ranges from yellow to red-brown. The roots are shallow, so be careful not to damage them if you cultivate the ground around the tree. (Zones 4–9)

Q. robur

Problems & Pests
The many possible problems are rarely serious: borers, canker, gypsy moth caterpillars, leaf gall, leaf miners, leaf rollers, leaf skeletonizers, leaf spot, powdery mildew, rust, scale insects, twig blight and wilt.

Oaks are important commercial trees. They are used for furniture, flooring, veneers, boat building and wine and whiskey casks.

Q. macrocarpa

Oregon-Grape
Oregon Grapeholly
Mahonia

Features: spring flowers, summer fruit, late-fall and winter foliage
Habit: upright, suckering, evergreen shrub **Height:** 2–6' **Spread:** 2–6'
Planting: B & B, container; spring, fall **Zones:** 5–9

OREGON-GRAPE MAY LOOK LIKE A HOLLY AT FIRST GLANCE, BUT it's actually an unrelated member of the barberry family. This Pacific Northwest native is a beautiful suckering evergreen, prized for its glossy foliage, pretty yellow flowers and purplish blue, grape-like fruit. Several dwarf cultivars make good groundcovers. The key to making Oregon-grape a good garden evergreen for Michigan is to site it properly. If unprotected from winter sun and wind, the foliage quickly scorches. I had to laugh when one author described winter-injured Oregon-grape as looking as if it was 'hit with a flamethrower.' It's an apt description, so plant with care.

Growing
Oregon-grape prefers **light to partial shade.** The soil should be of **average fertility, humus rich, moist** and **well drained.**

Provide **shelter** from winter sun and wind to prevent the foliage from drying out. Awkward shoots can be removed in early summer. Deadheading will keep the plant looking neat but will prevent the attractive, edible (though sour) fruit from forming.

Tips

Use Oregon-grape in shrub or mixed borders and in woodland gardens. Low-growing specimens can be used as groundcovers.

Recommended

M. aquifolium grows 3–6' tall, with an equal spread. Bright yellow flowers appear in spring and are followed by clusters of purple or blue berries. The foliage turns a lovely bronzy purple color in late fall and winter. '**Compactum**' is a low, mounding shrub with bronzy green foliage. It grows 24–36" tall and wide.

Problems & Pests

Rust, leaf spot, gall and scale insects may cause occasional problems. Plants in exposed locations may develop leaf scorch in winter.

The juicy berries are edible but very tart. They can be eaten fresh or used to make jelly, juice or wine.

M. aquifolium (both photos)

Peashrub

Caragana

Features: late-spring flowers, foliage, habit **Habit:** prickly, weeping (grafted) or upright, rounded deciduous shrub **Height:** 3–20' **Spread:** 3–18'
Planting: container, B & B, bare-root; spring or fall **Zones:** 2–7

PEASHRUB IS A GREAT SMALL TREE FOR ADDING CHARM AND character to the garden. The small, yellow, pea-like flowers appear in spring. They are a bonus for a plant primarily grown for its graceful habit, petite leaves and olive green bark. Weeping peashrub makes a beautiful, interesting specimen for an entrance area garden or patio garden.

Growing

Peashrub prefers **full sun** but tolerates partial or light shade. Soil of **average to high fertility** is preferred. This plant adapts to just about any growing conditions and tolerates dry, exposed locations.

Peashrub roots fix nitrogen in the soil, so this shrub has been used in soil-improvement programs.

Prune out awkward or damaged shoots as needed to maintain a neat shape. Rejuvenate unruly or overgrown plants by pruning them to within 6" of the ground. Don't prune weeping, grafted specimens to the ground. If you need to control the spread of a grafted specimen, prune back to near the graft at the top of the main trunk. If you prune below the graft, the weeping habit will be lost.

Tips

Peashrub is grown as a windbreak and as a formal or informal hedge. It can be included in borders, and weeping forms are often used as specimen plants.

Recommended

C. arborescens is a large, twiggy, thorny shrub that grows up to 20' tall, with a lesser spread. Branches may be upright or arching. Yellow, pea-like flowers are borne in late spring, followed by seedpods that ripen to brown in summer and rattle when blown by the wind. 'Pendula' has long, weeping branches. It is generally grafted to a standard that may be 3–6' in height, with an equal or greater spread. 'Walker' is a similar weeping form with fine, feathery foliage.

Problems & Pests

Aphids and leafhoppers may disfigure young foliage but are generally not a problem.

This tough, durable plant is native to Siberia and Mongolia. It is a good choice for difficult locations and regions, such as parts of the Upper Peninsula.

Pieris
Lily-of-the-Valley Shrub
Pieris

Features: colorful new growth, spring flowers **Habit:** compact, rounded, evergreen shrub **Height:** 2–8' **Spread:** 2–8' **Planting:** B & B, container; spring, fall **Zones:** 4–8

CLUSTERS OF WAXY, CREAMY WHITE BLOSSOMS ADORN THESE lovely broad-leaved evergreen shrubs in spring. The slightly fragrant blooms bear some resemblance to those of the herbaceous lily-of-the-valley *(Convallaria). Pieris* species are related to rhododendrons and require similar growing conditions. The Japanese species *(P. japonica)* has pendulous blooms and is the parent of more than 50 cultivars. The American species *(P. floribunda),* less common in gardens, has erect blossoms and only a few cultivars. Both are exceptionally beautiful plants.

The flower buds of pieris form in late summer in the year before flowering and provide an attractive show all winter.

Growing

Pieris grow equally well in **full sun** and **partial shade**. The soil should be of **average fertility, acidic, humus rich, moist** and **well drained**. *P. floribunda* is more pH adaptable than *P. japonica*. Provide a **sheltered** location with protection from the hot sun and drying winds.

P. japonica

Remove spent flowers once flowering is complete. Prune out awkward shoots at the same time.

Tips

Pieris can be used in a shrub or mixed border, in a woodland garden or as specimens. Try grouping them with rhododendrons and other acid-loving plants. With their year-round good looks, pieris are great shrubs to use in a protected entryway.

All parts of pieris plants, and even honey derived from the nectar, are extremely poisonous. Children have died from eating the leaves.

Recommended

P. floribunda (mountain pieris) is a compact mounding shrub. It grows 2–6' tall, with an equal or greater spread, and bears clusters of white flowers in spring. This species is resistant to lace bugs. (Zones 4–6)

P. japonica grows 4–8' tall and wide. It bears white flowers in long, pendulous clusters at the ends of the branches. **'Mountain Fire'** has bright red new growth that matures to chestnut brown. The flowers are white. **'Valley Rose'** has dark green foliage and pink flowers. **'Variegata'** has white flowers, and its green leaves have creamy white margins. There are also several dwarf cultivars that grow about 36" tall and wide. (Zones 5–8)

Problems & Pests

Canker, lace bugs, nematodes and root rot can cause occasional problems. Plants may suffer dieback if exposed to too much wind.

P. japonica 'Mountain Fire'

Pine
Pinus

Features: foliage, bark, cones, habit **Habit:** upright, columnar or spreading, evergreen tree **Height:** 2–120' **Spread:** 2–50' **Planting:** B & B, container; spring, fall **Zones:** 2–8

FROM THE TOWERING, PICTURESQUE MICHIGAN NATIVE WHITE pine to the shrubby, low, mounded mugo pine, this vast genus offers a wide array of interesting landscape plants. Large pines can be used to create rich green backdrops for your smaller ornamentals. Smaller species and cultivars can be mixed into the border to provide texture and interest year-round. For those who are new to tree gardening, there's an easy way to distinguish pines from other needled evergreens. Pine needles are grouped together in bundles, while spruce, fir and hemlock needles are borne singly.

Growing

Pines grow best in **full sun**. They adapt to most **well-drained** soils. These trees are not heavy feeders. Fertilizing will encourage rapid new growth that is weak and susceptible to pest and disease problems.

Generally, little or no pruning is required. Hedges can be trimmed in mid-summer. Pinch up to one-half the length of the 'candles,' the fully extended but still soft new growth, to shape the pine or to regulate growth.

Tips

Pines can be used as specimen trees, hedges or windbreaks. Smaller cultivars can be included in shrub or mixed borders.

Austrian pine *(P. nigra)* was long recommended as the pine most tolerant of urban conditions. Unfortunately, overplanting has led to severe disease problems, some of which can lead to a tree's death within a single growing season.

Recommended

P. aristata (bristlecone pine) is a fairly small, slow-growing pine with a conical or shrubby habit. It grows 8–30' tall and spreads 6–20'. It is not pollution tolerant but survives in poor, dry, rocky soil. The needles may dry out in areas exposed to winter winds. (Zones 4–8)

P. cembra (Swiss stone pine) has a dense, columnar habit. It grows 30–70' tall and spreads 15–25'. This slow-growing pine is resistant to white pine blister rust. (Zones 3–7)

P. cembra

P. mugo var. pumilio

P. mugo

Most pines' seeds are edible, though many are too small to bother with. Commercially available 'pine nuts' come from P. pinea *and other species.*

P. aristata

P. mugo (mugo pine) is a low, rounded, spreading shrub or tree. It grows 10–20' tall and spreads 15–20'. **Var. *pumilio*** (var. *pumilo*) is a dense variety that forms a mound 2–8' tall and wide. Its slow growth and small size make it a good choice for planters and rock gardens. (Zones 2–7)

P. parviflora (Japanese white pine) grows 20–70' tall and spreads 20–50'. It is conical or columnar when young and matures to a spreading crown. This species has been used to create bonsai. (Zones 4–8)

P. strobus (eastern white pine) is native to the eastern U.S. It is a slender, conical tree 50–120' tall and 20–40' in spread, with soft, plumy needles. It is sometimes grown as a hedge. Young trees can be killed by white pine blister rust, but mature trees are resistant. **'Fastigiata'** is an

attractive, narrow, columnar form that grows up to 70' tall. **'Nana'** is a dwarf cultivar that grows about 36" tall and spreads up to 6'. **'Pendula'** has long, ground-sweeping branches. It must be trained to form an upright leader when young to give it some height and shape; otherwise, it can be grown as a groundcover or left to spill over the top of a rock wall or slope. It develops an unusual soft, shaggy, droopy appearance as it matures. (Zones 3–8)

P. sylvestris (Scots pine, Scotch pine) grows 30–70' tall and spreads 20–40'. It is rounded or conical when young and develops an irregular, flat-topped, spreading habit when mature. Trees of this species vary in size, habit, needle color and needle length. Young Scots pine are popular as Christmas trees. (Zones 2–7)

Problems & Pests
Blight, blister rust, borers, caterpillars, cone rust, leaf miners, mealybugs, pitch canker, sawflies, scale insects and tar spot can all cause problems. The European pine-shoot moth attacks pines with needles in clusters of two or three.

The eastern white pine (P. strobus) *is Michigan's state tree, symbolizing one of our greatest industries. From 1870 to the early 1900s, Michigan led the U.S. in lumber production.*

P. cembra
P. strobus

Potentilla
Shrubby Cinquefoil
Potentilla

Features: flowers, foliage, habit **Habit:** mounding, deciduous shrub
Height: 12–40" **Spread:** 2–4' **Planting:** container; spring, fall **Zones:** 2–8

THE FACT THAT IT IS NATIVE TO MUCH OF THE NORTHERN
Hemisphere, including Michigan, speaks to the adaptability of potentilla.
This member of the rose family blooms over a long period each year, with
few of the problems associated with roses. Flower color ranges from yellow,
which is most typical, to orange, pink, red and white. The forms with red or
pink flowers are especially beautiful. These colors tend to fade in the summer
heat, but they brighten up with the cooler days of fall.

Growing

Potentilla prefers **full sun** but will tolerate partial or light shade. The soil should be of **poor to average fertility** and **well drained**. This plant tolerates most conditions, including sandy or clay soil and wet or dry conditions. Established plants are drought tolerant. Too much fertilizer or too rich a soil will encourage weak, floppy, disease-prone growth.

On mature plants, prune up to one-third of the old wood each year to keep the growth neat and vigorous. Though it tolerates more severe pruning, potentilla looks best if left to grow as an informal rounded or mounding shrub. Shearing back hard in spring will rejuvenate older, overgrown or ragged plants.

Tips

Potentilla is useful in a shrub or mixed border. The smaller cultivars can be included in rock gardens and on rock walls. On slopes that are steep or awkward to mow, potentilla can prevent soil erosion and reduce

'McKay's White'

the time spent maintaining a lawn. Potentilla can even be used to create a low, informal hedge.

If your potentilla's flowers fade in bright sun or in hot weather, try moving the plant to a more sheltered location. A cooler location that still gets lots of sun or a spot with some shade from the hot afternoon sun may be all your plant needs to keep its color. Colors should revive in fall as the weather cools. Plants with yellow or white flowers are the least negatively affected by heat and sun.

'Pink Beauty'

P. fruticosa
'Tangerine'

Recommended

P. fruticosa is the parent of many, many cultivars. The following are a few popular and interesting ones. **'Abbotswood'** is one of the best white-flowered cultivars. It grows 30–36" tall and spreads up to 4'. **'Goldfinger'** has large yellow flowers and a mounding habit. It grows up to 40" tall, with an equal spread. **'Gold Star'** has large yellow flowers and a spreading habit. It grows 24–36" tall and spreads 3–4'. **'McKay's White'** bears creamy white flowers, but it doesn't develop seed-heads. It grows 24–36" tall, with an equal spread. **'Pink Beauty'** bears pink semi-double flowers that stand up well in the heat and sun of summer. It grows 24–36" tall, with an equal spread. **'Princess'** ('Pink Princess') has light pink flowers that fade to white in hot weather. It grows about 36" tall, with an equal spread. **'Red Robin'** bears orangy red

flowers that hold their color best in summer if the plant is grown in light or partial shade. It grows about 24" tall and wide. **'Snowbird'** bears large, white semi-double flowers. This robust, somewhat spreading plant grows about 32" tall and spreads up to 4'. **'Tangerine'** has orange flowers that bleach to yellow if the plant is exposed to too much direct sunlight, so place it in partial or light shade. This cultivar grows 18–24" tall and spreads 3–4'. **'Yellow Gem'** has bright yellow flowers. It is a low, mounding, spreading cultivar that grows 12–18" tall and spreads up to 36".

'Abbotswood'

Problems & Pests

Though infrequent, occasional problems with mildew, fungal leaf spot or spider mites are possible.

Potentilla will tolerate excess lime in the soil and can handle extreme cold very well. Try this small shrub as a low-maintenance alternative to turfgrass.

'Tangerine'

Redbud
Cercis

Features: spring flowers, fall foliage **Habit:** rounded or spreading, multi-stemmed, deciduous tree or shrub **Height:** 20–30' **Spread:** 25–35' **Planting:** B & B, container; spring, fall **Zones:** 4–9

WITH ITS DARK GRAY BARK AND ZIGZAGGED BRANCHING, REDBUD creates wonderful garden architecture. Adding to its exotic charm are the unique, dark lavender flowers that emerge directly from the stems, branches and trunk well before the heart-shaped leaves appear. The overall effect is high art. Whether planted in a formal row or scattered along the edge of a woodland garden, this small tree looks at home and elegant in every situation.

Growing
Redbud grows well in **full sun, partial shade** or **light shade**. The soil should be a **fertile, deep loam** that is **moist** and **well drained**.

Pruning is rarely required. The growth of young plants can be thinned to encourage an open habit at maturity. Awkward branches can be removed after flowering. This plant has tender roots and does not like being transplanted.

Select a redbud from a locally grown source. Plants grown from seeds produced in the south are not hardy in the north.

Tips

Redbud can be used as a specimen tree, in a shrub or mixed border or in a woodland garden.

Recommended

C. canadensis (eastern redbud) is a spreading, multi-stemmed tree that bears red, purple or pink flowers in mid-spring, before the leaves emerge. The young foliage is bronze, fading to green over the summer and turning bright yellow in fall. **Var.** *alba* has white flowers. '**Forest Pansy**' has purple or pink flowers and dark reddish purple foliage that fades to green over the summer. The best foliage color is produced when this cultivar is cut back hard in early spring, but plants cut back this way will not produce flowers. This cultivar is less hardy than the species, to Zone 7 or a sheltered location in Zone 6. **Lavender Twist** ('Covey') is a new, fast-growing, hardy cultivar with a graceful, contorted weeping habit. The flowers are pale purple. '**Silver Cloud**' has foliage irregularly variegated with creamy white spots. It doesn't bear as many flowers as the species.

Problems & Pests

Blight, canker, caterpillars, dieback, downy mildew, leafhoppers, leaf spot, scale insects, weevils and *Verticillium* wilt are potential problems for redbud.

The common name describes the pointed flower buds, which are slightly deeper in color than the flowers.

C. canadensis (both photos)

Rhododendron
Azalea
Rhododendron

Features: late-winter to early-summer flowers, foliage, habit **Habit:** upright, mounding, rounded, evergreen or deciduous shrub **Height:** 1–10' **Spread:** 2–10' **Planting:** B & B, container; spring, fall **Zones:** 3–8

RHODODENDRONS AND AZALEAS ARE GROUPED TOGETHER botanically in the genus *Rhododendron*. Extensive breeding and hybridizing are making it more and more difficult to apply one label or the other. As a general rule, rhododendrons are robust, broad-leaved evergreen shrubs whose flowers have 10 stamens. Azaleas tend to be smaller plants, with smaller flowers and leaves than rhododendrons. Azaleas can be either evergreen or deciduous, and their flowers have 5 stamens. Both rhododendrons and azaleas are wonderful shrubs noted for their showy, colorful flowers and attractive foliage. If you choose the proper cultivars and plant them in well-drained, acidic soils, you will be rewarded with spectacular blooms and years of healthy growth.

Growing

Rhododendrons prefer **partial shade** or **light shade**. The deciduous azaleas typically perform best in **full sun** or **light shade,** while the evergreen azaleas tend to appreciate **partial shade**. A location **sheltered** from strong winds is preferable. The soil should be **fertile, humus rich, acidic, moist** and **well drained**. Rhododendrons are sensitive to high pH, salinity and winter injury.

Shallow planting with a good mulch is essential, as is excellent drainage. In heavy soils, elevate the crown of rhododendrons 1" above soil level when planting to ensure surface drainage of excess water. Don't dig near rhododendrons; their root system is shallow and resents being disturbed.

Dead and damaged growth can be removed in mid-spring. Spent flower clusters should be removed if possible. Grasp the base of the cluster between your thumb and forefinger and twist to remove the entire cluster. Be careful not to damage the new buds that form directly beneath the flowerheads. Spent flowerheads can also be carefully removed with hand pruners or scissors.

Kurume hybrid

Tips

In Michigan, rhododendrons grow and look better when planted in groups. Use them in shrub or mixed borders, in woodland gardens or in sheltered rock gardens. Be aware of the needs of rhododendrons, and take care to give them a suitable home with protection from the wind and full sun. In a protected location they should not need an unsightly burlap covering in winter.

The foliage and flowers of rhododendrons and azaleas are poisonous, as is honey derived from the nectar.

Northern Lights hybrid

Northern Lights 'Golden Lights'

Even without their flowers, rhododendrons are wonderful landscape plants. Their striking, dark green foliage lends an interesting texture to a shrub planting in summer.

PJM 'Aglo'

Recommended

R. catawbiense (Catawba rhododendron, mountain rosebay) is a large, rounded, evergreen species. It grows 6–10' tall, with an equal spread. Clusters of reddish purple flowers appear in late spring. **'Album'** has light purple buds and white flowers. **'Cilpinense'** has white flowers flushed with pink. **'English Roseum'** has light pink flowers. This cultivar is heat tolerant. **'Nova Zembla'** has purple-hued red flowers. It is also heat tolerant. (Zones 4–8)

R. **Girard Hybrids** are cold-hardy evergreen azaleas with large flowers in a wide variety of colors. Plants generally grow 18–24" tall and spread up to 3'. Many of these hybrids will survive in Zone 5 if given winter protection. **'Girard's Crimson'** is a compact plant that bears large, crimson flowers. **'Girard's Fuchsia'** bears ruffled, reddish purple flowers. **'Girard's Hot Shot'** bears plentiful, large, scarlet flowers. (Zones 6–8)

R. **Glenn Dale Hybrids** are ever-green azaleas developed in North America for hardiness and large blooms. They grow 2–6' tall and wide, and their late-spring to early-summer flowers are usually red, pink or white. 'Delaware Valley White' bears large white flowers. It grows up to 36" tall and spreads up to 4'. (Zones 6–8)

R. **Kurume Hybrids** are evergreen azaleas developed in Japan. These hybrids are slow growing and are popular for creating bonzai speci-mens. They bear small but plentiful flowers in a wide range of colors. 'Blaauw's Pink' bears salmon pink flowers in late spring and early sum-mer. This cultivar grows 3–5' tall, with an equal spread. (Zones 5–8)

R. mucronulatum (Korean rhodo-dendron) is a rounded to upright, deciduous shrub that grows 1–8' tall and spreads 3–8'. It bears pinky pur-ple flowers in early spring. 'Cornell Pink' bears bright pink flowers. (Zones 4–8)

R. **Northern Lights Hybrids** are broad, rounded, deciduous azaleas. They grow about 5' tall and spread about 36". They are very cold hardy and are excellent choices for gardens in northern Michigan. 'Apricot Surprise' has yellow-orange flowers. 'Golden Lights' has fragrant, yellow flowers. 'Orchid Lights' is a bushy, compact plant with light purple flowers. 'Rosy Lights' has fragrant, dark pink flowers. 'Spicy Lights' has fragrant, light orange-red flowers. 'White Lights' has fragrant, white flowers. (Zones 3–7)

PJM hybrid

R. **PJM Hybrids** are compact, rounded, dwarf, evergreen rhododen-drons. They grow 3–6' tall, with an equal spread. Flowers in a range of colors are produced in early to mid-spring. These hybrids are weevil resis-tant. 'Aglo' bears pink flowers with reddish throats. 'Olga Mezitt' bears peachy pink flowers. The leaves turn red in fall and winter. 'Regal' has a more spreading habit than the species and bears pink flowers. 'Victor' is compact and slow growing with pink flowers. (Zones 4–8)

Problems & Pests

Rhododendrons suffer few problems if planted in good conditions with well-drained soil. When plants are stressed, however, aphids, caterpil-lars, lace bugs, leaf galls, leafhoppers, petal blight, powdery mildew, root rot, root weevils, rust, scale insects, vine weevils, Japanese beetles and whiteflies can cause problems.

Rose-of-Sharon
Hardy Hibiscus
Hibiscus

Features: mid-summer to fall flowers **Habit:** bushy, upright, deciduous shrub
Height: 8–12' **Spread:** 6–10' **Planting:** B & B, container; spring, fall **Zones:** 5–9

ROSE-OF-SHARON, ALSO KNOWN AS HARDY HIBISCUS, MAKES
a bright color statement from late summer through to mid-fall, when few
other trees or shrubs are blooming. Big, bold flowers in white, pink, lavender,
violet or blue emerge daily over a period of weeks. Flower form ranges from
large, flat single blooms, to carnation-like doubles, to the newly created
anemone forms that combine the simplicity of the single flower with a lacy
center. Grow rose-of-Sharon as a bushy shrub or train it into a small patio
tree. The results are breathtaking.

Growing

Rose-of-Sharon prefers **full sun**. Though the plants tolerate partial shade, they become leggy and produce fewer flowers. The soil should be **humus rich, moist** and **well drained**.

Pinch young plants to encourage bushy growth. Train them to form a tree by selectively pruning out all but the strongest single stem and removing the side branches up to the height where you want the plant to bush out. The flowers form on the current year's growth; prune back tip growth in late winter or early spring for larger but fewer flowers.

Some cultivars are heavy seeders and can produce unwanted seedlings. To avoid this problem, shear off and dispose of the seed-heads right after blooming finishes.

'Red Heart'

Rose-of-Sharon attracts birds and butterflies and repels deer.

'Freedom'

'Purpurea Variegata'
Blue Satin

Tips

Rose-of-Sharon is best used in shrub or mixed borders. The leaves emerge late in spring and drop early in fall. Plant along with evergreen shrubs to make up for the short period of green.

This plant develops unsightly legs as it matures. Plant low, bushy perennials or shrubs around the base to hide the bare stems.

Recommended

H. syriacus is an erect, multi-stemmed shrub that bears dark pink flowers from mid-summer to fall. It can be trained as a small, single-stemmed tree. Many cultivars are available. **Blue Satin** ('Marina') is a vigorous plant that bears rich blue flowers. **Blush Satin** ('Mathilde') bears light pink flowers with red centers. **'Diana'** bears large white flowers. **'Freedom'** bears reddish pink semi-double flowers. **'Helene'** has

white flowers with red or pink petal bases. **Lavender Chiffon** ('Notwoodone') bears lavender flowers with a second ring of small lacy petals in the center. **'Purpurea Variegata'** is grown for its attractive cream-margined leaves. The purple flowers don't open fully. **'Red Heart'** bears white flowers with red centers. **Rose Satin** ('Minrosa') bears pink flowers with red centers. **Violet Satin** ('Floru') bears reddish violet flowers. The plants are vigorous and bloom for a long time in summer and fall. **White Chiffon** ('Notwoodtwo') bears white flowers with a small second ring of lacy petals in the center.

Problems & Pests

Rose-of-Sharon can be afflicted with aphids, bacterial blight, caterpillars, fungal leaf spot, mealybugs, mites, root rot, rust, scale insects, stem rot, *Verticillium* wilt and viruses.

'Diana'

A well-tended rose-of-Sharon is one of the most beautiful and prolific blooming shrubs for the late-season garden.

Lavender Chiffon with White Chiffon

Serviceberry
Saskatoon, Juneberry, Shadberry
Amelanchier

Features: spring or early-summer flowers, edible fruit, fall color, habit, bark
Habit: single- or multi-stemmed, deciduous large shrub or small tree
Height: 3–30' **Spread:** 3–30' **Planting:** B & B, container; spring, fall
Zones: 3–9

ONE OF OUR MOST BEAUTIFUL NATIVE TREES, COMMON serviceberry graces our woods and roadsides with a flurry of white spring flowers and autumn hues of yellow, orange and scarlet. The smooth pewter bark completes the package and is especially eye-catching in winter when draped with snow. All the serviceberries are excellent small to medium-sized trees for residential landscapes. Birds love them for their small, tasty, blueberry-like fruit. Gardeners love them for their simple, elegant beauty.

Growing

Serviceberries grow well in **full sun** or **light shade.** The soil should be **fertile, acidic, humus rich, moist** and **well drained.** *A. canadensis* will tolerate boggy soil conditions.

Serviceberry fruit can be used in place of blueberries in any recipe, having a similar but generally sweeter flavor.

Very little pruning is needed. Young plants, particularly multi-stemmed ones, can be pruned to encourage healthy, attractive growth and habit; only the strongest, healthiest stems should be allowed to remain. Dead, damaged, diseased and awkward branches can be removed as needed. If you prefer, some of the lower and interior branches can be removed to better display the structure and attractive bark.

A. alnifolia 'Regent'

Tips
Serviceberries make beautiful specimen plants or even shade trees in small gardens. Spring flowers, edible fruit, attractive fall color and an often artistic branching habit make these excellent trees all year long. The shrubbier forms can be grown along the edges of a woodland garden or in a border. In the wild, serviceberries are sometimes found growing near water sources, and they can make beautiful pondside or streamside plants.

Recommended
A. alnifolia (saskatoon serviceberry, alder-leaved serviceberry) is a large, rounded, suckering shrub 3–12' tall, with an equal spread. It bears clusters of white flowers in late spring, followed by dark purple fruit in summer. The foliage turns shades of yellow, orange and red in fall. **'Regent'** is a compact plant with attractive flowers, delicious fruit and good fall color. It grows 4–6' tall, with an equal spread. (Zones 3–8)

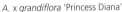

A. x *grandiflora* 'Princess Diana'

A. x *grandiflora* 'Robin Hill'

A. *canadensis*

A. arborea (common serviceberry, Juneberry) forms a small single- or multi-stemmed tree. This Michigan native grows 15–25' tall and spreads 15–30'. Clusters of fragrant white flowers are borne in spring. The edible fruit ripens to reddish purple in summer. The foliage turns in fall to shades ranging from yellow to red. (Zones 4–9)

A. canadensis (shadblow serviceberry) forms a large, upright, suckering shrub. It grows 6–20' tall and spreads 5–15'. White spring flowers are followed by edible dark purple fruit in summer. The foliage turns orange and red in fall. **'Prince William'** is an upright cultivar that grows about 8' tall and spreads about 6'. The new leaves emerge a reddish color, turning dark green in summer and orange to scarlet in fall. (Zones 3–8)

A. x *grandiflora* (apple serviceberry) is a small, spreading, often multi-stemmed tree. It grows 20–30' tall, with an equal spread. New foliage is often a bronze color, turning green in summer and bright orange or red in fall. White spring flowers are followed by edible purple fruit in summer. **'Autumn Brilliance'** is a fast-growing cultivar that reaches 25' in height and about 20' in spread. The leaves turn brilliant red in fall. This cultivar is hardy to Zone 3. **'Ballerina'** has bright red fall color. **'Princess Diana'** may be single- or multi-stemmed. It flowers prolifically in spring, and the foliage turns brilliant red in fall. It is also hardy to Zone 3. **'Robin Hill'** has pink buds that open to white flowers. It has an upright habit, spreading half as much as the species. (Zones 4–8)

A. laevis (Allegheny serviceberry) is native to Michigan. It has a spreading habit and grows about 25' tall, with an equal spread. The new leaves are reddish, turning green in summer. Fall color is scarlet. White mid-spring flowers are followed by sweet, dark blue fruit. **'Cumulus'** is a narrower, more upright cultivar that grows up to 30' tall and spreads up to 20'. It resists blight when not under stress. (Zones 4–8)

Problems & Pests
Problems with rust, fire blight, powdery mildew, leaf miners, borers and leaf spot can occur but are generally not serious.

A. arborea

The common name 'shadberry' may have come about because the spring flowers appear about the time shadfish spawn.

A. canadensis

Seven-Son Flower

Heptacodium

Features: habit, bark, flowers **Habit:** upright to spreading, multi-stemmed, deciduous shrub or small tree **Height:** 10–20' **Spread:** 8–15' **Planting:** B & B, container; spring, fall **Zones:** 5–8

SEVEN-SON FLOWER IS A REMARKABLE LARGE SHRUB OR SMALL tree that has recently found its way into North American gardens. This Chinese native has quickly made a name for itself with its attractive bark and showy, fragrant blooms. The white late-summer flowers are lovely, but it's the persistent sepals (outer flower parts) that put on the real show. These sepals turn bright red in fall, giving the appearance of a second bloom.

Each flower cluster is made up of seven small blooms, hence the common name.

Growing

Seven-son flower prefers **full sun** but tolerates partial shade. The soil should be of **average fertility, moist** and **well drained,** though this plant is fairly tolerant of most soil conditions, including dry and acidic soil.

Little pruning is required. Remove awkward branches in early spring, and prune out dead or damaged growth as needed. Seven-son flower can be grown as a multi-stemmed shrub or trained to form a small, single-stemmed tree.

Tips

This large shrub can be used in place of a shade tree on a small property. Planted near a patio or deck, the plant will provide light shade, and its fragrant flowers can be enjoyed in late summer. In a border it provides light shade to plants growing below it, and the dark green leaves make a good backdrop for bright perennial and annual flowers.

This unique plant has year-round interest and is well worth the time it may take to seek it out.

Seven-son flower's tolerance of dry and salty soils makes it useful where salty snow may be shoveled off walkways in winter and where watering will be minimal in summer.

Recommended

H. miconioides is a large, multi-stemmed shrub or small tree with peeling tan bark. The dark green leaves may become tinged with purple in fall. Clusters of fragrant, creamy white flowers are borne from late summer into fall. The persistent sepals turn dark pink to bright red in mid- to late fall and surround small, purple-red fruit.

Silverbell
Halesia

Features: late-spring to early-summer flowers, summer and fall foliage
Habit: spreading, rounded, deciduous tree **Height:** 20–40' **Spread:** 20–35'
Planting: B & B, container; spring, fall **Zones:** 5–9

THESE LITTLE-KNOWN TREES, NATIVE TO THE SOUTHEASTERN
United States, have been prized by plant enthusiasts and collectors but
largely ignored by the general gardening public. They may not be as flashy
as the flowering dogwoods, but these small understory trees are well worth
growing. The pure white, pendulous, bell-shaped flowers appear in May,
dangling in a line along the underside of each branch. The effect is most
appealing, especially in a woodland garden setting.

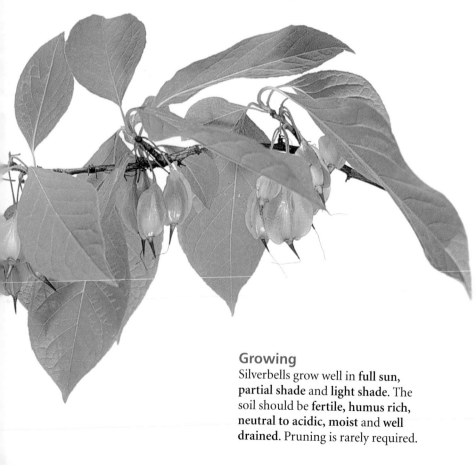

Growing
Silverbells grow well in **full sun,
partial shade** and **light shade**. The
soil should be **fertile, humus rich,
neutral to acidic, moist** and **well
drained**. Pruning is rarely required.

Tips

Silverbells make attractive, small to medium-sized specimen trees. They can also be used in a woodland garden or as backdrop plants in a shrub or mixed border.

Recommended

H. diptera (two-wing silverbell) is a small, rounded, often multi-stemmed tree that grows 20–30' tall, with an equal spread. It bears white flowers in early summer. In fall the foliage turns yellow. This species is not as common as *H. tetraptera*.

H. tetraptera (H. carolina var. *monticola)* (snowdrop tree, Carolina silverbell, mountain silverbell) is a rounded, spreading tree. It grows 25–40' tall and spreads 25–35'. The white flowers appear in spring, before the leaves emerge. Fall color is yellow. 'Rosea' has pink flowers. The intensity of the pink can vary greatly from plant to plant; some flowers are just tinged with pink and others are a much deeper hue.

H. tetraptera (both photos)

Problems & Pests

Occasional problems with root rot, wood rot and scale insects may occur.

Depending on the species, two or four narrow 'wings' (ridges) run down the length of each fruiting capsule, giving rise to the specific epithets diptera, *'two-winged,'* and tetraptera, *'four-winged.' The capsules hang from the branches almost all winter.*

Smokebush
Smoketree
Cotinus

Features: summer flowers, summer and fall foliage **Habit:** bushy, rounded, spreading, deciduous tree or shrub **Height:** 10–15' **Spread:** 10–15'
Planting: container; spring, fall **Zones:** 4–8

BELIEVE IT OR NOT, SMOKEBUSH IS A BIT OF A BORE WHEN IT'S IN bloom. The real show begins in mid-summer, after the minute flowers have faded. Thousands of tiny, feather-like hairs expand from the spent blooms, growing into pink, fluffy, smoke-like plumes. Cultivars with purple, red, yellow or green leaves are available. Smokebush is an easy-to-grow plant that adapts to poor, dry soils. In autumn, you will be rewarded with leaf color ranging from yellow to orange to red.

Growing

Smokebush grows well in **full sun** or **partial shade**. It prefers soil of **average fertility** that is **moist** and **well drained**. Established plants will adapt to dry, sandy soils.

You have a couple of options where pruning is concerned. Long, lanky growth develops from pruning cuts. To take advantage of this tendency, plants grown for foliage are often pruned to the ground each spring, encouraging a lush flush of colorful growth. Alternatively, to avoid the lanky growth on any smokebush, young plants can be lightly sheared or pruned, then left to develop and mature naturally.

Tips

Smokebush can be used in a shrub or mixed border, as a single specimen or in groups. It is a good choice for a rocky hillside planting. You can train smokebush to take a tree form.

Recommended

C. coggygria develops large, puffy plumes of flowers that start out green and gradually turn pinky gray. The green foliage turns red, orange and yellow in fall. '**Daydream**' develops many pink plumes. The habit is more dense than that of the species. '**Royal Purple**' (purple smokebush) has dark purple foliage and purple-gray flowers. '**Young Lady**' flowers from a young age and for a long period in summer.

Problems & Pests

Verticillium wilt and powdery mildew are possible problems. The purple-leaved forms are more likely to be affected by mildew.

'Royal Purple'

Try encouraging a clematis to wind its way through the spreading branches of a smokebush.

C. coggygria

Spirea

Spiraea

Features: summer flowers, habit **Habit:** round, bushy, deciduous shrub
Height: 1–10' **Spread:** 1–12' **Planting:** container; spring, fall **Zones:** 3–9

SPIRAEA IS A USEFUL AND DIVERSE GENUS OF PLANTS GROWN FOR
their flowers, foliage, form and fall color. The flowers are typically either
white or light pink, but a few selections have nearly red flowers. These easy-
growing shrubs thrive in most full-sun situations. Japanese spirea and its
varieties are the most popular because they are low, mounding plants that
become covered with loads of blooms in early to mid-summer. Many Japanese spirea selections have bright yellow foliage, and nearly all of them have
superb red fall leaf color. Lightly shear them back after they've finished
blooming, and you'll often be graced with a second flush of flowers.

Growing

Spireas prefer **full sun**. The soil should be **fertile, moist** and **well drained**.

Pruning is necessary to keep spireas tidy and graceful. The tight, shrubby types require less pruning than the larger, more open forms, which may require heavy renewal pruning in spring.

The appropriate pruning method depends on the flowering time for any given species. Those that bloom in spring and early summer usually form their flowers the previous year. These plants should be pruned immediately after flowering is complete. Cut out one-third of the old stems to encourage new, young growth.

Plants that flower later in summer or in fall usually form flowers during the current year. Cut these plants to within 12" of the ground in early spring, as the buds begin to swell, to encourage lots of new growth and flowers later in the season.

S. japonica 'Neon Flash'

Tips

Spireas are used in shrub or mixed borders, in rock gardens and as informal screens and hedges.

Recommended

S. betulifolia (birch-leaf spirea) is a dense, mound-forming shrub that grows 2–4' tall, with an equal spread. It bears clusters of small white flowers in early to mid-summer. The foliage turns golden yellow and bronze in fall and provides a long-lasting colorful display. 'Tor' has purple fall foliage. (Zones 3–9)

S. japonica 'Little Princess'

S. japonica (Japanese spirea) forms a clump of erect stems. It grows 4–6' tall and spreads up to 5'. Pink or white flowers are borne in mid- and late summer. Many cultivars and hybrids have been developed from this species. **Var.** *albiflora (S. albiflora;* Japanese white spirea) is a low, dense, mounding shrub. It grows 24–36" tall, with an equal spread, and bears white flowers in early summer. **'Anthony Waterer'** grows 3–4' tall and spreads 3–5'. The new foliage is reddish, turning blue-green over summer and red again in fall. **'Gold Flame'** grows 24–36" tall and 2–4' wide. The new foliage emerges red and matures to yellow-green, with red, orange and yellow fall color. **'Goldmound'** has bright yellow foliage and bears pink flowers in late spring and early summer. **'Little Princess'** forms a dense mound 18" tall and 3–6' wide. The flowers are rose pink. **'Magic Carpet'** grows 12–18" tall, with an equal spread. It has new red growth that stands out above the older gold and lime green foliage. The flowers are dark pink. **'Neon Flash'** bears vivid pink flowers. It grows up to 36" tall and wide. **'Shirobori'** ('Shirobana') grows 24" tall and wide. Both pink and white flowers appear on the same plant. (Zones 3–9)

S. nipponica (Nippon spirea) is an upright shrub with arching branches. It grows 3–8' tall, with an equal spread. White flowers appear in mid-summer. **'Snowmound'** (snowmound Nippon spirea) is grown more commonly than the species. The spreading, arching branches are covered with flowers in early summer. This cultivar grows 3–5' tall, with an equal spread. (Zones 4–8)

S. japonica 'Magic Carpet'

S. thunbergii (Thunberg spirea) is a dense, arching shrub. It grows 3–5' tall and spreads 3–6'. Small clusters of flowers appear along the stems in spring, before the leaves emerge. '**Mount Fuji**' has small, narrow leaves, each with a white stripe down the center. '**Ogon**' has narrow yellow leaves that turn bronzy in fall. (Zones 4–8)

S. x vanhouttei (bridal wreath spirea, Vanhoutte spirea) is a dense, bushy shrub with arching branches. It grows 6–10' tall and spreads 10–12'. White flowers are borne in clusters in early summer. (Zones 3–8)

S. betulifolia 'Tor' in fall color

Problems & Pests
Aphids, dieback, fire blight, leaf spot and powdery mildew can cause occasional problems.

Spireas belong to the rose family. Under a magnifying glass, their flowers indeed resemble tiny roses.

S. x vanhouttei

Spruce
Picea

Features: foliage, cones, habit **Habit:** conical or columnar, evergreen tree or shrub
Height: 3–80' **Spread:** 3–20' **Planting:** B & B, container; spring, fall **Zones:** 2–8

THIS DIVERSE GROUP OF SHORT-NEEDLED EVERGREENS OFFERS
many useful, garden-worthy plants. Colorado blue spruce may be the best
known of the bunch, but there are hundreds of others to choose from.
Spruce trees readily produce branch mutations, or 'witch's brooms,' which
when propagated become new cultivars of varied size, shape, habit and color.
With the plethora of varieties and cultivars, forms can range from dwarf,
bushy shrubs to tall, stately trees. Dwarf and weeping forms are ideal for the
home landscape, whether grown in rock gardens, perennial beds or shrub
borders.

Growing

Spruce trees grow best in **full sun**. Dwarf Alberta spruce prefers **light shade**
and a **sheltered** location. The soil should be **deep, well drained** and **neutral to
acidic.** Pruning is rarely needed.

Spruces are best grown from small, young stock because they dislike being
transplanted when larger or more mature.

Tips

Spruce trees are used as specimens and windscreens. The dwarf and slow-growing cultivars can also be used in shrub or mixed borders.

Oil-based pesticides such as dormant oil can take the blue out of your blue-needled spruce.

Recommended

P. abies (Norway spruce) is a fast-growing, pyramidal tree with dark green needles. It grows 70–80' tall and spreads about 20'. This species is wind tolerant. **'Nidiformis'** (nest spruce) is a slow-growing, low, compact, mounding form. It grows about 3–4' tall and spreads 3–5'. (Zones 2–8)

P. abies 'Nidiformis'

Try using a dwarf, slow-growing cultivar, such as dwarf Alberta spruce, for plant sculpture and bonsai.

P. abies

P. glauca 'Conica'

P. pungens 'Mission Blue'

P. glauca (white spruce) is native to Michigan and many other northern states. This conical tree with blue-green needles grows 40–60' tall and spreads 10–20'. It can grow up to 160' tall in the wild. **'Conica'** (dwarf Alberta spruce, dwarf white spruce) is a dense, conical, bushy shrub that grows 6–20' tall and spreads 3–8'. This cultivar works well in planters. (Zones 2–6)

P. omorika (Serbian spruce) is a slow-growing, narrow, spire-like tree with upward-arching branches and drooping branchlets. Two white stripes run the length of each needle. This tree grows 30–50' tall and spreads 10–15'. **'Nana'** is a dwarf cultivar, growing 3–8' tall, with a dense, conical or pyramidal habit. (Zones 4–8)

Spruce is the traditional Christmas tree in Europe.

P. pungens (Colorado spruce) is a conical or columnar tree with stiff, blue-green needles and dense growth. This drought-tolerant, hardy tree grows 30–60' tall, with a spread of 10–20'. **Var.** *glauca* (Colorado blue spruce) is similar to the species, but with blue-gray needles. Cultivars have been developed from this variety, and some are smaller. **'Hoopsii'** grows up to 60' tall. It has a dense, pyramidal form and even more blue-white foliage than var. *glauca.* **'Mission Blue'** is a broad-based, compact form 3–8' tall, with bold blue foliage. (Zones 2–8)

P. pungens 'Hoopsii'

Problems & Pests

Possible problems include aphids, caterpillars, gall insects, needle cast, nematodes, rust, sawflies, scale insects, spider mites and wood rot.

Stradivarius used spruce to make his renowned violins. The resonant, lightweight but tough wood is still preferred for violins, guitars, harps and the sounding boards of pianos.

P. glauca

St. Johnswort
St. John's Wort
Hypericum

Features: tidy habit, attractive foliage, summer to fall flowers **Habit:** rounded, deciduous or evergreen shrub **Height:** 2–4' **Spread:** 2–4' **Planting:** container; spring **Zones:** 4–8

WITH THE INCREASED INTEREST IN HERBAL REMEDIES, COMMON St. Johnswort *(H. perforatum)* has become known as a treatment for mild depression. Of greater interest to the home gardener are the ornamental species, which are a miracle cure for a dull summer landscape. Masses of bright yellow flowers with numerous showy, hair-like stamens add sunshine to the summer garden. These are easy-to-grow, drought-tolerant shrubs that deserve greater use.

Growing
St. Johnsworts grow best in **full sun** but can tolerate partial shade. **Well-drained** soil of **average fertility** is preferred, but these plants adapt to most soil conditions except wet soils. They tolerate drought and heavy, rocky or very alkaline soils.

Flowers form on new wood, so do any pruning in spring. Little pruning is required, though plants can be cut back to within 6–12" of the ground if they need renewing.

Tips

St. Johnsworts make good additions to mixed or shrub borders, where the late-summer flowers can brighten up a planting that is looking tired or faded in the heat of summer. These durable shrubs are also useful for difficult areas where the soil is poor and watering is difficult.

Recommended

H. frondosum (golden St. Johnswort) forms a rounded, upright mound. This deciduous species grows 2–4' tall and wide. Bright yellow flowers are borne in mid- and late summer. The long, dense stamens give each flower a fuzzy, bushy appearance. 'Sunburst' is a more compact cultivar with blue-green foliage. It grows up to 36" tall and wide. The flowers are larger and are produced longer into fall than those of the species. (Zones 5–8)

H. kalmianum (Kalm St. Johnswort) is a bushy evergreen shrub that is native to Michigan. It grows 24–36" tall, with an equal spread. Yellow flowers are borne from mid- to late summer. 'Ames' is a compact cultivar that bears plentiful small, yellow flowers. 'Gemo' is a dense, mounded, deciduous shrub that grows 3–4' tall. It has willow-like leaves and bears small, bright yellow flowers in summer. The fall color is yellow. (Zones 4–8)

Problems & Pests

Occasional problems may occur with scale insects, rust, leaf spot and thrips.

H. kalmianum 'Ames'

Many medicinal and magical properties have been attributed to species of St. Johnswort. The flowers have also been used to produce yellow or red dyes.

H. frondosum 'Sunburst'

Sumac

Rhus

Features: summer and fall foliage, summer flowers, late-summer to fall fruit, habit
Habit: bushy, suckering, colony-forming, deciduous shrub **Height:** 2–25'
Spread: equal to or greater than height **Planting:** container; spring, fall
Zones: 3–9

SUMACS INCLUDE MANY FINE LANDSCAPE PLANTS, MOST OF which are native to the U.S. and most of which have dramatic red autumn foliage. These plants are all relatively easy to grow and are adaptable to difficult growing conditions. Staghorn sumac is a small tree with large, almost tropical-looking leaves and showy red fruit spikes. It is best suited for naturalized areas. Fragrant sumac is a shrubby plant with small leaves and superb orange and red fall color. It is well suited for mass plantings. Sumac cultivars are even more desirable for landscaping purposes than the species.

Growing

Sumacs develop the best fall color in **full sun** but tolerate partial shade. The soil should be of **average fertility, moist** and **well drained**. Once established, sumacs are very drought tolerant.

These plants can become invasive. Remove suckers that come up where you don't want them. Cut out some of the oldest growth each year and allow some suckers to grow in to replace it. If the colony is growing in or near your lawn, you can mow down any young plants that pop up out of bounds.

Tips

Sumacs can be used to form a specimen group in a shrub or mixed border, in a woodland garden or on a sloping bank. Both male and female plants are needed for fruit to form.

When pulling up suckers, be sure to wear gloves to avoid getting the unusual, onion-like odor all over your hands.

The fruits are edible. For a refreshing beverage that tastes like pink lemonade, soak the ripe fruits in cold water overnight and then strain and sweeten to taste.

Recommended

R. aromatica (fragrant sumac) is native to Michigan. It forms a low mound of suckering stems 2–6' tall and 5–10' wide. This species tolerates hot, dry exposed conditions. It can be used to prevent erosion on hills too steep for mowing. The foliage turns red or purple in fall. 'Gro-Low' is a groundcover growing about 24" tall and spreading up to 8'. (Zones 3–9)

R. aromatica

R. typhina (*R. hirta;* staghorn sumac) is also native to Michigan. This suckering, colony-forming shrub has branches covered with velvety fuzz. It grows 15–25' tall and spreads 25' or more. Fuzzy, yellow blooms are followed by hairy, red fruit. 'Laciniata' ('Dissecta') has finely cut leaves that give the plant a lacy, graceful appearance. This cultivar is more compact than the species, growing 6' high and spreading 10'. (Zones 3–8)

Problems & Pests

Blister, canker, caterpillars, dieback, leaf spot, powdery mildew, scale insects, wood rot and *Verticillium* wilt can afflict sumacs.

R. typhina 'Laciniata'

Summersweet Clethra
Sweet Pepperbush, Sweetspire
Clethra

Features: fragrant summer flowers, habit, fall foliage **Habit:** rounded, suckering deciduous shrub **Height:** 2–8' **Spread:** 3–8' **Planting:** B & B, container; spring **Zones:** 3–9

SUMMERSWEET CLETHRA IS ONE OF THE VERY BEST shrubs for adding fragrance to the garden. It blooms in late July and into August. The species typically has white flowers, which are lovely, but new selections are available with light pink or deep pink blooms. Several new dwarf cultivars will allow you to use summersweet clethra in the front of the border, where you can really enjoy its rich, sweet fragrance.

Summersweet clethra is useful in damp, shaded gardens, where the late-season flowers are much appreciated.

Growing

Summersweet clethra grows best in **light or partial shade**. The soil should be **fertile, humus rich, acidic, moist** and **well drained**.

Prune up to one-third of the growth back to the ground in early spring. Deadhead if possible to keep the plant looking neat. Dwarf cultivars typically require little if any pruning.

'Ruby Spice'

Tips

Although not aggressive, this shrub tends to sucker, forming a colony of stems. Use it in a border or in a woodland garden. The light shade along the edge of a woodland is an ideal location.

Recommended

C. alnifolia is a large, rounded, upright, colony-forming shrub. It grows 3–8' tall, spreads 3–6' and bears attractive spikes of white flowers in mid- to late summer. The foliage turns yellow in fall. **'Hummingbird'** is a compact plant that grows 24–40" tall, with a spread similar to that of the species. **'Rosea'** ('Pink Spires') bears pink flowers. It grows up to 8' tall and wide. **'Ruby Spice'** bears deep pink, fade-resistant flowers. **'September Beauty'** bears large white flowers later in the season than other cultivars or than the species. **'Sixteen Candles'** is a dense dwarf cultivar that grows 24–30" tall.

Problems & Pests

This plant is generally trouble free, though some fungal infections, such as root rot, can occur.

'Hummingbird'

Sweetgum
Liquidambar

Features: habit, fall color, spiny fruit, corky bark **Habit:** pyramidal to rounded, deciduous tree **Height:** 60–80' **Spread:** 40–50' **Planting:** B & B; spring **Zones:** 5–9

A COMMONLY USED TREE IN THE SOUTHERN AND WESTERN U.S., sweetgum is a large, relatively fast-growing tree with an upright pyramidal habit and excellent orange and red fall color. It is rarely grown in Michigan, mostly because there are questions about its hardiness. The tree is native from southern Ohio to northern Florida, and hardiness varies depending upon which end of the range the mother stock comes from. Hardy cultivars have been selected, though, and this tree is well worth growing if you have the space.

Growing

Sweetgum grows equally well in **full sun** or **partial shade,** but it develops the best color in full sun. The soil should be of **average fertility, slightly acidic, moist** and **well drained.** This tree requires lots of room for its roots to develop. The foliage may develop late after excessively cold winters.

Little pruning is required. Remove dead, damaged, diseased or awkward branches in spring or early summer.

Tips

Sweetgum is attractive as a shade tree, street tree or specimen tree, or as part of a woodland garden. The spiny fruit makes sweetgum inappropriate near patios, decks, walkways or other areas where people may walk in bare feet or get hit by falling fruit.

Recommended

L. styraciflua is a neat, symmetrical, pyramidal or rounded tree with attractive star-shaped leaves. Spiny, capsular fruits drop off the tree over the winter and often into the following summer. The fall color of the glossy dark green leaves varies, often from year to year, from yellow to purple or brilliant red. Corky ridges may develop on young bark but disappear as the tree ages. '**Moraine**' is a fast-growing, cold-hardy cultivar. It is hardy to the warmer parts of Zone 4. Fall color is brilliant red.

'Rotundiloba' is not as cold hardy as the species. Its leaf lobes have rounded tips, and, more important, it does not bear any fruit. This admirable feature alone makes it worth growing in Zone 6 gardens. Let's hope other fruitless cultivars with better cold hardiness will appear in garden centers in the future.

Problems & Pests

Occasional problems with leaf spot, rot, scale insects, caterpillars and borers can occur. Iron chlorosis can occur in too alkaline a soil.

Sweetspire
Virginia Sweetspire
Itea

Features: habit, fragrant flowers, fall color **Habit:** upright to arching, deciduous shrub **Height:** 2–10' **Spread:** 3–10' or more **Planting:** container; spring **Zones:** 5–9

MANY AMERICAN NATIVE SHRUBS HAVE BEEN IGNORED AS GARDEN plants. Not so with sweetspire. This lovely summer bloomer has found a following in recent years, and with good reason. Its lightly fragrant, pendulous white blooms are highly decorative and emerge at a time when few other shrubs are blooming. And if you're looking for a plant with superb fall leaf color, look no further. Sweetspire's bright green leaves transform to rich hues of burgundy and scarlet in late autumn. It is at its best when planted in big drifts or used for covering slopes.

Growing

Sweetspire grows well in all light conditions from **full sun to full shade**. Plants grown in full sun develop the best fall color. The habit will be more upright in shade and more arching in sun. The soil should be **fertile** and **moist,** though sweetspire is fairly adaptable and well-established plants are quite drought tolerant.

One-third of the older growth can be removed to the ground each year once flowering ends. Do not prune in early spring or you will lose the current season's flower buds.

Tips

Sweetspire is an excellent shrub for low-lying and moist areas of the garden. It grows well near streams and water features. It is also a fine choice for plantings near decks, patios and pathways, where the scent of the fragrant flowers can be enjoyed.

Recommended

I. virginica is an upright to arching, suckering shrub native to the south-eastern U.S. It usually grows 3–5' tall but can grow up to 10' tall, with an equal or greater spread. Spikes of fragrant white flowers appear in mid-summer, and the leaves turn shades of purple and red in fall. **'Henry's Garnet'** bears many long, white flower spikes in early summer and consistently develops dark red-purple fall color. It grows 3–4' tall, with an equal or greater spread. **Little Henry** ('Sprich') is a compact cultivar 24–36" tall and 36" wide, with a low, mound-forming habit. It bears bright white flower spikes in summer and develops bright red fall color.

Problems & Pests

Sweetspire may suffer infrequent problems with aphids or leaf spot.

The colorful fall leaves usually persist on the plant until freezing weather sets in. They may last all winter in a very mild year.

Little Henry

'Henry's Garnet'

Thornless Honeylocust

Gleditsia

Features: summer and fall foliage, habit **Habit:** rounded, spreading, deciduous tree **Height:** 16–100' **Spread:** 16–70' **Planting:** B & B, container; spring, fall **Zones:** 4–8

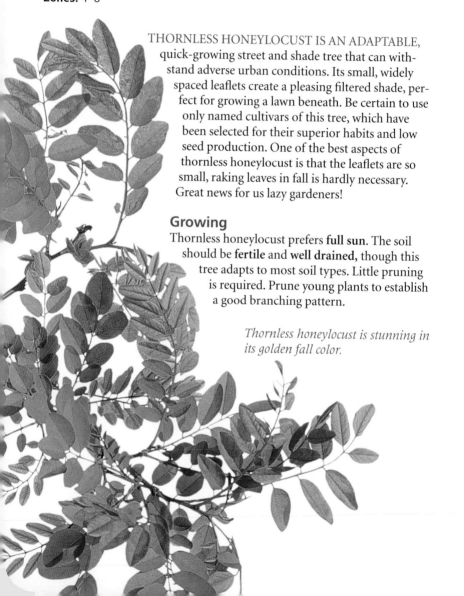

THORNLESS HONEYLOCUST IS AN ADAPTABLE, quick-growing street and shade tree that can withstand adverse urban conditions. Its small, widely spaced leaflets create a pleasing filtered shade, perfect for growing a lawn beneath. Be certain to use only named cultivars of this tree, which have been selected for their superior habits and low seed production. One of the best aspects of thornless honeylocust is that the leaflets are so small, raking leaves in fall is hardly necessary. Great news for us lazy gardeners!

Growing

Thornless honeylocust prefers **full sun.** The soil should be **fertile** and **well drained,** though this tree adapts to most soil types. Little pruning is required. Prune young plants to establish a good branching pattern.

Thornless honeylocust is stunning in its golden fall color.

Tips

Use thornless honeylocust as a specimen tree. Though it is often used as a street tree, this species is a poor choice for narrow streets because the vigorous roots can break up pavement and sidewalks.

Recommended

G. triacanthos var. *inermis* is a spreading, rounded tree up to 100' tall and up to 70' in spread. The fall color is a warm golden yellow. The flowers are inconspicuous, but the long, pea-like pods that develop in late summer persist into fall and sometimes still dangle from the branches after the leaves have fallen. This variety is thornless and many cultivars have been developed from it. **'Emerald Kaskade'** is a small, weeping tree with dark green foliage. It grows about 16' tall, with an equal spread. **'Halka'** has a rounded habit with less pendulous branches than the species. It grows about 40' tall, with an equal spread. **'Imperial'** has a spreading habit with graceful branching. It grows up to 35' tall. **'Skyline'** is an upright cultivar that grows about 45' tall, with a spread of 35'. **'Sunburst'** is fast growing and broad spreading. It grows 30–40' tall and spreads 25–30'. The foliage emerges bright yellow in spring and matures to light green over the summer.

Problems & Pests

Aphids, borers, canker, caterpillars, heart rot, leaf spot, mites, powdery mildew, tar spot and webworm can cause problems.

G. triacanthos var. *inermis*

The twisted, hanging pods of thornless honeylocust contain a sweet, edible pulp. Do not, however, confuse this species with black locust (Robinia pseudoacacia, *p. 328) or Kentucky coffee tree* (Gymnocladus dioica), *which are poisonous.*

'Sunburst'

Trumpetcreeper
Campsis

Features: habit, summer flowers **Habit:** clinging, deciduous vine **Height:** 30–60'
Spread: 30–60' **Planting:** container; any time **Zones:** 4–9

THESE FAST-GROWING, TWINING VINES WILL COVER JUST ABOUT
any structure in less than five years. Large, showy flowers are
the main feature of trumpetcreepers. The clusters of
bright reddish orange, trumpet-like blooms appear
in July and August. Use these vines to hide a
cyclone fence, or grow them over rock piles
or trellises. They will attract lots
of attention, and a few
hummingbirds as well.

Growing
These heat-tolerant vines grow well in **full sun, partial shade** or **light shade,**
but they flower best in full sun. Any soil is fine, but the richer the soil, the
more invasive trumpetcreepers can be.

These vines are perfect for people who love to do a lot of pruning. They are very fast growing and can quickly take over entire gardens if not kept in check. Prune them back hard each spring to encourage lots of new growth, which is where the summer flowers appear.

Tips

Trumpetcreepers will cling to any surface—a wall, a tree, a fence, a telephone pole. Once you have one of these vines, you will probably never get rid of it. One plant can provide a privacy screen quickly or can be grown up an exterior wall or over the porch of a house. They can be used on arbors and trellises but will need frequent pruning to stay attractive and in bounds.

Recommended

C. radicans is valued for its fast growth and for the attractive, dark orange, trumpet-shaped flowers it bears for a long period in summer. It can reach 30–60' in height and spread. **'Crimson Trumpet'** has bright red flowers. **'Flava'** bears yellow flowers. (Zones 4–9)

C. x *tagliabuana* 'Madame Galen'

C. x *tagliabuana* (Tagliabue trumpetcreeper) is similar to *C. radicans* but is not as hardy and not as invasive. This species grows up to 30' tall and bears many bright orange flowers. Michigan gardeners will need to plant this species in a spot sheltered from wind. **'Madame Galen'** is a more prolific bloomer and is hardy to Zone 5. (Zones 6–9)

Problems & Pests

Problems with powdery mildew, scale insects, leaf spot and whiteflies can occur but are rarely serious.

C. radicans

Tulip Tree
Tulip Poplar
Liriodendron

Features: early-summer flowers, foliage, fruit, habit **Habit:** large, rounded, oval, deciduous tree **Height:** 70–100' **Spread:** 33–50' **Planting:** B & B; spring **Zones:** 4–9

THE TULIP TREE, OR TULIP POPLAR, IS A LARGE, FAST-GROWING species native from Michigan to Florida. It's an interesting tree but too large for most residential landscapes. The leaves are a curious shape, and the greenish yellow flowers do bear a resemblance to tulips. I have always been impressed by the massive, straight, nearly flawless trunk of this tree and by its clear yellow autumn color. Driving through the Smoky Mountains in autumn you can spot the tulip tree's yellow fall color and distinctive form from miles away.

Growing

Tulip tree grows well in **full sun** or **partial shade**. The soil should be **average to rich, slightly acidic** and **moist**. This tree needs plenty of room for its roots to grow. Frequent periods of drought may eventually kill it.

Little pruning is required. Remove dead, damaged or diseased growth as needed, and prune awkward growth in winter.

Tips

This beautiful, massive tree needs lots of room to grow. Parks, golf courses and large gardens can host this tree as a specimen or in a group planting, but its susceptibility to drought and need for root space makes it a poor choice as a specimen, shade or street tree on smaller properties.

Recommended

L. tulipifera is native to the eastern U.S. It is known more for its unusually shaped leaves than for its tulip-like flowers because the blooms are often borne high in the tree and go unnoticed until the falling petals litter the ground. The foliage turns golden yellow in fall. The leaves of '**Aureomarginata**' have yellow-green margins.

Problems & Pests

Aphids and sooty mold can be common. Borers, leaf miners, scale insects, leaf spot and powdery mildew may also afflict tulip tree. Drought stress can cause some of the leaves to drop early.

L. tulipifera (both photos)

The genus name Liriodendron *comes from the Greek and means 'lily tree.'*

Viburnum

Viburnum

Features: flowers, summer and fall foliage, fruit, habit **Habit:** bushy or spreading, evergreen or deciduous shrub **Height:** 2–15' **Spread:** 2–15' **Planting:** bare-root, B & B, container; spring, fall **Zones:** 2–9

THE VIBURNUMS ARE AMONG THE MOST DIVERSE AND USEFUL flowering shrubs. Gardeners appreciate them because they offer showy flowers, fragrance, good growth habits, vivid ornamental berries and attractive autumn leaf color. The Korean spice viburnum is one of the best loved because it has gorgeous, fragrant blooms and rich burgundy autumn color. As a general rule, viburnums are easy to grow and adapt to most soils. The wonderful decorative fruit attracts birds and glowing comments alike. Depending on the variety, fruit color ranges from bright yellow to bright pink, rich red and deep blue.

Growing

Viburnums grow well in **full sun, partial shade** or **light shade**. The soil should be of **average fertility, moist** and **well drained**. Viburnums tolerate both alkaline and acidic soils.

Little pruning is needed. Remove awkward, dead, damaged or diseased branches as needed. Fruiting is better when more than one plant of a species is grown.

Tips

Viburnums can be used in borders and woodland gardens. They are a good choice for plantings near patios, decks and swimming pools.

The edible but very tart fruits of *V. opulus* and *V. trilobum* are popular for making jellies, pies and wine. They can be sweetened somewhat by freezing or by picking them after the first frost or two.

V. dilatatum Cardinal Candy

Although cranberry sauce is traditionally made with the fruit of the American cranberry (Vaccinium macrocarpon), *the fruit of* Viburnum trilobum *makes an acceptable alternative. The large seeds must be strained out of the viburnum sauce.*

V. opulus

V. x burkwoodii

V. nudum 'Winterthur'

Recommended

V. x burkwoodii (Burkwood viburnum) is a rounded shrub that is evergreen in warm climates, but not in Michigan. It grows 6–10' tall and spreads 5–8'. Clusters of pinkish white flowers appear in mid- to late spring and are followed by red fruits that ripen to black. (Zones 4–8)

V. carlesii (Korean spice viburnum) is a dense, bushy, rounded, deciduous shrub. It grows 3–8' tall, with an equal spread. White or pink, spicy-scented flowers appear in mid- to late spring. The fruits are red, ripening to black. The foliage may turn red in fall. **'Cayuga'** bears large flower clusters with pink buds that contrast with the fragrant white flowers. It grows 4–5' tall, with an equal spread. This cultivar resists disease. (Zones 5–8)

V. dentatum (arrowwood viburnum) is an upright, arching, deciduous shrub that is native to Michigan. It grows 6–15' tall, with an equal spread. Clusters of white flowers appear in late spring or early summer, followed by dark blue fruit in fall. This shrub is hardy and durable and adapts to almost any soil conditions. **Blue Muffin** ('Christom') is a compact cultivar that flowers prolifically and bears clusters of bright blue fruit. It grows 5–7' tall, with an equal spread. **Chicago Lustre** ('Synnestvedt') has glossy, dark green foliage. (Zones 2–8)

V. dilatatum (linden viburnum) is an open, upright, deciduous shrub. It grows 8–10' tall and spreads 6–10'. Clusters of white late-spring or early-summer flowers are followed by bright red berries in fall. The foliage turns bronze, red or burgundy in fall. **Cardinal Candy** ('Henneke') bears plentiful flowers and fruit and is hardy to Zone 4. It grows 5–6' tall, with an equal spread. **'Michael Dodge'** bears yellow fruit that contrasts with the bright red fall foliage. (Zones 5–7)

V. lantana (wayfaring tree) is a large, multi-stemmed, deciduous shrub or small tree 10–20' tall and 10–15' wide. Clusters of white flowers are borne in late spring and early summer, followed by green fruits that ripen to orange and red before finally turning black in fall. **'Mohican'** is a compact cultivar that grows 10–12' tall. The fruit stays red longer than that of the species. (Zones 3–8)

V. nudum (smooth witherod) is a bushy, spreading, deciduous shrub that grows 12–15' tall and spreads about 6'. It bears clusters of white flowers in early summer, followed by pink fruits that ripen to blue then black. The pink and blue fruits are present at the same time, creating a striking contrast. **'Winterthur'** flowers and fruits prolifically, and the foliage turns bright red in fall. (Zones 5–9)

V. dilatatum 'Michael Dodge'

Many species of birds are attracted to viburnums for the edible fruit and the shelter they provide.

V. opulus 'Roseum'

V. plicatum var. tomentosum
'Mariesii'

The long, straight stems of V. dentatum *have been used to make arrow shafts, giving rise to the common name arrowwood.*

V. opulus (*V. opulus* var. *opulus*; European cranberrybush, guelder-rose) is a rounded, spreading, deciduous shrub that grows 8–15' tall and spreads 8–12'. The flower clusters consist of an outer ring of showy sterile flowers surrounding the inner fertile flowers, giving the plant a lacy look when in bloom. The fall foliage and fruit are red. **'Compactum'** ('Nanum') is dense and slow growing, reaching 2–5' in height and spread. **'Roseum'** ('Sterilis'; European snowball bush) bears large clusters of white flowers but does not form fruit. (Zones 3–8)

V. plicatum (Japanese snowball viburnum) is a bushy, upright, deciduous shrub with arching stems. It grows 10–15' tall and spreads 12–15'. Ball-like clusters of white flowers appear in late spring. The fall color is reddish purple. **'Mary Milton'** bears pink flowers and has bright red fall foliage. **Var. *tomentosum*** (doublefile viburnum) has graceful, horizontal branching that gives the shrub a layered effect. It grows 8–10' tall and spreads 8–12'. The leaves have fuzzy undersides. Clusters of inconspicuous fertile flowers surrounded by showy sterile flowers blanket the branches. Several cultivars have been developed from this variety. **'Mariesii'** has more distinctly layered branches. **'Molly Schroeder'** bears lacy clusters of pink flowers. It blooms in spring and again in fall. **'Summer Snowflake'** bears clusters of white flowers from late spring until fall. (Zones 5–8)

V. plicatum var. tomentosum 'Molly Schroeder'

V. sargentii (Sargent viburnum) is a large, bushy, deciduous shrub. It grows 10–15' tall, with an equal spread. The early-spring blossoms consist of clusters of inconspicuous fertile flowers surrounded by showy sterile flowers. The fall color is yellow, orange and red. 'Onondaga' has purple stems and red to pink fertile flowers ringed with showy, pinkish white sterile flowers. The purple-green foliage turns red in fall. (Zones 3–7)

V. trilobum (*V. opulus* var. *americanum;* American cranberrybush, highbush cranberry) is a dense, rounded, deciduous shrub that is native to much of central North America, including Michigan. It grows 8–15' tall, with a spread of 8–12'. Early-summer clusters of showy sterile and inconspicuous fertile flowers are followed by edible red fruit. The fall color is red. This species is resistant to aphids. 'Compactum' is a smaller, more dense shrub that grows 5–6' in height and width. Its flowers and fruit resemble those of the species. (Zones 2–7)

V. sargentii 'Onondaga'

Problems & Pests
Aphids, borers, dieback, downy mildew, gray mold, leaf spot, mealybugs, powdery mildew, scale insects, treehoppers, *Verticillium* wilt, weevils and wood rot can affect viburnums.

Viburnums look lovely in the shade of evergreen trees. Their richly textured foliage complements shrubs and perennials that bloom in late spring.

V. dentatum Blue Muffin

Virginia Creeper
Boston Ivy
Parthenocissus

Features: summer and fall foliage, habit **Habit:** clinging, woody, deciduous climber **Height:** 30–70' **Spread:** 30–70' **Planting:** container; spring, fall **Zones:** 3–9

WHEN WE THINK OF IVY-COVERED WALLS, odds are that we're probably visualizing Boston ivy (*P. tricuspidata*). This easy-growing vine offers a wonderfully lush texture for softening brick or cement. Its leaves are a rich green, transforming in autumn into a blaze of red and burgundy. Virginia creeper *(P. quinquefolia)* is a hardy native species. It's perhaps not as refined as the Japanese Boston ivy, but its fall foliage is vastly superior, with brighter colors ranging from hot pink to blood red. Virginia creeper looks fantastic growing over a rock pile or climbing up a tree. Both species can take the edge off the most rigid hardscape features.

Growing
These vines grow well in any light from **full sun to full shade.** The soil should preferably be **fertile** and **well drained.** The plants will adapt to clay or sandy soils.

These vigorous growers may need to be trimmed back frequently to keep them where you want them.

Virginia creepers can cover the sides of buildings and help keep them cool in the summer heat. Cut plants back to keep windows and doors accessible.

Tips

Virginia creeper and Boston ivy can cover an entire building, given enough time. They do not require support because they have clinging rootlets that can adhere to just about any surface—even smooth wood, vinyl or metal. Give the plants lots of space and let them cover a wall, fence or arbor. Note that when a vine is pulled off, the sticky ends leave little marks that can be hard to remove or even paint over.

P. quinquefolia (both photos)

These vines can be used as groundcovers. When grown this way they will spread 50' but will grow up to only 12" tall.

The fruits are poisonous.

Recommended

P. quinquefolia (Virginia creeper, woodbine) is a clinging, woody climber that can grow 30–50' tall. This species is native to Michigan and most of the eastern half of the U.S. The dark green foliage turns flame red in fall. Each leaf is divided into five leaflets. 'Dark Green Ice' has glossy dark green foliage. (Zones 3–9)

P. tricuspidata (Boston ivy, Japanese creeper) is also a clinging, woody climber. It grows 50–70' tall. The three-lobed leaves turn red in fall. 'Fenway Park' has new yellow foliage that matures to green in summer then turns red in fall. 'Lowii' has dainty little leaves and brilliant red fall color. (Zones 4–8)

Problems & Pests

Aphids, bacterial leaf scorch, canker, dieback, downy mildew, grape-leaf beetle, leafhoppers, leaf skeletonizers, leaf spot, powdery mildew, scab and scale insects can cause trouble.

Weigela
Weigela

Features: late-spring to early-summer flowers, foliage, habit **Habit:** upright or low, spreading, deciduous shrub **Height:** 1–9' **Spread:** 3–12' **Planting:** bare-root, container; spring, fall **Zones:** 3–8

GREAT STRIDES HAVE BEEN MADE WITH WEIGELA CULTIVARS OF late, and the plant now offers much more than a spring blast of flower power. New breeding efforts have provided cultivars with attractive yellow, purple or variegated foliage for season-long interest. Flower colors include pink, red, purple and white. Weigela is an easy-to-grow, adaptable flowering shrub that will brighten up any garden. As an added bonus, plants will often rebloom if lightly sheared after the first flush of flowers fades.

Growing
Weigela prefers **full sun** but tolerates partial shade. For the best leaf color, grow purple-leaved plants in full sun and yellow-leaved plants in partial shade. The soil should be **fertile** and **well drained.** Weigela will adapt to most well-drained soil conditions.

Once flowering is finished, cut flowering shoots back to strong buds or branch junctions. One-third of the old growth can be cut back to the ground at the same time.

Tips
Weigela can be used in a shrub or mixed border, in an open woodland garden or as an informal barrier planting.

Recommended
W. florida is a spreading shrub with arching branches. It grows 6–9' tall and spreads 8–12'. Dark pink flowers in clusters appear in late spring and early summer. 'Carnaval' bears red, pink and white flowers on the same plant. **French Lace** ('Brigela') has lime green to yellow leaf margins. The flowers are dark reddish pink. **Midnight Wine** ('Elvera') is a dwarf plant that grows up to 12" tall. The foliage is purple and the flowers are pink. 'Minuet' is a compact, spreading shrub 24–36" tall and about 3–4' in spread. The dark pink flowers have yellow throats. The foliage is a purplish green that matures to dark green over the summer. This cultivar is hardy in Zones 3–7. 'Red Prince' is an upright shrub. It grows 5–6' tall, spreads about 5' and is hardy in Zones 4–7. Bright red flowers appear in early summer, with a second flush in late summer. 'Variegata' is a compact plant about 5' tall, with an equal spread. The flowers are pale pink and the leaves have creamy white margins. It is hardy to Zone 5. **Wine and Roses** ('Alexandra') has dark purple foliage and vivid pink flowers. (Zones 3–8)

Problems & Pests
Scale insects, foliar nematodes, twig dieback and *Verticillium* wilt are possible, but usually not serious, problems.

This shrub's name honors German botanist Christian Weigel (1748–1831).

French Lace

Hummingbirds adore weigela and are often spotted sipping nectar from the tubular flowers.

Wine & Roses

White Forsythia
Korean Abelialeaf
Abeliophyllum

Features: fragrant late-winter or early-spring flowers **Habit:** suckering, deciduous shrub **Height:** 3–5' **Spread:** 3–5' **Planting:** container; spring or fall **Zones:** 5–8

THIS LITTLE-KNOWN FLOWERING SHRUB IS NOT ACTUALLY A *Forsythia* at all. It is an unrelated Korean species that happens to have similarly shaped flowers and blooms at the same time. While on a plant-hunting trip to Korea, I learned that it is illegal to sell this plant in its home country. It's an endangered species there, and the government is trying to protect it. Our Korean friends were quite surprised when we told them we sell thousands every year! White forsythia is easy to grow but requires a bit of pruning and shearing to build a full-bodied plant.

Growing

White forsythia prefers **full sun** but tolerates very light shade. The soil should be of **average fertility** and **well drained.** This shrub adapts to most well-drained soils.

Prune in spring as soon as flowering is complete. Prune right back to within 6" of the ground every two or so years to keep plants looking their best.

Tips

White forsythia tends to develop a tangled mass of twigs. The showy early-spring flowers make up for its deficiencies when not in bloom.

Though it's not ideal in a small garden, gardeners with a bit more space can include this plant in a corner with true forsythia, witchhazel and crocuses to create a wonderful early-season show. White forsythia can also be included in a sunny border or in a naturalized garden.

Recommended

A. distichum is a spreading, suckering shrub that bears creamy white flowers in late winter or early spring. The foliage may turn purple in fall. This plant can survive in Zone 4, but the flower buds may be frost killed during severely cold winters. '**Roseum**' bears light pink flowers.

Blooming shrubs such as white forsythia are a welcome sight in early spring, signaling that a long winter is finally over.

'Roseum'

A. distichum

Wisteria

Wisteria

Features: late-spring flowers, foliage, habit **Habit:** twining, woody, deciduous climber **Height:** 20–50' or more **Spread:** 20–50' or more **Planting:** container; spring, fall **Zones:** 4–9

WHEN IN BLOOM, THESE TWINING VINES ARE simply spectacular. The large, pendulous clusters of fragrant violet blooms look as elegant as the most expensive jewels. Wisterias are large, vigorous vines that do best when grown up a heavy wood or steel support. They look great on a sturdy arbor, or when trained up steel pipe to form a small tree. Cultivars offer flower colors ranging from white to pink, purple and blue. Seedlings can take years to flower, so choose one of the cultivars, which have been propagated from adult wood and are quicker to bloom.

Growing

Wisterias grow well in **full sun** or **partial shade**. The soil should be of **average fertility, moist** and **well drained.** Vines grown in too fertile a soil will produce lots of vegetative growth but very few flowers. Avoid planting wisteria near a lawn where fertilizer may leach over to your vine.

The first two or three years of growth will establish the main framework of sturdy stems. Once the vine is established, side shoots can be cut back in late winter to within three to six buds of the main stems. Trim the entire plant back in mid-summer if the growth is becoming rampant. Grown on a large, sturdy structure, wisteria can simply be left to its own devices, but be prepared for it to escape once it runs out of room.

To propagate wisteria, bend a length of vine down and bury it in a pot of good potting soil. Hold the branch in place with a rock if required. The buried section will root and can then be cut from the main plant. The roots have taken when you can no longer pull the buried section out of the pot with a gentle tug.

Tips

These vines require something to twine around, such as an arbor or other sturdy structure. You can also train a wisteria to form a small tree. Try to select a permanent site; wisterias don't like being moved once established.

These vigorous vines will send up suckers and can root wherever branches touch the ground. Regular and frequent pruning will help prevent your wisteria from getting out of hand.

All parts of wisteria plants, especially the seeds, are poisonous.

Recommended

W. floribunda (Japanese wisteria) grows 25–50' tall, or taller. Long, pendulous clusters of fragrant blue, purple, pink or white flowers appear in late spring before the leaves emerge. Long, bean-like pods follow. (Zones 4–9)

W. sinensis (*W. chinensis;* Chinese wisteria) can grow 20–30' tall, or taller. It bears long, pendent clusters of fragrant blue-purple flowers in late spring. 'Alba' has white flowers. (Zones 5–8)

Problems & Pests

Aphids, crown gall, dieback, leaf miners, leaf spot, mealybugs and viral diseases may cause occasional problems.

Witchhazel
Hamamelis

Features: flowers, foliage, habit **Habit:** spreading, deciduous shrub or small tree
Height: 6–20' **Spread:** 6–20' **Planting:** B & B, container; spring, fall **Zones:** 3–9

ON A COOL, MISTY MARCH DAY IN BELGIUM, I HAD A GLIMPSE OF
heaven as I walked the estate of my friend Jelena De Belder. She has been
breeding, evaluating and introducing witchhazels for more than 30 years.
Every way we walked, yellow, orange, red and even purple spider-like blooms
filled the air with perfume. Witchhazels, and particularly the *intermedia*
hybrids, are wonderful small trees with exotic elegance. The colors of the fall
foliage are stunning, in shades of orange, red and purple. Everything about
these plants makes them desirable. Americans have yet to fully appreciate
witchhazels, but I'm sure in time that will change.

*The branches can be cut in winter
and forced into bloom indoors.*

Growing

Witchhazels grow well in **full sun** or **light shade**. The soil should be of **average fertility, neutral to acidic, moist** and **well drained**. Pruning is rarely required. Remove awkward shoots once flowering is complete.

Tips

Witchhazels work well individually or in groups. They can be used as specimen plants, in shrub or mixed borders or in woodland gardens. As small trees, they are ideal for space-limited gardens.

The unique flowers have long, narrow, crinkled petals that give the plant a spidery appearance when in bloom. If the weather gets too cold, the petals will roll up, protecting the flowers and extending the flowering season.

H. x *intermedia* 'Arnold Promise'

H. virginiana with *Hydrangea*

H. virginiana

Recommended

H. x *intermedia* is a vase-shaped, spreading shrub. It grows 10–20' tall, with an equal spread. Clusters of fragrant yellow, orange or red flowers appear in mid- to late winter. The leaves turn attractive shades of orange, red and bronze in fall. **'Arnold Promise'** has large, fragrant, bright yellow or yellow-orange flowers. **'Diane'** ('Diana') bears dark red flowers in late winter, and its fall foliage is yellow, orange and red. **'Jelena'** has a horizontal branching habit. The fragrant flowers are coppery orange and the fall color is orange-red. **'Pallida'** is a more compact plant, growing to 12' tall and wide. It bears very fragrant bright yellow flowers. **'Ruby Glow'** is a vigorous, upright shrub with deep orange flowers. (Zones 5–9)

Witchhazel branches have been used as divining rods to locate water and gold.

H. x *intermedia* 'Jelena'

H. vernalis (vernal witchhazel) is a rounded, upright, often suckering shrub. It grows 6–15' tall, with an equal spread. Very fragrant yellow, orange or red flowers are borne in early spring. The foliage turns bright yellow in fall. (Zones 4–8)

H. virginiana (common witchhazel) is a common Michigan native. It is a large, rounded, spreading shrub or small tree 12–20' or more in height, with an equal spread. Yellow fall flowers are often hidden by the foliage that turns yellow at the same time, but this species is attractive nonetheless. (Zones 3–8)

H. vernalis

Problems & Pests

Aphids, leaf rollers, leaf spot, powdery mildew, scale insects and wood rot are possible, but rarely serious, problems.

A witchhazel extract was used traditionally as a general remedy for burns and skin inflammations. Today it is often sold as a mild astringent for skin care.

H. virginiana

Yellowwood
American Yellowwood
Cladrastis

Features: summer and fall foliage, spring flowers, bark, habit **Habit:** rounded, low-branching, deciduous tree **Height:** 30–50' **Spread:** 30–55'
Planting: B & B; spring **Zones:** 4–8

YELLOWWOOD IS A SUPERB MEDIUM-SIZED TREE THAT IS WELL suited to residential landscapes. This beautiful species remains attractive in all seasons. In spring the branches are graced with 10–16" long, pendulous clusters of fragrant white flowers. Fresh, bright green leaves make the tree a standout in summer. The autumn foliage is a pleasing butter yellow. And throughout the winter months, yellowwood's smooth, gray bark and broad, rounded habit lend grace and beauty to the garden.

The bean-like seedpods and the seeds they contain are not edible.

Growing

Yellowwood grows best in **full sun**. The soil should be **fertile, moist** and **well drained**. Alkaline soil is preferable, but yellowwood adapts well to acidic soil. Plant trees when they are young and don't move them again because they resent having their roots disturbed.

Remove dead, diseased, damaged or awkward growth in summer; the sap tends to run profusely if yellowwood is pruned in winter or spring.

Tips

Yellowwood is a beautiful flowering shade tree appropriate for large properties. Do not plant it close to houses or other buildings because the wood is fairly weak and can break in a strong wind.

Recommended

C. lutea (C. kentukea) is an attractive, wide-spreading tree with bright yellowish green leaves. In late spring and early summer, the branches are covered with long, drooping clusters of white or pink, pea-like flowers. The leaves turn bright yellow in fall. Yellowwood's bark is smooth and gray, much like beech bark.

The genus name Cladrastis *comes from the Greek* klados, *'branch,' and* thraustos, *'fragile,' referring to the brittle wood of this tree.*

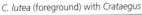

C. *lutea* (foreground) with *Crataegus*

Yew

Taxus

Features: foliage, habit, red seed cups **Habit:** evergreen; conical or columnar tree or bushy or spreading shrub **Height:** 2–50' **Spread:** 3–30' **Planting:** B & B, container; spring, fall **Zones:** 4–7

YEWS ARE PERHAPS THE MOST COMMONLY PLANTED EVERGREENS in Michigan, and with good reason. These tough, easy-to-grow plants adapt to all but wet, poorly drained growing sites. They also have attractive dark green needles and take well to shearing or pruning. Yews are extremely long-lived and if left unpruned will eventually take a tree form. Maintaining yews as shrubs is easy because they grow relatively slowly, so annual pruning keeps their size in check. Avoid the excessive shearing that can make these otherwise pleasantly fluffy-looking shrubs appear stiff and boxy.

Growing

Yews grow well in any light conditions from **full sun to full shade**. The soil should be **fertile, moist** and **well drained**. Yews tolerate soils of any acidity, most urban pollution and windy or dry conditions. They dislike soil contaminated with road salt and very wet soil. Do not plant them near downspouts or other places where water collects.

Hedges and topiary can be trimmed back in summer and fall. Yews can be cut back very hard to reduce their size or to rejuvenate them. New growth will sprout from old wood after a hard pruning.

Tips

Yews can be used in borders or as specimens, hedges, topiary and groundcovers. There are separate male and female plants, and both must be present for the attractive red arils (seed cups) to form.

Recommended

T. cuspidata (Japanese yew) is a slow-growing, broad, columnar or conical tree. It grows 30–50' tall and spreads 20–30'. **'Capitata'** is a pyramidal form that can grow up to 50' tall if left unpruned. **'Green Wave'** is a spreading, mound-forming plant that grows 3–4' tall and spreads up to 5'.

T. x media 'Densiformis'

T. x media (English Japanese yew), a cross between *T. baccata* (English yew) and *T. cuspidata*, has the vigor of English yew and the cold hardiness of Japanese yew. It forms a rounded, upright tree or shrub 2–25' in height, depending on the cultivar. **'Brownii'** is globe-shaped and about 5' in height and spread. **'Densiformis'** is a wide, dense, rounded shrub 3–4' tall and 6–8' wide. **'Hicksii'** is an open, columnar tree 15–25' tall and 5–10' wide. This narrow, upright yew is a good choice in colder climates. **'Sentinalis'** is an even narrower upright form. It grows about 10' tall, with a spread of 24–30". **'Tauntonii'** is a spreading cultivar that is both cold and heat hardy, suffering very little foliage browning in either situation. It grows 3–4' tall and spreads up to 6'.

Problems & Pests

Root rot can occur in wet, poorly drained soils, and scale insects are possible but not serious problems.

T. cuspidata 'Green Wave'

Yucca
Adam's Needle
Yucca

Features: summer flowers, foliage, habit **Habit:** rounded rosette of long, stiff, spiky, evergreen leaves **Height:** 24–36"; up to 6' in flower **Spread:** 24–36"
Planting: container; spring, fall **Zones:** 5–9

I DUG UP A YUCCA AND THREW IT ALONGSIDE MY compost pile four years ago, and it's still alive and thriving. If you tend to kill every plant you grow, try yucca for sure success. This unusual evergreen is native to the southern U.S., but it's perfectly hardy in Michigan. In fact, it has naturalized in some areas of the state. Its desert-like appearance can seem out of place in shrub borders or foundation plantings, so use it with care. I think yucca— especially variegated yucca—looks great in the perennial garden or rock garden.

Growing

Yucca grows best in **full sun** but tolerates partial shade. Any **well-drained** soil is suitable. This plant is very drought-tolerant.

Yucca fruits are rarely seen in Michigan. The yucca moth, which pollinates the flowers, is uncommon outside the plant's native range.

Pruning is not needed, but the flower spikes can be removed when blooming is finished, and dead leaves can be removed as needed.

Tips

Yucca is used as a specimen, usually in groups or in planters, to give a garden a southern appearance. In pots, planters and urns this plant also makes a strong architectural statement.

Recommended

Y. filamentosa has long, stiff, finely serrated, pointed leaves with threads that peel back from the edges. It is the most frost-hardy *Yucca* species available. '**Bright Edge**' has leaves with yellow margins. '**Golden Sword**' has leaves with yellow centers and green margins.

Problems & Pests

Cane borers, fungal leaf spot and scale insects can cause problems.

'Bright Edge'

The striking white flowers are edible raw or cooked and are said to taste like Belgian endive.

'Golden Sword'

Zelkova
Japanese Zelkova
Zelkova

Features: habit, summer and fall foliage **Habit:** vase-shaped to broadly spreading, deciduous tree **Height:** 50–80' or more **Spread:** 50–80' **Planting:** B & B; spring or fall **Zones:** 5–9

THIS ASIAN SPECIES HAS GAINED A PASSIONATE FOLLOWING ON the East Coast but is still relatively uncommon in Michigan. It will undoubtedly see much greater use as more and more gardeners learn about this lovely vase-shaped tree. Zelkova not only has an attractive form, it boasts elegant, clean, rich green foliage. In autumn, the leaves develop rich hues of yellow, orange, red and purple. With time the bark matures into a pleasing patchwork of gray and brown.

The mature, exfoliating bark of zelkova provides interest in the winter landscape.

Growing

Zelkova grows well in **full sun** or **partial shade**. The soil should be **fertile, humus rich, moist** and **well drained**. Young trees are sensitive to wind, drought and cold, but established plants tolerate these conditions. Prune in fall or winter to encourage neat, even growth.

Tips

Zelkova is a medium-sized tree with attractive habit and foliage. It is well suited as a residential shade tree or for street plantings.

Recommended

Z. serrata grows 50–80' tall, or taller, with a spread of 50–80'. It is vase-shaped when young and develops a broader, more spreading habit as it matures. It also develops exfoliating bark as it matures. Inconspicuous flowers are produced in early spring. The dark green leaves turn yellow or orange, and sometimes red, in fall. 'Green Vase' maintains a vase-shaped habit and develops a strong, straight trunk. It grows up to 70' tall

'Variegata'

and spreads up to 50'. **'Variegata'** has leaves with narrow white margins. **'Village Green'** is a hardy, fast-growing, pest- and disease-resistant tree. It develops red fall color. This cultivar is hardy to the warmer parts of Zone 4. There is also a dwarf cultivar of *Z. serrata*, but it is difficult to find in North America.

Problems & Pests

This tree is in the elm family, but it is quite resistant to Dutch elm disease. Zelkova may have some trouble with canker, elm-leaf beetles and scale insects.

Z. serrata in fall color

OTHER TREES & SHRUBS TO CONSIDER

Taxodium distichum

Robinia pseudoacacia 'Frisia'

BALD CYPRESS
Taxodium distichum

Conical, coniferous, deciduous or semi-evergreen tree 50–130' tall and 20–30' wide. Becomes more open and asymmetrical with age. Bright green foliage turns orangy brown in fall. In or near swampy areas, this tree forms gnome-like 'knees' (pneumatophores), which are knobby roots that poke up out of the water and allow the roots to breathe. (Zones 4–9)

Bald cypress prefers **full sun** or **partial shade** and **moist, acidic** soil but adapts to many soil conditions. Alkaline soil can cause the foliage to turn yellow (chlorotic). Bald cypress has a deep taproot but transplants easily when young. This tree is a bit large for most home gardens but makes a good choice in waterlogged soils. Use as a large specimen individually or in groups.

BLACK LOCUST
Robinia pseudoacacia

Upright, suckering and self-seeding deciduous tree 30–50' tall and 20–40' wide. Features fast growth, spiny shoots and dangling clusters of fragrant white flowers in early summer. Several cultivars are available, including 'Frisia,' with yellow-green foliage, and 'Purple Robe,' with pinky purple flowers. (Zones 3–8)

Black locust prefers **full sun** and adapts to any soils that aren't constantly soggy. It tolerates infertile or salty soils, drought and pollution, though it does best in **average to fertile, moist** soil. Avoid growing in exposed locations because heavy wind can cause the weak branches to break. Best used in difficult situations, where other trees have failed to thrive.

BLACK TUPELO
Nyssa sylvatica

Pyramidal to rounded deciduous tree 30–50' tall and 20–30' wide. The glossy dark green leaves of this Michigan native turn brilliant shades of yellow, orange, red and purple in fall. Not frequently found in cultivation owing to transplanting difficulties, but availability should improve as more nurseries produce container-grown trees. (Zones 4–9)

Black tupelo grows well in **full sun** or **partial shade** and in **average to fertile, neutral to acidic, well-drained** soil. Plant trees when they are young; the roots resent being disturbed. This beautiful specimen tree is suitable for a medium-sized property, but it resents polluted conditions and shouldn't be used as a street tree.

Nyssa sylvatica
Enkianthus campanulatus

ENKIANTHUS
Enkianthus campanulatus

Large, bushy deciduous shrub or small tree 10–15' tall and wide. Bears small, white, red-veined, pendulous, bell-shaped flowers in spring. Foliage turns fantastic shades of yellow, orange and red in fall. (Zones 4–7)

Enkianthus grows well in **full sun, partial shade** or **light shade** with **fertile, humus-rich, moist, acidic, well-drained** soil. A beautiful shrub to include in the understory of a woodland garden, enkianthus makes a good companion for rhododendrons and other acid-loving plants.

Actinidia kolomikta
Leucothoe cultivar

Hardy Kiwi
Actinidia

Vigorous, twining deciduous vines that reach 15–30'. Grown for their attractive small, edible fruit and ornamental foliage. Both male and female vines are needed in order for fruit to form on the females. Flowers are inconspicuous but fragrant. *A. arguta* (Zones 3–8) grows vigorously and quickly fills in, providing a dense screen of foliage. Male vines of *A. kolomikta* (Zones 4–8) have foliage variegated with green, white, pink or red.

Hardy kiwi vines grow best in **full sun** and in **fertile, well-drained** soil. They require **shelter** from strong winds. These vigorous growers may need pruning to keep them in bounds. Prune in late winter. Provide a sturdy structure, such as a pergola, an arbor or a fence, for them to twine around.

Leucothoe
Leucothoe fontanesiana

Graceful evergreen shrub 3–6' tall and 3–10' in spread, with arching branches. Plentiful, tiny, white spring flowers are borne in drooping clusters and are often hidden by the foliage. Leucothoe is also admired for its glossy green foliage highlighted with red or bronze at the tips and along the margins. The cultivar 'Rainbow' has attractive foliage mottled with cream and pink. (Zones 5–8)

Leucothoe grows well in **light shade, partial shade** or **full shade,** with **shelter** from the wind and with **fertile, acidic, humus-rich, moist** soil. It makes a good companion for other acid-loving plants, such as rhododendrons and kalmia, in shaded borders and woodland gardens.

Cut the lovely, colorful foliage of leucothoe and use it in indoor arrangements.

LONDON PLANETREE
Platanus x *acerifolia*

Broad, rounded or pyramidal, large deciduous tree with wide-spreading branches. The bark flakes off, leaving the smooth trunk and branches with an attractive multi-colored surface. London planetree was long popular as a pollution-tolerant street tree, but overplanting has led to problems with anthracnose and powdery mildew. Use resistant cultivars, such as 'Columbia' and 'Liberty.' (Zones 4–8)

London planetree grows well in **full sun** and in just about any soil conditions. This magnificent tree looks best where it has plenty of space to grow and spread, but it tolerates heavy pruning and can be grown as a hedge. Trees can be pruned back hard every two or so years to keep them small enough for an urban home garden.

Platanus x *acerifolia* (above & below)

PERSIAN PARROTIA
Parrotia persica

Small to medium-sized, single- or multi-stemmed deciduous tree 20–40' tall and 15–30' or more wide. Branches form an attractive layered pattern. The glossy green leaves have undulating margins. Foliage emerges red in spring and turns shades of bronzed purple, red, orange or yellow in fall. The exfoliating bark creates a mottled, multi-colored pattern on the trunk and branches. (Zones 4–8)

Persian parrotia grows best in **full sun** but tolerates partial shade. It prefers **average to fertile, moist, slightly acidic, well-drained** soil. It tolerates alkaline soil but produces less colorful fall foliage. This beautiful tree rarely needs pruning; remove damaged or awkward growth as needed. Though not exceptionally tall, Persian parrotia is quite wide-spreading. It makes a stunning addition to a medium-sized yard.

Ligustrum amurense

PRIVET
Ligustrum amurense

Upright or arching, deciduous or semi-evergreen shrub 12–15' tall and 8–15' wide. Commonly used as a hedge because it is fast-growing and inexpensive; also makes an attractive border specimen when left unpruned. Susceptible to minor pest and disease problems that can disfigure the appearance. (Zones 3–8)

Privet grows equally well in **full sun** or **partial shade.** It can be grown in any **well-drained** soil, tolerating even polluted urban conditions.

Trim privet hedges twice a summer. Specimen plants need almost no pruning; remove damaged or awkward branches as needed. Occasional problems with aphids, scale insects, leaf miners, root rot, canker and leaf spot can occur.

Legend has it that the name privet comes from 'privy,' whose malodors were said to have been masked by plantings of this pungent-flowered shrub.

Stewartia pseudocamellia

STEWARTIA
Stewartia pseudocamellia

Broad, columnar or pyramidal deciduous tree 20–40' tall, with an equal spread. Attractive white flowers with showy yellow stamens are borne in mid-summer. Leaves turn shades of yellow, orange and red in fall. Scaly, exfoliating bark gives the trunk a gray, orange, pink and red-brown mottled surface. Bark may take several years to develop the mottling. (Zones 5–7)

This tree grows well in **full sun** or **light shade,** with **average to fertile, humus-rich, neutral to acidic, moist, well-drained** soil. Provide **shelter** from strong winds. Plant when the tree is young and avoid moving it once planted. Stewartia makes an attractive shade tree in a smaller garden; group plantings look stunning in larger gardens.

Willow
Salix

Many species and cultivars of fast-growing deciduous shrubs with attractive habits and sometimes colorful stems or foliage. *S. alba* 'Flame' is a large shrub about 15' tall and wide, with dark red young stems (Zones 2–8). *S. elaeagnos* (Zones 4–7), commonly called rosemary willow, is a delicate arching shrub that shows off the white undersides of its narrow green leaves in a breeze. It grows to about 12' tall and wide. *S. integra* 'Hakuro Nishiki' (Zones 5–8) has white and pink mottling on light green foliage and grows 3–5' tall and wide.

Willows grow best in **full sun** with **moist** but **well-drained** soil. Coloring is best on young growth, so 'Flame' should be cut back to within 6" of the ground every couple of years to keep the stem color bright. Other willows can also be cut back this way if they need rejuvenating.

The many possible pests won't trouble these fast growers if the plants are grown in appropriate conditions.

S. integra 'Hakuro Nishiki'

Cut a few winterhazel branches in January or February, and put them in a vase indoors to force them into very early bloom. The fragrant flowers will foreshadow spring delights to come.

Winterhazel
Corylopsis spicata

Open, wide-spreading deciduous shrub 4–10' tall and 6–10' wide. Bears 6" long tassels of pale yellow flowers in mid-spring, before the leaves emerge. (Zones 5–8)

Winterhazel grows well in **full sun, partial shade** or **light shade** and in **fertile, humus-rich, moist, well-drained** soil. The growing site should be **sheltered** from winter winds. Pruning is rarely required but can be done in late spring once flowering is complete. Winterhazel is useful in borders or as a specimen.

Corylopsis spicata

TREE HEIGHT LEGEND: Short: < 25' • Medium: 25–50' • Tall: > 50'

SPECIES
by Common Name

SPECIES by Common Name	FORM						FOLIAGE							
	Tall Tree	Med. Tree	Short Tree	Shrub	Groundcover	Climber	Evergreen	Deciduous	Variegated	Blue/White	Purple/Red	Yellow/Gold	Dark Green	Light Green
Aralia			•	•				•	•				•	
Arborvitae		•	•	•			•					•	•	
Aronia				•				•					•	
Barberry				•				•	•	•	•	•	•	
Bearberry				•	•		•						•	
Beautyberry				•				•						
Beauty bush				•				•						
Beech	•	•						•	•		•	•	•	
Birch	•	•						•				•		
Black jetbead				•				•						
Boxwood				•			•							
Bush honeysuckle				•				•						
Butterfly bush				•				•	•					
Caryopteris				•				•				•		•
Cherry	•	•	•	•				•			•		•	•
Cotoneaster			•	•	•		•	•						
Crabapple		•	•					•						
Daphne				•			•	•	•	•		•	•	
Dawn redwood	•							•				•	•	
Deutzia				•				•						
Dogwood		•	•	•				•	•					
Elderberry			•	•				•			•	•	•	•
English ivy					•	•	•		•	•				
Euonymus		•	•	•	•	•	•	•	•	•		•	•	•
False cypress	•	•	•	•			•					•	•	
False spirea				•				•						
Fir	•	•	•	•			•			•			•	
Firethorn				•	•	•	•	•					•	
Flowering quince				•				•						
Forsythia				•				•						•

	FEATURES								BLOOMING					SPECIES by Common Name
Form	Flowers	Foliage	Bark	Fruit/Cones	Scent	Spines	Fall Color	Winter Interest	Spring	Summer	Fall	Zones	Page Number	
	•	•		•		•				•		4–8	74	Aralia
•		•	•	•	•			•				2–9	76	Arborvitae
	•		•				•	•	•	•		3–8	80	Aronia
	•	•				•			•			4–8	82	Barberry
•	•	•		•			•	•	•			2–7	84	Bearberry
				•						•		5–10	86	Beautyberry
	•								•			4–8	88	Beauty bush
•		•	•				•					4–9	90	Beech
•	•	•	•				•	•	•			2–9	94	Birch
•	•			•					•	•		4–8	98	Black jetbead
•		•			•			•				4–9	100	Boxwood
•		•					•		•	•		3–8	104	Bush honeysuckle
•	•				•					•	•	5–9	106	Butterfly bush
	•	•			•					•		5–9	110	Caryopteris
•	•		•	•	•		•	•	•	•		2–9	112	Cherry
•	•		•	•			•	•		•		4–9	120	Cotoneaster
•	•	•	•	•	•		•	•	•			4–8	124	Crabapple
	•	•			•				•			4–7	130	Daphne
•		•	•	•			•	•				4–8	134	Dawn redwood
•	•									•		4–9	136	Deutzia
•	•	•	•	•			•	•	•	•		2–9	138	Dogwood
•	•	•		•			•			•		3–9	142	Elderberry
•		•					•	•				5–9	146	English ivy
•		•	•				•	•				4–9	148	Euonymus
•		•		•				•				4–8	152	False cypress
	•	•								•		2–8	156	False spirea
		•		•	•			•				3–7	158	Fir
•	•	•				•				•		5–9	160	Firethorn
	•			•	•	•			•			5–9	162	Flowering quince
	•								•			3–9	164	Forsythia

TREE HEIGHT LEGEND: Short: < 25' • Medium: 25–50' • Tall: > 50'

SPECIES by Common Name	FORM						FOLIAGE							
	Tall Tree	Med. Tree	Short Tree	Shrub	Groundcover	Climber	Evergreen	Deciduous	Variegated	Blue/White	Purple/Red	Yellow/Gold	Dark Green	Light Green
Fothergilla				•				•	•				•	
Fringe tree			•	•				•						•
Ginkgo	•	•						•						•
Goldenchain tree			•			•		•						
Golden rain tree		•						•						
Hawthorn		•	•	•				•					•	
Hazel			•	•				•			•	•	•	
Heather				•	•		•					•	•	•
Hemlock	•	•	•	•			•						•	
Holly	•	•	•	•			•	•					•	
Hornbeam	•	•	•					•						•
Horsechestnut	•	•	•					•						
Hydrangea			•	•		•		•	•				•	•
Japanese hydrangea vine						•		•		•			•	
Japanese pagoda-tree		•	•					•						
Juniper	•	•	•	•	•	•	•			•		•	•	
Kalmia			•				•							
Katsura-tree	•	•						•			•	•		
Kerria				•				•	•					•
Larch	•	•						•						•
Lilac		•	•	•				•	•					
Linden	•	•	•					•						
Magnolia		•	•	•				•						
Maple	•	•	•	•				•			•	•	•	•
Mock-orange				•				•				•		
Ninebark				•				•			•	•	•	
Oak	•	•						•					•	
Oregon-grape				•	•		•						•	
Peashrub			•	•				•						•
Pieris				•			•			•	•	•	•	

Form	Flowers	Foliage	Bark	Fruit/Cones	Scent	Spines	Fall Color	Winter Interest	Spring	Summer	Fall	Zones	Page Number	SPECIES by Common Name
•	•				•		•		•			4–9	168	Fothergilla
•	•		•	•	•			•		•		4–9	170	Fringe tree
•		•	•	•	•		•	•				3–9	172	Ginkgo
•	•			•					•	•		5–7	174	Goldenchain tree
•	•	•		•			•			•		5–8	176	Golden rain tree
•	•	•	•	•		•	•	•	•	•		3–8	178	Hawthorn
•	•	•	•	•				•	•			3–9	182	Hazel
•	•	•			•				•			5–7	186	Heather
•		•		•				•				3–8	188	Hemlock
•		•				•		•				3–9	190	Holly
•			•				•					3–9	194	Hornbeam
•	•	•		•			•		•	•		3–9	196	Horsechestnut
•	•	•	•				•			•	•	3–9	198	Hydrangea
•	•	•								•		5–8	204	Japanese hydrangea vine
•	•				•	•		•		•		5–7	206	Japanese pagoda-tree
•		•		•	•	•		•				3–9	208	Juniper
	•	•						•	•	•		4–9	212	Kalmia
•		•			•		•	•				4–8	214	Katsura-tree
•	•		•				•	•	•			4–9	216	Kerria
•		•		•			•					1–7	218	Larch
	•	•			•				•	•		2–8	220	Lilac
•	•	•			•					•		2–8	224	Linden
•	•	•	•	•	•			•	•			3–9	226	Magnolia
•	•	•	•	•			•	•	•			2–9	230	Maple
	•				•					•		3–8	236	Mock-orange
•	•	•	•					•	•	•		2–8	238	Ninebark
•		•	•	•			•	•				2–9	240	Oak
•	•	•				•	•	•	•			5–9	244	Oregon-grape
•	•	•		•					•			2–7	246	Peashrub
•	•	•						•	•			4–8	248	Pieris

TREE HEIGHT LEGEND: Short: < 25' • Medium: 25–50' • Tall: > 50'

SPECIES by Common Name	Tall Tree	Med. Tree	Short Tree	Shrub	Groundcover	Climber	Evergreen	Deciduous	Variegated	Blue/White	Purple/Red	Yellow/Gold	Dark Green	Light Green
Pine	•	•	•	•			•		•				•	•
Potentilla				•	•			•						
Redbud		•	•	•				•	•		•			•
Rhododendron				•			•	•					•	
Rose-of-Sharon			•	•				•	•					
Serviceberry		•	•	•				•						
Seven-son flower		•	•	•				•						
Silverbell		•	•					•						
Smokebush			•	•				•			•			
Spirea				•				•	•	•	•	•	•	•
Spruce	•	•	•	•			•			•			•	
St. Johnswort				•			•	•						
Sumac				•	•			•						
Summersweet clethra				•				•						
Sweetgum	•							•					•	
Sweetspire				•				•						
Thornless honeylocust	•	•	•					•				•	•	•
Trumpetcreeper						•		•						
Tulip tree	•							•	•				•	
Viburnum				•			•	•						
Virginia creeper						•		•				•	•	
Weigela				•				•	•		•	•	•	
White forsythia				•				•						
Wisteria						•		•						
Witchhazel			•	•									•	
Yellowwood		•						•				•		•
Yew		•	•	•			•						•	
Yucca				•			•							
Zelkova	•							•	•					

	FEATURES								BLOOMING					SPECIES by Common Name
Form	Flowers	Foliage	Bark	Fruit/Cones	Scent	Spines	Fall Color	Winter Interest	Spring	Summer	Fall	Zones	Page Number	
•		•	•	•	•			•				2–8	250	Pine
•	•	•		•						•	•	2–8	254	Potentilla
•	•	•				•	•		•			4–9	258	Redbud
•	•	•					•		•	•		3–8	260	Rhododendron
	•	•					•			•	•	5–9	264	Rose-of-Sharon
•	•	•	•	•			•	•	•	•		3–9	268	Serviceberry
•	•	•		•	•		•	•		•	•	5–8	272	Seven-son flower
•	•	•					•		•	•		5–9	274	Silverbell
•	•	•					•			•		4–8	276	Smokebush
•	•	•					•					3–9	278	Spirea
•		•		•				•				2–8	282	Spruce
•	•	•								•	•	4–8	286	St. Johnswort
•	•	•		•			•			•		3–9	288	Sumac
	•	•			•		•			•		3–9	290	Summersweet clethra
•		•	•	•	•							5–9	292	Sweetgum
•	•				•		•			•		5–9	294	Sweetspire
•		•		•						•		4–8	296	Thornless honeylocust
•	•									•		4–9	298	Trumpetcreeper
•	•	•					•			•		4–9	300	Tulip tree
•	•	•		•			•	•	•	•		2–9	302	Viburnum
•		•					•					3–9	308	Virginia creeper
	•	•							•	•		3–8	310	Weigela
	•				•			•	•			5–8	312	White forsythia
•	•	•			•				•	•		4–9	314	Wisteria
•	•	•					•	•	•		•	3–9	316	Witchhazel
•	•	•	•		•		•		•			4–8	320	Yellowwood
•		•		•				•				4–7	322	Yew
•	•	•						•		•		5–9	324	Yucca
•		•	•	•				•				5–9	326	Zelkova

GLOSSARY

B & B: abbreviation for balled-and-burlapped stock, i.e., plants that have been dug out of the ground and have had their rootballs wrapped in burlap

Bonsai: the art of training plants into miniature trees and landscapes

Bract: a modified leaf at the base of a flower or flower cluster; bracts can be showy, as in flowering dogwood blossoms

Candles: the new, soft spring growth of needle-leaved evergreens such as pine, spruce and fir

Crown: the part of a plant at or just below the soil where the stems meet the roots; also, the top of a tree, including the branches and leaves

Cultivar: a *culti*vated plant *var*iety with one or more distinct differences from the species; e.g., *Hedera helix* is a botanical species, of which 'Gold Heart' is a cultivar distinguished by leaf variegation

Deadhead: to remove spent flowers in order to maintain a neat appearance, encourage a longer bloom and prevent the plant from expending energy on fruit production

Dieback: death of a branch from the tip inwards; usually used to describe winter damage

Dormancy: an inactive stage, often coinciding with the onset of winter

Double flower: a flower with an unusually large number of petals, often caused by mutation of the stamens into petals

Dripline: the area around the bottom of a tree, directly under the tips of the farthest-extending branches

Dwarf: a plant that is small compared to the normal growth of the species; dwarf growth is often cultivated by plant breeders

Espalier: the training of a tree or shrub to grow in two dimensions

Gall: an abnormal outgrowth or swelling produced as a reaction to sucking insects or diseases

Genus: a category of biological classification between the species and family levels; the first word in a scientific name indicates the genus, e.g., *Pinus* in *Pinus mugo*

Girdling: a restricted flow of water and nutrients in a plant caused by something tied tightly around a trunk or branch, or by a cut that encircles the trunk or branch

Grafting: a type of propagation in which a stem or bud of one plant is joined onto the rootstock of another plant of a closely related species

Heartwood: the wood in the center of a stem or branch consisting of old, dense, non-functional conducting tissue

Hybrid: a plant created by natural or human-induced cross-breeding between varieties, species or genera; hybrids are often sterile but may be more vigorous than either parent and have attributes of both. Hybrids are indicated in scientific names by an x, e.g., *Forsythia* x *intermedia*

Inflorescence: a flower cluster

Leader: the dominant upward growth at the top of a tree; may be erect or drooping

Nodes: the places on the stem from where leaves grow; when cuttings are planted, new roots grow from the nodes under the soil

pH: a measure of acidity or alkalinity ranging from 0 to 14 (0 is very acidic, 7 is neutral and 14 is very alkaline); soil pH influences nutrient availability for plants

Pollarding: a severe form of pruning in which all younger branches of a tree are cut back virtually to the trunk to encourage bushy new growth

Procumbent, prostrate: terms used to describe plants that grow along the ground

Rhizome: a modified stem that grows horizontally underground

Rootball: the root mass and surrounding soil of a container-grown or dug-out plant

Single flower: a flower with a single ring of typically four or five petals

Species: the original plant from which cultivars are derived; the fundamental unit of biological classification, indicated by a two-part scientific name, e.g., *Pinus mugo* (*mugo* is the specific epithet)

Standard: a shrub or small tree grown with an erect main stem; accomplished either through pruning and training or by grafting the plant onto a tall, straight stock

Subspecies (*abbrev.* subsp.): a naturally occurring, regional form of a species, often geographically isolated from other subspecies but still potentially able to interbreed with them

Sucker: a shoot that comes up from a root, often some distance from the plant; it can be separated to form a new plant once it develops its own roots

Topiary: the training of plants into geometric, animal or other unique shapes

Variegation: describes foliage that has more than one color, often patched or striped or bearing differently colored leaf margins

Variety (*abbrev.* var.): a naturally occurring variant of a species; below the level of subspecies in biological classification

Resources

Barnes, B.V. and W.H. Wagner. 1981. *Michigan Trees.* University of Michigan Press, Ann Arbor.

Billington, C. 1977. *Shrubs of Michigan.* Cranbrook Institute of Science, Bloomfield Hills.

Dirr, M.A. 1997. *Dirr's Hardy Trees and Shrubs: An Illustrated Encyclopedia.* Timber Press, Portland, Oregon.

Editors of Sunset Books and Sunset Magazine. 1997. *Sunset National Garden Book.* Sunset Books, Menlo Park, California.

Ellis, B.W. and F.M. Bradley, eds. 1996. *The Organic Gardener's Handbook of Natural Insect and Disease Control.* Rodale Press, Emmaus, Pennsylvania.

Fiala, J.L. 1988. *Lilacs: The Genus* Syringa. Timber Press, Portland, Oregon.

Galle, F.C. 1997. *Hollies: The Genus* Ilex. Timber Press, Portland, Oregon.

Phillips, R. and M. Rix. 1989. *The Random House Book of Shrubs.* Random House, New York.

Thompson, P. 1992. *Creative Propagation: A Grower's Guide.* Timber Press, Portland, Oregon.

Tripp, K.E. and J.C. Raulston. 1995. *The Year in Trees: Superb Woody Plants for Four-Season Gardens.* Timber Press, Portland, Oregon.

- International Society of Arboriculture www.isa-arbor.com/

- Michigan State University Extension www.msue.msu.edu/mastergardener/

- Spring Meadow Nursery www.springmeadownursery.com/

- University of Connecticut database of trees, shrubs and vines www.hort.uconn.edu/plants/

- National list of gardens and arboretums www.colorchoiceplants.com/gardens.htm

INDEX OF PLANT NAMES